the complete
nail technician

HAIRDRESSING AND BEAUTY INDUSTRY AUTHORITY SERIES

HAIRDRESSING

Mahogany Hairdressing: Steps to Cutting, Colouring and Finishing Hair *Martin Gannon and Richard Thompson*
Mahogany Hairdressing: Advanced Looks *Richard Thompson and Martin Gannon*
Essensuals, Next Generation Toni & Guy: Step by Step
Professional Men's Hairdressing *Guy Kremer and Jacki Wadeson*
The Art of Dressing Long Hair *Guy Kremer and Jacki Wadeson*
Patrick Cameron: Dressing Long Hair *Patrick Cameron and Jacki Wadeson*
Patrick Cameron: Dressing Long Hair Book 2 *Patrick Cameron*
Bridal Hair *Pat Dixon and Jacki Wadeson*
Trevor Sorbie: Visions in Hair *Kris Sorbie and Jacki Wadeson*
The Total Look: The Style Guide for Hair and Make-up Professionals *Ian Mistlin*
Art of Hair Colouring *David Adams and Jacki Wadeson*
Start Hairdressing: The Official Guide to Level 1 *Martin Green and Leo Palladino*
Hairdressing – The Foundations: The Official Guide to Level 2 *Leo Palladino and Jane Farr*
Professional Hairdressing: The Official Guide to Level 3 *Martin Green and Leo Palladino*
Men's Hairdressing: Traditional and Modern Barbering *Maurice Lister*
African-Caribbean Hairdressing *Sandra Gittens*
Salon Management *Martin Green*

BEAUTY THERAPY

Beauty Therapy – The Foundations: The Official Guide to Level 2 *Lorraine Nordmann*
Professional Beauty Therapy: The Official Guide to Level 3 *Lorraine Nordmann, Lorraine Appleyard and Pamela Linforth*
Aromatherapy for the Beauty Therapist *Valerie Ann Worwood*
Indian Head Massage *Muriel Burnham-Airey and Adele O'Keefe*
The Official Guide to Body Massage *Adele O'Keefe*
An Holistic Guide to Anatomy and Physiology *Tina Parsons*
The Encyclopedia of Nails *Jacqui Jefford and Anne Swain*
Nail Artistry *Jacqui Jefford, Sue Marsh and Anne Swain*
The Complete Nail Technician *Marian Newman*
The World of Skin Care: A Scientific Companion *Dr John Gray*
Safety in the Salon *Elaine Almond*

the complete nail technician

SECOND EDITION

MARIAN NEWMAN

HABIA

THOMSON™

Australia • Canada • Mexico • Singapore • Spain • United Kingdom • United States

THOMSON

The complete nail technician, second edition

Copyright © Thomson Learning 2005

The Thomson logo is a registered trademark used herein under licence.

For more information, contact Thomson Learning, High Holborn House, 50–51 Bedford Row, London, WC1R 4LR or visit us on the World Wide Web at http://www.thomsonlearning.co.uk

British Library Cataloguing-in-Publication Data
A catalogue record for this book is available from the British Library

ISBN-13: 978-1-84480-139-X
ISBN-10: 1-84480-139-X

First edition published by Thomson Learning 2002
Reprinted 2002
Reprinted 2003
This edition published by Thomson Learning 2005
Reprinted 2005 by Thomson Learning

Typeset in the UK by Meridian Colour Repro Ltd, Pangbourne-on-Thames
Printed in China by C+C Offset Printing.

Images on title page and half-title page courtesy of Odyssey Nail Systems, Robin Derrick and Rimmel, and Darren Feist and *Sunday Times Style*.

contents

foreword

Marian Newman is one of the most inspirational people I have ever met.

When I first met Marian in 1995 she was the leading force and passion driving the nail industry forward. Her direct approach, never afraid to question or challenge pre-conceived ideas, has given her an immense knowledge of the industry. She is recognised today by her peers and the media as the most influential person in UK nails.

Marian creates many of the beautiful nails that are used on the covers of fashion magazines; one look at her work and you will soon see why she is so much in demand from film stars and celebrities all over the world. Marian is clearly an inspiration who never stops promoting the industry over and above her own work.

The second edition of *The Complete Nail Technician* is an absolute must for anyone in the industry. From basics to master techniques – it's here for all budding nail technicians and industry professionals who want to see what happens when learning never stops.

Alan Goldsbro
Chief Executive Officer
HABIA

acknowledgements

The author and publishers would like to thank the following people and organisations for their assistance in producing this book:

Tracey Stephenson
Marco Benito
Beauty Express
Grafton International
HABIA
Nail Creations
Tom Wandrag (for retouching the pictures)
Oxford Designers and Illustrators

Four years on from the first edition and more lovely people giving endless support: Tracey, one of the most dedicated technicians I know, for the time spent on the step by steps; Marco for his talent and trust in me; many, many beauty journalists who have helped to create a profile for me that I only dreamt of. There are too many to mention them all, but very special thanks to Kathy Phillips and Alessandra Steinherr; my bookers at Streeters London (www.streeterslondon.com) who help keep me in work (Lindsey, Helen and Paul); Alan Goldsbro who is always an ear to moan to and a wise councellor and Nick Knight, still the best photographer in the world (says me and many other people too!) for his continuing loyalty and support. His skill, attention to detail, dedication and unbelievable creativity have been an inspiration. Thanks also to his wife and agent, Charlotte, who makes things happen!
I must mention my very good friend, Sam McKnight. He hasn't helped to improve my nail skills or anything like that, but he is very special and helps to give me inspiration.

Again, and far from least, an even more long suffering husband, Malcolm, who continues to trust, believe, help and support me in everything I choose to do. I have him and my children, Katy, Elizabeth and Tom, who are all magic. How lucky can a person get!

about this book

The Complete Nail Technician is a book written by a technician for technicians; a technician who has experienced, first hand, every aspect of the job. It provides all the necessary information for those just starting to learn the skill and also provides a 'one stop shop' for experienced technicians in a vast range of generic information that is often hard to find as most information is produced by product companies and specifically relates to their products.

All the **National Occupational Standards** requirements are included, but are broken down into a natural progression of learning and reinforcement. If the book is followed in sequence, the learner will become a proficient technician. The experienced technician will be able to look up invaluable information and facts.

The book concentrates on the commercial aspect of the work of a nail technician and provides the information necessary to provide a good service for a wide variety of clients. It provides the background, impartial technical information and practical skills for every service option of nail treatments for clients while stressing the importance of manicure as a treatment option for every client.

The nail technician is a profession in its own right and is becoming more popular all the time. For the right person, it is rewarding, challenging and lucrative. The right person is the one who takes the profession seriously and embarks on a lifetime of learning.

chapter 1

STARTING OUT:
YOU AND YOUR INDUSTRY

Learning objectives

In this chapter you will learn about:

- **a brief history of the nail industry**
- **the education and qualifications available today**
- **the career routes open to a technician**
- **the benefits and pitfalls of each career route**
- **how to start your career**
- **how to promote your services**

INTRODUCTION

This chapter introduces the world of 'nails'. It is an amazingly fast-growing section of the service industry that includes beauty and hair. What used to be an 'add-on' service for some therapists and hairdressers is now a booming business that has its own identity, with many dedicated salons all over the country. There are even many nail salons that offer beauty or hair treatments as an 'add-on' service to their main business of 'nails'. This chapter provides a brief history of the industry, describes the training available and the possible career routes for the nail technician.

ARTIFICIAL NAILS: A BRIEF HISTORY

The art of lengthening nails has been around for centuries, and in many cultures long nails are a symbol of wealth. The ancient Egyptians had shapes made from gold, bone or ivory that could be attached to the end of the finger to indicate wealth and class. Far Eastern cultures have, over the centuries, displayed their social standing by growing their own nails to extreme lengths. The ability to grow nails or wear extended decorations on fingers is meant to show that the person does not do any manual work and has servants or slaves to attend to all their needs.

There are lots of people who have been doing 'nails' for 30 years who claim to have been the first to offer artificial nail services in the UK and Europe. They are probably all correct if their concept of the UK and Europe is scaled down to mean their own particular area. Artificial nails as a practice appeared almost simultaneously in many places, but it was in the US before any other country where it became big business. The idea of creating artificial nails came from the dental and hearing aid industries, as inventive people started experimenting with the **polymers** and **adhesives** that dental technicians used to create crowns, moulds and other dental appliances. These materials, when mixed, could be formed into a strong solid structure that could go into the mouth, but could also be moulded onto a nail to lengthen or protect it! Small quantities could be applied with a brush and shaped to look like a natural nail. Pigments were already being added to match the colours of teeth or skin, and a method of etching tooth enamel to allow the material to bond could be modified to work with nails.

The earliest experiments and resultant artificial nails used a **monomer** and polymer mix applied to the nail and extended over a supporting form. This structure hardened and, when the support was removed, was then shaped to look like a natural extension of the nail plate. These dental materials were chemicals that came under the 'family' name of **acrylics**: thus the acrylic artificial nail was created. All materials subsequently used also belong to the acrylic family, but the term 'acrylic nails' has stuck to the method of using a **liquid** monomer and **powder** polymer.

Plastic nail shapes that could be stuck onto natural nails with an adhesive had been available for some time so it was not long before the shape of these was adapted to create the support for the acrylic structure. Lots of other tools and equipment were used or created to assist this skill. Even dental drills found their way into the equation, as the early acrylics could be so hard that help was needed to shape the nails. An industry grew up to provide nail technicians with a whole range of accessories.

THE MODERN NAIL TECHNICIAN

Education and skills training

In the US, technicians utilised these new materials very well and the public loved the resulting long, painted nails. Eventually colleges included teaching the skill in their cosmetology courses and each of the States included it in their licensing legislation, as it became essential to regulate the practice. This is the situation that remains in the US today; students in cosmetology learn the art of artificial nails and, if they want to be a commercial practitioner, they have to achieve their State licence. Each State has different requirements but, essentially, training is usually carried out in a college environment and a set number of hours learning and practising must be completed, followed by a practical exam. Once they have passed this, individuals receive their licence and this allows them to work and purchase products.

The nail companies obviously want to sell their products and many of them provide a 'post-graduate' training service to provide qualified technicians with advanced skills and an understanding of their particular product range. Of course this does not apply to all companies, as many find selling to the wholesale outlets and mail order via trade magazines sufficient.

The education programme offered by some nail product companies can be likened to the skin care companies that provide application techniques and product knowledge to the qualified beauty therapists who will be using their ranges. It can be an important aspect of the product range as correct usage is essential for optimum results and there are usually some techniques that have been developed to make a specific product range different from that of a competitor.

It was this type of post-graduate training, typically of one or two days' duration, that was imported from the US to the UK along with the products. It was training that was designed for qualified technicians who had already learned the basic skills. These short courses were offered in the UK to anyone who was interested in buying products and hundreds of 'technicians' were created who had no theoretical knowledge of the nail and skin, hygiene requirements, legislation or any of the basic information provided in a full qualifying course.

For many years this has been the accepted practice; it has always been assumed that 'nails' is an additional service that can be learned in under a week and has a good profit margin. Fortunately for the future of the industry, it has been becoming apparent that there is more to it than that. A therapist or hairdresser can learn how to apply nails but not in the same way as learning a new massage technique or a new hair colour range. It is more like adding aromatherapy to a therapist's services or a stylist learning how to perm. Many clients will only ever go to a specialist and many are happy to have one person provide all treatments. There will always be plenty of room for both types of technicians.

As the industry grows, so does the number of nail salons. It is becoming an industry in its own right, recognised by employers, insurers and local authorities. 'Nails' has its own magazines and trade shows, and it now has its own qualifications.

The industry is an exciting place to work in, as it is still so new. It is developing and growing, and opportunities for those working within it are becoming wider. 'Nails' is a creative and practical skill and, as such, needs education, practice and dedication. It cannot be learned in a day or two. There are some 'natural' technicians who have good co-ordination and an 'eye' for form, shape, balance and symmetry. Others need to learn how to use the tools and materials and develop their 'eye'. Good training and education is the first step; a dedication to practise is the second; the acceptance that no one ever stops learning and improving is the final step to a whole new career and skill.

Qualifications

The qualification structure evolves over time and now the professional nail industry has full qualifications dedicated to the required skills.

The Occupational Standards are a set of requirements drawn up with the help of professionals in the sector, following an analysis of the sector's needs, and approved by a wide range of relevant establishments and individuals. They are a set of skills, knowledge and understanding that those experienced in the sector believe are the minimum requirements for an individual working in the sector and providing treatments for paying clients. They also make sure that individuals have a knowledge and understanding in areas such as health and safety, legislation and customer service issues. In brief, when the skills, knowledge and understanding have been achieved, the individual is qualified for employment.

The standards are used in a variety of ways to measure skills but, most importantly for the purposes of this book, they are used to create recognised qualifications that students and experienced individuals who do not already possess a suitable qualification can achieve for the purposes of employment, further education, insurance purposes and local authority licensing. They can also be used in most EU countries as proof of competence.

The National Vocational Qualification (**NVQ**) is understood by most people as a recognised and widely available qualification (they are known as SVQs in Scotland). The Occupational Standards are used to create these NVQs. In Beauty Therapy, of which Nail Technology is a part, there are currently 3 levels. (Level 4 is in the process of being created, but will be aimed more towards business management and is unlikely to include any specialist nail units.)

Level 1 could be described as a qualification for assistants in a salon. An assistant would be able to carry out basic consultations and treatments and help Therapists or Technicians to prepare for other treatments. This is a general qualification and the individual would probably be expected to continue their education, although this is not mandatory.

Level 2 is a qualification for beauty therapists or nail technicians and will allow them to work unsupervised. Fortunately for the nail industry there is now a full Level 2 qualification dedicated to nails: the 'Nails Route'. There are certain general subjects to be achieved, such as health and safety issues and the expected set of skills required of a nail technician: providing manicure and pedicure treatments, applying artificial nails and providing a nail art service.

Level 3 is the advanced qualification for therapists and technicians. The 'Nails Specialist' syllabus also has general areas of knowledge covering aspects of the salon that are more appropriate to supervisory duties. The nails sections, for both artificial nails and nail art, are more advanced.

NVQs are awarded by a number of awarding bodies, City & Guilds and UTCT being just two.

Some awarding bodies also have their 'own brand' qualification structure. These are perfectly acceptable for employment and insurance purposes. They are usually in the form of smaller 'certificates' or 'diplomas' specialising in specific fields. There are several in the area of nail technology. For example, City & Guilds have a series of Specialist Awards: Advanced Certificate in Nail Technology. When a candidate has achieved a set number of these Certificates they are awarded with a Diploma.

This book covers all the necessary knowledge for the specialist nail qualifications, regardless of level, the title of the qualification or the awarding body. It is based on the Occupational Standards and they are based on all the essential skills, knowledge, information and understanding required by a beginner in the field of nails or an experienced technician needing a reference or to revise areas of their work. The book, however, goes a little further and it discusses the skills and knowledge necessary for earning a living in the sector. It also deals with real situations and scenarios in the commercial world.

Winning nails   Marco Benito

CAREER ROUTES

Doing 'nails' is not just about sitting behind a desk and buffing for 8 hours a day. A qualified and experienced technician has a wide range of choices available. The best starting point to choosing one of these routes, however, is to put in the time at that desk. Nails is a public service and experience of working with the public is invaluable. Eight career routes are common today: mobile technician; working from home; being self-employed or employed in a salon; running a salon of your own; teaching or demonstration work; or being a media technician. We shall briefly look at all of these.

For information and help on all the career routes, an excellent website is www.habia.org. The sales department has numerous publications for all personnel and businesses. There are many other useful sections and it is a generally interesting site to explore.

All technicians must get public and products liability insurance, whether they are employed or not. If a client decides to take legal action they could sue the salon and the individual technician separately. This type of insurance is inexpensive and will protect the technician from most situations involving products, whether as a result of an accident or an allergic reaction, for example. It often covers for accidental damage to property and loss of products and tools. This form of insurance is readily available from trade associations and some trade publications.

Mobile technicians

Like hairdressing and most beauty treatments, 'nails' can be a service that can be carried out in a client's home, as the equipment can be carried. It is a popular career route for newly-trained technicians as start-up costs are low. There are many technicians who have made a successful career with a good income this way.

Requirements: A qualification that is suitable for insurance purposes and local authority licensing if needed, for example the NVQ Unit in Beauty Therapy Level 3 (Nails Specialist). Experience is not essential as this may be the way a newly-qualified technician can gain practice.

Plus points:

- Low start-up costs (no property deposits/mortgages, legal costs, decoration, salon equipment)
- Low overheads (no rent, council taxes, utility bills)
- Flexible working time (no set opening times).

Minus points:

- Lots of travelling time that is not paid for
- Client expectation of lower charges
- Lots of kit carrying
- Less than ideal working situation (working on a dining room or kitchen table).

Things to consider:

- The cost of a car, petrol and car insurance when used for business and carrying your kit (make sure you are insured to do this as not all insurance policies cover business use and you may find you are not insured if you are travelling to a client)
- Maintaining good working standards without the stimulus of salon colleagues
- Working in unfavourable conditions that could cause back strain
- Problems of promotion of services, advertising
- Working in a salon is invaluable experience and advisable for a beginner
- Perception: however good the service, a mobile service is frequently perceived as having a lower professional status. There are many mobile technicians who do not bother with basic requirements like insurance, and over time this has led to a public view that 'mobile' can mean 'amateur'.

Where to start: Anyone thinking of starting to work in this way should approach it as a business and seek advice from those who understand financial matters. A bank manager can often recommend or be aware of schemes to help a business start up. The Citizens Advice Bureau (CAB) often has information that is useful and the Inland Revenue has many leaflets for self-employed people.

When you have decided what services you plan to offer you will need to create a price list (see Chapter 3 p.81) and you must decide how you are going to promote your services. This need not be expensive. Leaflets handed out to all your friends and family with a request to pass them onto their friends and colleagues can sometimes start the ball rolling. You could put them through letterboxes in your local area. In addition, you can have some small posters printed and ask to put them up in local shops, waiting rooms of doctors and dentists, village halls (especially if they hold women's interest group meetings), on supermarket notice boards, etc. For a little extra money, you can place a small advert in the classified section of your local paper or, if you have some money to invest in your new business, you could have a larger boxed advert.

Display your work to promote the salon   Marco Benito

Monitor the effectiveness of each method you try, as there is no point in continuing with a method that does not bring you clients.

When designing cards, posters and price lists the best piece of advice is to look at examples everywhere you go, including adverts in magazines. Notice the ones that grab your attention, their colour and layout. Notice the words that make you think you must try that product or service or rush out and buy it. Look at notice boards and shop windows and see if one thing stands out more than others.

Think very carefully about how you will organise yourself and your kit for travelling around. You will need to carry enough equipment for all the services you offer but not so much that you need several boxes and bags. Remember your client may be on the fourth floor with no lift! You need to remember all the rules of hygiene and you and your kit must look immaculate at all times. You may find that your kit evolves over time as you discover better ways to arrange it, but start off with well-thought out planning and carry spares of everything in your car.

Working from home

A salon can be set up in a private home instead of commercial premises.

Requirements: A qualification that is suitable for insurance purposes and local authority licensing if needed, such as the NVQ Unit mentioned above. Experience is not essential as this may be the way a newly qualified technician can gain practice.

Plus points:

- Low overheads
- No travelling
- Can be good for a working parent
- Flexible hours
- Salon atmosphere can be achieved.

Minus points:

- Strangers brought into home
- Lack of stimulus from salon colleagues
- Can disrupt family life.

Things to consider:

- Local authority permission needs to be gained to run a business from a residential property

- Good working practices and hygiene need to be adhered to, as odours from products and dust can affect the whole house

- Is access to the salon going to affect the family or the security of the home?

- As with a mobile technician, this should be set up as a proper business.

Where to start: Careful thought must be given to the salon set-up. Make sure there is sufficient space for what you plan to do and make sure all the necessary health and safety rules are followed. Thoroughly research the best furniture and equipment for the space you have and plan every detail. Consult the HABIA website for health and safety help.

Promotion of your services is essential. See the suggestions above for the Mobile Technician.

Self-employed in a salon

Clients of most salons, whether hair or beauty, will often ask if the salon 'does nails'. Working as a technician in a salon on a self-employed basis can prove to be a good relationship for the technician and the salon. A nail desk takes up so little space that it can usually be squeezed into most salons.

Requirements: These will be the same as for a mobile technician, but a salon may require experience. It is worth getting personal public and product liability insurance. The salon may have appropriate insurance, but it may not cover a person who is not employed by them and it is not always easy to get a sight of the policy to make sure it is relevant for you.

Plus points:

- Existing potential clients in a commercial environment

- Potential for good promotion, with salon staff having their nails done by you

- Professional atmosphere (hopefully!)

- Less lonely than working alone

- Possibility of sharing promotion and advertising costs and benefits.

Minus points:

- Salon owner may be too demanding

- Staff may not like 'nails' and be unhelpful in making recommendations.

Things to consider:

- Care must be taken in making a financial arrangement with the salon owner. Being self-employed is a common arrangement, but it has implications for VAT (if appropriate) and your position with the Inland Revenue. It is often difficult to get definite answers to questions on tax, but the problem usually lies with the salon owner rather than the technician. The technician must ensure that all legal rules for a self-employed person are followed – that is to say, payment of income tax and National Insurance and the keeping of accurate accounts.

- There are several financial arrangements that salon owners can use for this 'rent a space' idea. A weekly or monthly fixed rent is one way; the rent can often be high for a technician just starting out but, when the technician becomes busy, it may appear low to the salon owner who can see how much business the technician is doing. Under this arrangement, it is best to keep payments from clients separate so that both parties have an accurate record of client payments.

- Another possibility is to share clients' payments as a form of rent, for example 40 per cent to the salon and 60 per cent to the technician. This can help the technician in the early days as there is no rent to pay if there are no clients, but a lot of 'rent' will be paid when the technician becomes busy. It can, however, cause tax problems for the owner. There is sometimes an added complication if a salon owner provides the nail products. In this instance, the percentage of payments as 'rent' are usually reversed.

- As with a mobile or home-based technician, this is a business, and should be set up properly.

Where to start: Research the salons in your area. Find out what services they offer and see how busy they are. Before you approach a proprietor, make sure there is enough room for a nail desk and have a plan of what you would like to offer in that salon. Think of how you can impress the proprietor so that they cannot afford to miss out on what you can offer them. Have some projected figures ready of how many clients you could accommodate in a day and an estimated turnover. Decide how much you can invest in your new venture, for example, have pictures of the equipment you would like to work with and will provide, how much you are willing to pay for promotional materials, etc. Convince the proprietor that you are serious about making your proposal work for you and the salon and it is worth their while giving you a chance.

Employed in a salon

Many employers now require qualified technicians who can provide specialist services for their clients. Many therapists and hairdressers can do 'nails', but they are often too busy or do not like doing it. Also, as nail work is a practical skill, it needs to be done frequently and with enjoyment to result in good work. It can often make sense for a busy salon to employ a specialist technician.

Requirements: Qualifications are required and, depending on the salon, experience may be necessary. A potential employer may ask you to carry out a trade test where you can demonstrate your skills. This can be nerve-wracking, but just imagine you are dealing with a new client. Again, it is worth having personal insurance, as a client can sue both technician and salon and having the correct cover will give you peace of mind.

Plus points:

- Guaranteed income
- The salon handles all promotion
- No worries about products, stock and equipment
- Colleagues to work with.

Minus point:

- No independence.

Things to consider:

- Many salons in the service industries pay a basic salary and then commission on treatments and sales on top. In this way, therapists and technicians are encouraged to work well and keep their clients.
- If the 'nails' service is new to the salon, the onus would be on the technician to make it work. As long as the salon is prepared to promote the treatments, the technician should produce good work and keep their clients happy and rebooking.

Where to start: Write yourself a CV if you do not already have one. There are many ways of writing a good CV and, if you do not have experience of this, get a book from the library and find an example that suits you.

Look in the local papers and trade magazines for vacancies or contact specialist employment agencies that often advertise in trade magazines.

When going for an interview, try to have examples of your work such as before and after pictures or examples of nail art you have done on tips. Make sure your appearance is clean and tidy and that your own nails are immaculate. If possible, do some research on the salon to find out what they offer already and be knowledgeable about their services and products. If nails are new to the salon, have plenty of ideas about how to promote a nail service.

Opening a salon

There are nail salons opening all over the country now and many of them are very successful. Clients often prefer to go to a specialist for a specific service and 'nails' is no exception.

Requirements: Some salon owners have no experience of the services offered and rely on their staff. For working owners it is advisable to have experience of working in a commercial environment together with practical experience. A salon owner will have to deal with difficult clients and no amount of training in a school or college can be a substitute for experience. It is also advisable to have some knowledge of the legal requirements for salons – PAYE, National Insurance, the responsibilities of employers, bookkeeping, retailing and promotion, health and safety of staff and premises.

Plus points:

● Total control

● Satisfaction of owning your own business.

Minus points:

● Large financial investment required

● Potential problems with staffing

● Permanent commitment

● The need to work long hours or stand in for staff to cover sickness and holidays.

Things to consider:

Salons do not have to be traditional   Marco Benito

● As with any new business, there is a great deal of work to do before the doors of the salon open. This work, such as researching the area, creating a viable business plan, making any necessary applications to the local authority, decorating the salon, printing promotional material, recruiting staff and so on, must be done thoroughly and time taken to get it right. So many businesses fail because the groundwork has not been properly done.

● Your own business is an exciting prospect and will have a better chance of succeeding if you have spent some time working in a good salon. This experience is invaluable and ensures that a lot of mistakes can be avoided.

Where to start: Never underestimate the value of professional advice. If you are starting a business for the first time, get as much professional help and advice as you can. This does not have to cost much money. Speak to your bank, as they may recommend schemes to help new businesses. Also, you will probably have a Business Link in your area and they have many different types of help for new businesses, including help with creating your business plan, marketing and promotion. Do not rush into it and take time to plan every detail.

Consult the HABIA website. The Business Advice and Guidance section has a very useful free download: HABIA Guide to Business Success for Beauty Therapy Salons. Plus the Official Health & Safety Implementation Pack available in the Online Store is an invaluable tool for salons.

Teaching

The way in which the nail industry has grown has produced a lot of 'nail' trainers, both good and bad. It has been traditional for product companies to have trainers in various parts of the country, usually on a self-employed basis and often connected with sales of the products. Many training schools have opened (and many have closed) on the strength of income received from short courses and product sales. Private schools and colleges of further education who offer qualifications in beauty therapy often have the facility to teach 'nail' qualifications and many bring in technicians to teach the subject rather than relying on their beauty therapy lecturers. Usually, a minimum of 3 years' industry experience is required to provide training on behalf of a product company. When teaching candidates for formal qualifications, most teachers need to have achieved, at least, the qualification of Assessor (your local FE college will have details on how to achieve this). This requires a minimum of 5 years' industrial experience, that is working in a commercially active salon for 5 years before becoming an Assessor and holding the relevant qualifications in the sector. All Assessors must also undertake Continuing Professional Development (CPD) throughout their career.

Plus points:

- Can be carried out part-time and provide additional income and interest
- A very good way of maintaining high standards
- Job satisfaction (and often frustration) in teaching new skills to students
- If connected to a product company, there is involvement with the industry as a whole.

Minus points:

- Full-time teaching of 'nails' is hard to find
- If self-employed and connected to a company, there is no guaranteed income.

Things to consider:

- A good technician does not necessarily make a good teacher, and vice versa.
- To become a good teacher, it is worth learning teaching skills in addition to 'nail' skills. If working in a college, it is usually necessary to be a qualified Vocational Assessor.
- Part-time teaching can often fit very well with working in a salon. You will be bringing real experience to your students, supplementing your income and gaining variety in your working life.

Where to start: Product companies usually expect a minimum number of years' experience, and teaching for formal qualifications requires 5 years' experience before the relevant Assessor qualification can be achieved.

If company training is an option, send an up-to-date CV to the company with a covering letter explaining that you are interested in becoming a trainer. If formal teaching is preferred, it is important to understand that, in order to achieve the Assessors qualification, actual teaching needs to be done. Therefore a teaching job must be found first. Some product companies provide teaching for formal qualifications, as does a division of the trade association, Association of Nail Technicians (ANT). They could be approached in the same way as above. Also FE colleges that run courses in Beauty Therapy often have vacancies for specialist teachers, especially those with extensive experience in a nail salon. Both product companies and colleges will be able to advise you on how to achieve an Assessors qualification.

Sales/demonstrator

Product companies often have a salesperson who visits salons to sell and demonstrate products and technicians who demonstrate on stands at trade shows.

Requirements: A skilled technician with a good understanding of how products work would be suited to this job. Experience in sales would also be a bonus.

Personality is very important; this job needs an outgoing person who communicates well with people. Qualifications are always desirable and personal insurance is recommended. It is unlikely that a set period of experience would be required, but it is obviously preferable.

Plus points:

● Variety of work

● Involvement in the wider industry

● Usually part-time, so could fit around clients.

Minus points:

● Full-time jobs are rare

● Part-time jobs may be casual (that is, only when required).

Things to consider:

● There are not many companies that are large enough to employ full-time sales reps. Many have part-time technicians who are either employed or self-employed and work on a commission basis. Demonstrators are often technicians connected with the company who are prepared to work at trade shows.

Where to start: Research the companies to see what they sell and who to. Look out in trade magazines for vacancies. Have a good CV prepared.

Media technicians

The nail industry is beginning to achieve a higher profile in the market and people are becoming more aware of 'nails' as part of grooming and fashion. A separate person to do 'nails' on photographic shoots and catwalk shows is now acceptable (if the budget allows).

Requirements: A high level of skill, creativity and imagination is needed. Insurance is essential. Patience, adaptability and discretion are essential commodities. The level of skill is more important than time spent working, but this technician will often be called upon to solve many different problems and nothing takes the place of experience.

Plus points:

● Wide variety of work

● Chance of meeting and working with famous people

● High fees for some types of work

● High profile for technician.

Minus points:

● Work not regular

● Long hours of waiting around following frantic working sessions

● Dealing with sometimes difficult people

● Carrying a very heavy kit

● Working very long hours on some jobs

● Lots of free or low-paid work in order to achieve the recognition needed to get paid work.

Things to consider: At the present time, there are very few technicians who get 'published' in the media. Lots appear in trade magazines. Media work is a very different world and technicians need to be like make-up artists and hairdressers who can help create images for advertising, editorial work and fashion shows. A portfolio of work needs to be compiled to show prospective employers. As a general 'rule of thumb', work that receives credits (that is, the person's name with the pictures) is usually low-paid or even free; work that does not receive credit is usually paid for by way of a fee. It is advisable to use the services of an agent as most magazines, advertising agencies, designers and photographers are used to using an agent to arrange the creative team. Agents obviously charge a fee, but the potential earnings of this kind of work are very high.

Where to start: There are many 'special occasion' opportunities for technicians. These may be weddings, fancy dress parties, local fashion shows held by shops or colleges. Keep a lookout for local activities and approach relevant outlets (e.g. fancy dress hire shops, fashion shops, colleges) to offer your services. Keep pictures of work you have done.

A way of gaining experience for this type of work is to contact hair and make-up agencies, usually based in London but there are some provincial ones, to find out if they represent any technicians. If they do, offer to assist the technician. There is not usually any payment for this type of work but the experience will be invaluable.

This list of career routes is not exhaustive; there are many variants and combinations. The nail industry is an exciting place to be and there is a place for everyone. Artificial nails is not the only skill and treatment involved; there are many who specialise in natural nail care, and it seems that the majority of European women prefer natural nails to artificial ones, even if they have used the artificial variety to help them on their way.

The most important message is that recognised qualifications, practice, dedication and a lifetime of learning are essential for real success.

SUMMARY

This chapter has sketched the education and skills training required by a modern nail technician and outlined the eight most common career paths the technician can follow, highlighting the advantages and disadvantages of each.

chapter 2

ANATOMY AND PHYSIOLOGY AS RELATED TO NAIL TREATMENTS

Learning objectives

In this chapter you will learn about:

- why anatomy and physiology is important knowledge for technicians
- the structures and functions of the skin
- an understanding of the skin as an organ and its relevance in all nail treatments
- the basic structure and functions of the cardiovascular system
- the basic structure and functions of the lymphatic system
- the basic structure and functions of the skeletal system
- the basic structure and functions of the muscular system
- the basic structure and functions of the nervous system
- some common conditions relating to each of the body systems
- the nail unit in depth

INTRODUCTION

This chapter provides all the essential theoretical information about the skin and nails, the parts of the body that are affected by the application of artificial nails. It covers all the requirements of the Occupational Standards and puts nail treatments in the context of the potential problems of an individual client.

ESSENTIAL KNOWLEDGE

Hairdressers learn about the structure of hair, how it grows and where it comes from; beauty therapists learn about the structure of skin, the underlying muscles and bones and the basic workings of the human body. They do this in order to understand the area that is being treated, how to vary treatments for individuals, how to recognise potential problems and how to put right something that has gone wrong. Nail technicians must do the same. They must learn about the area of the human body they deal with. This will ensure that they work safely, understand when and how to adapt treatments, give the best possible advice to their clients and know how to deal with problems.

Areas of the body are not isolated. The body functions because several systems within the human body work together. When one of these systems does not work properly, many areas of the body and other systems are affected. The main 'systems' in the human body are: nervous system; cardiovascular system (heart, lungs and circulation); digestive system; skeletal system; endocrine system (glands); urinary system; and reproductive system. Many organs are concerned with and form part of these systems and, when they all function correctly and efficiently, we have a healthy body.

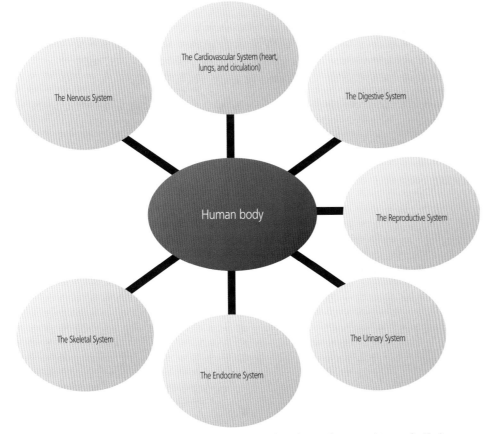

Although it is not necessary to have an in-depth understanding of all the workings of the human body, it is useful to have a basic understanding of how all areas affect the parts relevant to a nail technician. It can help to explain such things as how a poor diet can affect nail growth, why a 'systemic' disorder (a disorder of the body as a whole but arising from one of the systems) can be noticed in the nails.

A **natural nail** is an adaptation of the skin and is surrounded by skin. By understanding how the skin is formed and why, helps us to understand how a nail is created and what may be happening if the nail is growing less than perfectly. The hands and feet are a collection of bones, connected by muscles, nourished by a blood supply and surrounded by skin. A thorough knowledge of this part of the body is a good basis for a nail technician because it will:

- help you to *recognise any disorders* and understand what may have caused them
- assist your understanding of how these specific parts of the body function
- demonstrate a knowledge and understanding of the area being worked on during treatments by answering any question the client may ask; this will *promote professionalism and generate confidence*
- help you to choose the *most suitable products* for the client and *understand their effects* on the skin and nails.

THE SKIN

The skin is the largest organ of the human body and plays many essential roles. It weighs 6–10 lb (3–4 kg) and measures approximately 20 sq feet in an adult. It is protective, helps with temperature control and is involved in one of the senses: touch. It is a giant, washable, stretchable, tough, waterproof sensory apparatus covering your whole body.

A body's skin has basically the same structure all over, but with some local variations, e.g. thickness, blood and nerve supply, colour, etc. Hair and nails are made of modified skin cells.

Cross-section through the skin

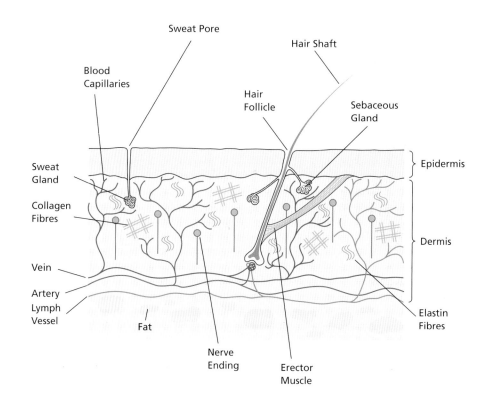

Functions

The skin performs eight main functions for the body.

1. Protection

Skin provides a waterproof coat that acts as a barrier to protect the body from dirt, minor injuries, bacterial infection and chemical attack. It does this in a number of ways.

- The first barrier is a mixture of oil (**sebum**) and **sweat** which forms a slightly acidic film over the skin's surface. This discourages the growth of **bacteria** and **fungus**. The sebum, the natural oil produced by sebaceous glands in the hair **follicles** of the skin, creates a waterproof coating which helps prevent the skin lose essential water and, to a certain extent, also prevents the skin from absorbing too much water. This effect is minimal, as the skin can be quite absorbent, especially when it suffers from dryness.

- The second barrier is the uppermost layer of the skin (**stratum corneum**) that can act as a filter against invading bacteria. The healthy construction of this barrier provides good protection but it is very easily damaged. It relies on a good level of natural moisture to hold the **keratinised** skin cells together. On the hands, especially, this moisture is very often lost through environmental damage (detergents, water and so on).

- The third barrier is the production of a pigment called **melanin** in the skin; this protects lower-level tissues against **ultraviolet (UV) light** damage.

- In addition to these barriers, the skin has an early warning system against invasion by a chemical that the body will not tolerate or is sensitive or allergic to. Irritation on any part of the skin is usually a sign that an **allergic reaction** is starting. If an **allergen** (substance that is causing the reaction) is promptly removed, the reaction should subside. This reaction is more common when a substance is applied to the skin as part of a treatment, but can also be the result of a substance getting inside the body either by **ingestion** (via the mouth) or **inhalation** (by breathing it in).

2. Sensation

There are several different nerve endings carried in the skin that respond to heat, cold, touch, pressure and pain.

3. Heat regulation

The skin helps to keep the body at a constant temperature of 37°C. It is able to do this in several ways: by dilation or constriction of the blood vessels (**capillaries**) near the surface of the skin thus retaining heat or allowing it to escape; through sweat, produced by the sweat glands, which evaporates and cools the body; and by having fat in the **subcutaneous layer** that insulates the body.

4. Excretion

Perspiration and some waste products, such as water and salt, are lost through the skin.

TIP ✓

The best moisture for the skin is its own natural level of water. Helping to prevent the loss of natural moisture is the best treatment.

5. Secretion

Sebum, which moisturises and protects, is produced in the **sebaceous glands.**

6. Vitamin D formation

The skin is able to produce **vitamin D** through the action of ultraviolet light. This vitamin is essential to the absorption of calcium in the digestive system.

7. Storage

The skin stores fat and water that can be used by any part of the body as necessary.

8. Absorption

Some substances can be absorbed through the skin and will stay in that area or enter the blood stream and be carried throughout the body. (The effect of over absorption can be seen after a good soak in the bath!) This absorbency can be useful when applying nourishing products to the skin but it can also be quite the reverse: the skin can sometimes allow penetration of harmful substances. **Absorption** through the skin is one of the routes of entry to the human body for chemicals, together with inhalation and ingestion. The skin should be protected when using potentially harmful substances so that the chances of absorption are minimised.

Classes of skin

There are two main classes of skin; both of which can be found on the hands and feet. (The other types are the **mucous membrane** that lines the inside of the body's orifices and **mucocutaneous** skin, which is found at the junction of the mucous membrane, hairy skin, lips and tongue). We are mainly concerned here with the two major types.

Thick, hairless skin

Hairless skin is found on the palms of the hands and the soles of the feet. As the name suggests, this type does not have any hair follicles and therefore has no oil-producing glands, which makes it prone to dryness. It has many sweat glands, which assist in gripping objects, and heightens sensitivity. Certain layers of the skin in this type are thicker and ridged to allow for wear and tear and to give a 'non-slip' surface. It has an **epidermis** of about 1.5mm in thickness and a **dermis** of about 3mm.

Thin, hairy skin

Hairy skin covers much of the body and, along with the many structures found in all skin, has hair follicles. Its epidermal layer is about 0.07mm in thickness (half the thickness of hairless skin) and a dermis of about 1–2mm.

Layers of skin

It can be seen from the earlier diagram that there are three main layers of skin: the epidermis, the dermis and the subcutaneous layer. In carrying out hand, feet and nail treatments, we are more concerned with the structure of the epidermis although the dermis does play some part.

The epidermis

Cells in the epidermis: The epidermis is of special interest as nails are evolutionary adaptations of this cell-producing area, as are hair, hooves, horns, scales and feathers. It is this layer that is treated in manicures and pedicures and an improvement to the condition of this layer is what is most sought by clients who request a manicure.

The epidermis consists of layers of skin cells in various stages of development, growth, adaptation and death. The adaptation will depend on where in the body the skin is situated:

- in a hair follicle the cells will form a hair
- in the **matrix** of the nail, they will form a **nail plate**
- in areas exposed to ultraviolet light, they will produce more melanin
- on the palms of the hands and soles of the feet, the clear layer (**stratum lucidum**) will be much thicker.

This progression of cells takes place from the lower level of the epidermis up through to the surface of the skin. The cells go through many changes during this journey. The progression of a skin cell in an area of skin that does not require any adaptations and is normal and healthy takes around 4–6 weeks. Skin disorders or other general health problems can influence this process. The little skin cell ends up keratinised, flat and non-living and part of the protective stratum corneum. It is eventually shed from the skin and often found in house dust (or the inside of a pair of tights!).

Layers in the epidermis

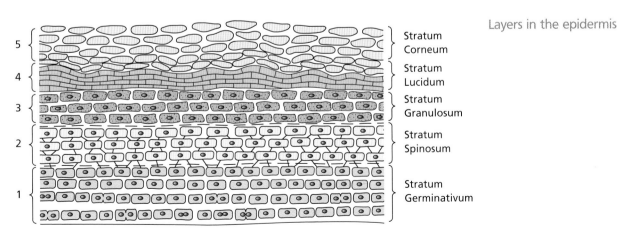

5 Stratum Corneum
4 Stratum Lucidum
3 Stratum Granulosum
2 Stratum Spinosum
1 Stratum Germinativum

Dermis

Layers in the epidermis:

1 The base layer or **stratum germinativum** is where the skin cells are formed and is responsible for the growth of the epidermis. These cells contain melanin and the early stages of **keratin**, which is a protein, and will eventually form either a protective layer on the top of the skin or be adapted to form nails or hair.

The cells here are continually dividing and reproducing themselves. This is a process called **mitosis**. The cells are plump, surrounded by the porous cell membrane, full of cellular fluid called **cytoplasm** and with an active nucleus that is responsible for cell reproduction and function and carries the genes inherited from our parents.

As these cells divide and reproduce themselves, they are pushed up and into the next layer of the epidermis.

2 The **stratum spinosum**, or prickle-cell layer, is where most of the cells have developed spines that connect them to surrounding cells. The nucleus is becoming less active as reproduction has slowed down or stopped.

Some of the cells have adapted into **melanocytes** that produce the pigment melanin. These are the cells that help protect the lower layers of the skin from ultraviolet damage from the sun. The amount of melanocytes depends on our skin colour. Black skins that have evolved from very hot countries, for example, have significantly more melanin for maximum protection. Fairer-skinned people who tend to come from the colder countries have much less pigment. Fair-skinned people who have been sunbathing or using a sunbed have developed extra melanocytes for their protection and this is what appears as a suntan. Sunburn is where too much radiation from the sun has been on the skin before melanocytes have been formed to protect it. This radiation has been able to penetrate to lower levels and could cause problems in later life. There is a great deal of advice becoming available now as the effects of overexposure to the sun's radiation are further understood.

The amount of melanin can vary in the same area of skin. Patches of darker skin can be evident, sometimes on the back of the hands, the face or chest. This can be due to an overproduction of melanin and is stimulated by ultraviolet radiation, but is more usually caused by a hormone imbalance, for example during pregnancy or when taking a contraceptive pill. In older people, 'liver spots' on the back of the hand are caused by minor **sun damage** throughout their life. Freckles are also the result of sun damage and are often found on lighter skin as this type is more prone to suffer from overexposure.

There is an opposite effect to the overproduction of melanin that results in lighter patches on the skin. This is called **vitiligo** or **leucoderma**, and it is where the skin has lost its ability to produce melanin. There is also a condition where the whole of the skin is unable to produce melanin, called **albinism**. People with this condition have very light skin and their hair and eyes lack colour.

None of these conditions is infectious, but the skin often needs extra protection and the hands are the areas that tend to suffer the most.

3 The **stratum granulosum**, or granular layer, is where the cells are beginning to die. They appear much less plump and the nucleus begins to break up. The cytoplasm (or cellular fluid) is thickening and becoming granular where keratin is beginning to form.

4 The stratum lucidum, or clear layer, is an adapted layer that is found only on the palms of the hand and soles of the feet – that is, the thick hairless class of skin. This extra layer gives specific characteristics to these areas. The hands and feet need to grip: the hands to hold things and the feet to grip the ground. This clear layer helps to form the dips and ridges in our hands and feet that are known as our 'finger or hand prints' (our feet also have the same 'prints'). The skin in these areas does not produce sebum (natural oil) as it does not have any hair follicles: oil would make our hands and feet slippery. This area of skin only produces sweat from millions of sweat glands. A small amount of sweat, together with the ridges and dips, helps our grip. Too much sweat makes our skin slippery and is usually a hormonal effect arising from an emotional moment such as fright or nervousness. Some people produce an excess amount of sweat on the palms of their hands. If 'slippery' hands are noticed, then the technician should take extra care in preparing the nail (see Chapter 5).

5 The stratum corneum, or cornified layer, is the uppermost layer of skin. The cells have flattened, lost their nucleus and all the cytoplasm and have become keratinised. The flat cells are held together in a type of 'brick-wall' arrangement by intercellular cement, which is mostly composed of lipids, a natural fat produced by the skin together with sebum and sweat and keratin bonds. This forms a wonderful barrier and protection for the skin but it is easily damaged, especially on the hands.

As newly keratinised cells are pushed up, the older flakes of dead skin are shed in a process called **desquamation** in which the bonds are broken down. This will happen naturally but can be speeded up by environmental excesses such as pollution or hard water that break down the intercellular cement.

There are many conditions that affect this whole cycle and there are skin disorders that can speed up the process, such as **psoriasis**, or slow it down.

It is very important for a nail technician to understand this process just described, for two reasons. First it shows us why the skin surrounding the nail and that on the hand must be cared for and, second, it is the basis of how nails are formed.

Below the epidermis is another part of the skin that is very different and much thicker; this is called the dermis.

The dermis

This layer carries the many structures that exist within the skin, such as nerves, blood capillaries, nerve endings, sweat ducts that open onto the surface of the skin as pores and sebaceous glands that open into hair follicles. It helps to serve the epidermis by carrying a vast network of capillaries and it gives the epidermis structural support.

TIP

Women, in particular, sometimes find patches of darker skin at the sides of their neck. This is often due to a reaction of the sun on the area of skin that has perfume sprayed on to it regularly. Also hormonal disturbances, such as taking the contraceptive pill, pregnancy and the menopause, can cause discoloration of the cheeks or the face.

Fibres in the dermis:

One of the main features of the dermis is the network of strong fibres, of which there are two types: **collagen** and **elastin**. They are both made of protein.

Collagen acts as a support to the skin, keeps it firm and gives it a plump, youthful appearance. Elastin gives the skin its elastic properties, allowing it to move and stretch but then return to its original position. In young skin, both types of fibres are plentiful, but as the skin ages, the fibres start to break down and are not replaced so readily. A lack of collagen allows the skin to form into wrinkles between muscles and a lack of elastin allows the skin to become softer and less firm.

The skin on the back of the hands does not always demonstrate a person's exact biological age as it is prone to misuse and damage and can look older than necessary. The skin of the face is usually given more care and can often appear younger than the person's actual age. The skin on the backs of the hands has very little support in the way of muscles and stored fat. It does, however, have some very strong tendons that move the fingers and large blood vessels that supply the hand. As the elastin and collagen become less effective, owing to age and damage from ultraviolet light and weather, the tendons and blood vessels become more apparent and thus add to the ageing appearance.

Other structures in the dermis:

- Nerves. The dermis carries a vast network of nerve endings that send a whole host of messages back to the brain where the messages are 'decoded' and any work that the body needs to do is undertaken. Nerves give us our sense of touch and our fingertips are some of the most sensitive areas of our body because they have a large number of sensory nerves. In addition to the ability to feel, the nerves also provide a form of protection. If extreme heat is touched, sensory nerves send an emergency message to the brain; the brain recognises the emergency and sends another message, via the nervous system, to the muscles that will then move the relevant area of the body away from danger. The type of nerve that sends a message to a muscle is a motor nerve. This procedure can take place in a fraction of a second.

- Blood vessels. These make up a network of fine arteries, veins and capillaries that carry blood around the body to maintain the health of all the organs, including the skin. Blood carries nutrients (food) and oxygen to every cell in the body and removes waste products. The blood plays several essential roles in the working of the whole body. With regard to the skin, its main role is connected with heat regulation. If the body is becoming too hot, the blood vessels dilate (become bigger) in the skin. This assists heat loss. The reverse happens if the body is becoming cold: the vessels constrict, keeping the blood deeper within the body to conserve heat.

  If the skin is damaged by a superficial cut, the tiny capillaries are severed and the skin bleeds. Some of the cells that make up the blood are capable of forming together and creating a clot that blocks the ruptured vessels

TIP ✔

A gentle pinch to the skin on the backs of the hands demonstrates age and skin condition. A young and hydrated skin recovers immediately. Older and/or dehydrated skin takes longer to recover. Experiment on different ages of skin to discover the difference.

and prevent further blood loss. The redness seen around a cut or other damage is an increase in the blood supply that helps the cells to repair themselves.

Increased blood supply in the skin causing redness without any obvious damage could be the body's defence mechanism in action. A harmful item (such as a splinter) or chemical could have entered the skin and be causing an irritation. Cells within the dermis called mast cells release a chemical called **histamine** that increases the blood supply to the area and attempts to destroy the invader. This defence mechanism can progress from a slight redness, to itching and even to blisters and swelling. If the allergen (the substance that is causing the allergic reaction) or irritant is removed at the first hint of trouble, the reactions will often subside. If not, the condition can continue and result in a painful and distressing type of **dermatitis**.

- Lymph vessels. Like the network of blood vessels, another system carries a fluid called **lymph** around the body. Lymph is similar in many ways to blood, in that it circulates to all the cells and carries a certain amount of nutrients, but its main role is as our body's defence mechanism. The lymph fights and removes bacteria and other invasive substances and carries excess fluid away from cells and surrounding tissue. The lymphatic fluid is 'filtered' by lymph glands situated all over the body. When the body is fighting an infection glands, often in the neck, can feel swollen and tender.

The lymphatic system does not have a pump to move it around in the way that the blood has the heart. It relies, instead, on muscular movement to push it along. The flow of lymph can sometimes be sluggish and excess fluid and waste can build up in certain areas.

There are no lymph glands sited near the feet and gravity will often cause excess fluid to collect in this area. The nearest glands are at the top of the leg in the groin and behind the knee. The nearest glands to the hands are on the inside of the elbows. Massage in these areas, with movements towards the glands, can help to increase circulation and reduce excess fluid in the hands and feet.

- Sweat glands. **Sweat glands**, with their own blood supply, are sited in the dermis and a tube, or duct, leads directly from the gland through the dermis and epidermis to open onto the surface and is seen as a pore in the skin. There are more sweat glands on the palms of the hands and soles of the feet than anywhere else on the body.

The most common type of gland, **eccrine glands**, are found all over the body and help to regulate the body's heat by secreting small amounts of sweat all the time. This function also helps to regulate the body's salt levels and eliminates some waste products. It helps to keep the skin hydrated and is part of the acid mantle that helps protect the skin. The level of sweat produced can be affected by the nervous system, for example emotions can raise the level, you may have noticed how anxiety often makes your palms very sweaty.

Another, less common type, are **apocrine glands**, which are situated under the arm and groin. The sweat secreted from these has a different chemical composition and hormones control its production.

- Hair follicles. Another structure found in the dermis of the skin are **hair follicles** (with the exception of the palms of the hands, the soles of the feet and the lips). A follicle is a long sack-like shape where epidermal tissue extends from the surface of the skin down through the epidermis and dermis to its own blood supply. At the base of the follicle is an area called the germinal matrix where certain epidermal cells are 'instructed' by their nucleus to adapt their growth and form together to create a hair. As in the epidermis, the new cells push the older ones upward and the hair grows up the follicle and out through the surface of the skin. Different types of hair grow on different areas of the skin. Although the same structure, the hairs have different characteristics, for example hair on the head has a longer life span than the hair of an eyelash. This is why eyelashes only grow to a certain length before falling out.

- Sebaceous glands. Connected to the follicle is another structure: the sebaceous gland. This secretes a natural oil, sebum, onto the hair shaft and the skin's surface. The oil helps to lubricate the hair shaft and plays an important role in the skin's protective functions. It helps create a waterproof barrier and therefore keep moisture in the cells of the skin and it also, together with sweat, creates a slightly acidic covering on the skin that acts as a bactericide and discourages the growth of unwanted micro-organisms. This covering is known as the **acid mantle**.

- pH values. For the skin to remain healthy it needs to maintain the degree of acidity created by the sebum and sweat. If this changes too much the skin can become dry and if it changes drastically the skin is damaged. A scale called the **pH value** measures acidity and alkalinity. Low numbers (1–6) are acidic and high numbers (6–14) are alkaline. A value of 7 is neutral. Examples of acids can be found in citrus fruits, such as lemons. This level of acidity would not damage the skin unless it were left on it for a period of time. Fruit acids are usually the base of a popular ingredient in skin care: **AHA** (alpha hydroxy acids). These can be useful in skin care as they help to remove dead skin cells and debris from the surface of the skin and generate cell renewal in areas that need assistance, such as the face and backs of the hands. **Acids** with low pH values would 'burn' the skin, causing extreme irritation and blisters.

At the other end of the scale are the **alkalines** that can have a similar effect on the skin. The milder alkalines are often used in skin treatments. Sodium hydroxide is sometimes used to soften and remove unwanted skin cells, for example in a cuticle remover. Soap is alkaline and is very drying to the skin. Extreme alkalines, such as household bleach, will damage skin in the same way that acids will.

The pH value of the skin is naturally 5.5–5.6 – that is, slightly acidic, and skin preparations that are called 'pH balanced' will have a similar pH value.

Another structure attached to the hair follicle is a tiny muscle, the arrector pili muscle. When this contracts it causes the hair to stand upright in the skin. It does this to help trap heat and also as a response to some emotional reactions. The effect is usually known as 'goose bumps'.

Below the level of the dermis is a layer of stored fat. This fat is a supply of energy for the body and also helps contain heat within the body.

Common conditions of the skin

- One of the most common skin conditions a nail technician is likely to come across is dermatitis. This literally means an inflammation of the skin and is non-specific (meaning the cause of the inflammation is not necessarily known). It is caused by an irritant to the skin or other part of the body activating the body's immune system so that white blood cells fight the invasion. Removing the cause can cure it.

- Eczema, on the other hand, has symptoms very similar to dermatitis, in that it is an inflammation of the skin, but it is usually a genetic condition.

- Psoriasis is a condition where there is an overproduction skin cells and scaly patches of dry, dead skin can be seen.

There is a more detailed discussion of skin conditions in Chapter 4.

BLOOD CIRCULATION

Blood needs to be carried to every cell of the body. It is the internal transport system that keeps the body functioning. It links every part of the body with every other part.

- The blood carries food in the form of nutrients extracted from the digestive system and oxygen from the lungs to every cell, where they are converted into the fuel necessary to the functioning of the cell.

- Waste products produced by every cell are carried away: **carbon dioxide** to the lungs, and the other waste products to the liver and kidneys where they are extracted from the blood.

- Many different glands around the body secrete hormones. These are controlled by the brain and are the chemical messengers that instruct the organs and tissues how and when to function. Hormones are transported by the blood system.

- The body's defence mechanism to fight the invasion of foreign bodies, such as bacteria, viruses, harmful chemicals, etc. is also a major function of the blood. Cells in the blood are able to recognise any invasion and decide whether it needs fighting or whether it is harmless. If it needs to be fought, other cells in the blood attack and, if necessary, bring other systems of the body into the fight to help defend against disease or damage.

- Blood circulation also helps with the control of heat. It distributes heat evenly around the body and, when necessary, helps it to cool down by dilating (opening) vessels near the skin surface to lose some heat, or contracting those vessels to keep the heat nearer the centre of the body.

- If the skin is damaged by a superficial cut, the tiny capillaries are severed and the skin bleeds. Some of the cells that form blood are capable of forming together and creating a clot that blocks the ruptured vessels and prevents further blood loss. The redness seen around a cut or other damage is an increase in the blood supply as it helps the cells to repair themselves.

The heart

The circulation of the blood needs a pump: the **heart**, a four-chambered, muscular organ. The muscles of the heart are of a special type; instead of being individual fibres bundled together, they are connected so that a contraction in one area stimulates a wave of contractions throughout. Its muscle function is controlled by the autonomic nervous system, that is it happens without any conscious effort on our part.

The upper right chamber (right **atrium**) of the heart receives de-oxygenated blood that has travelled all around the body providing oxygen to the cells via two major **veins**: the superior and inferior **vena cava**. This travels into the lower right chamber (right **ventricle**) where strong muscles pump it directly to the lungs, close by, via the **pulmonary** arteries. The blood, low in oxygen but high in carbon dioxide that has been collected from the cells, collects oxygen from the tiny air sacks in the lungs that are filled when we breathe in and releases the carbon dioxide into the air sacks that is then dispersed when we breathe out.

When the blood has passed through the lungs, it is delivered back to the upper left chamber of the heart (left atrium) via the pulmonary veins. This blood, high in oxygen and low in carbon dioxide, passes into the lower left chamber (left ventricle) where very powerful muscles send it on its journey around the body again via a huge blood vessel, the **aorta**.

The heart beats on average 70–80 times a minute in a healthy body. This pump starts when we are an embryo in the womb and continues until we die. Quite literally, our lives depend on it!

The blood travels along three main types of vessels: **arteries**, **veins** and **capillaries**.

1 Arteries are the vessels that carry the blood away from the heart (remember: A = artery and away). The blood is oxygenated and bright red. The structure of the artery has a thick muscular wall that helps maintain the pressure of blood in order for it to travel to all areas of the body. If an artery is cut, this pressure causes the blood to pump out with each heartbeat. Arteries are usually situated deeper within the body to protect them from this kind of damage.

2 Veins carry blood that is returning from all parts of the body to the heart. These vessels do not have the muscular walls of arteries but they do have 'non-return' valves to keep the blood flowing in one direction, that is to the heart. The movement of the blood is mainly affected by the movement of the muscles in the areas around the veins and by the flow generated by the heart. This is one important reason why exercise and movement is essential for a healthy body. There are more veins than arteries and many are situated closer to the surface of the skin. If a vein is cut, the blood is seen to well out rather than the way it pumps out of an artery.

3 Capillaries are the link between the arteries and veins and allow the blood to reach every cell in the body. They are tiny, thread-like vessels with very thin walls and they branch out to every extremity. Their walls are so thin that the nutrients and oxygen carried in the blood are able to pass through the wall and into the tissue fluid that bathes the spaces between

---

TIP ✓

Some general terms when relating to the positioning within the body:
Distal: furthest away from the body
Proximal: closest to the body
Lateral: at the side
Medial: middle
Anterior: front
Posterior: back

cells. Red blood cells are too large to pass through the capillary walls, just the clear blood plasma carrying the nutrients is transferred. These substances, which are essential for life, flow naturally through the wall from an area of high level (the blood) into an area with a lower level (the tissues). Waste materials from the cells, in the same way, flow from the tissues into the blood to be carried away for elimination.

For the purposes of manicure and pedicure, an understanding of how the blood circulation works is required. However, you will only need to remember the main arteries and veins in the hand, arm, leg and foot.

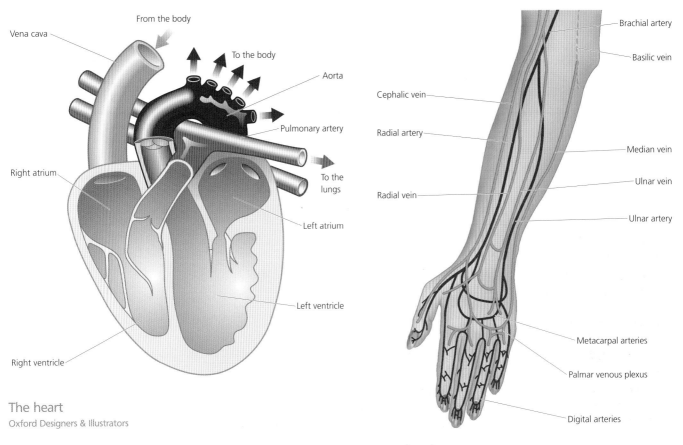

The heart
Oxford Designers & Illustrators

Hand and arm
Oxford Designers & Illustrators

Hand and arm

The artery that serves the arms branches indirectly from the aorta and is known as the **brachial artery**. It runs down the middle of the inside of the upper arm, quite deep, to just below the elbow where it branches into:

- The **radial artery** running down the thumb side of the lower arm where it supplies oxygenated blood to that side of the hand and the back of the hand. It is commonly used as a pulse point as it is quite close to the surface in the wrist and the beat of the heart can be felt.

- The **ulnar artery** that runs down the other side of the lower arm, crosses the wrist and supplies that side of the hand and the palm.

There are interconnections between the radial and ulnar arteries that form the **palmar arches**: known as the deep and superficial arches. Branches from these serve the main areas of the hand (metacarpal arteries) and more branches run down the fingers (**digital arteries**) to end under each nail to supply the nail unit with blood.

The hand and arm are served by more veins than arteries to carry away the deoxygenated blood from the area. The deeper veins have the same names as the relevant arteries, that is the **radial vein** serving the thumb side of the hand and lower arm and the **ulnar vein** serving the outside of the hand and lower arm, plus the digital, metacarpal and palmar veins.

In addition to the major vessels, there are veins closer to the skin, known as superficial veins. Many of these can be seen through the skin on the back of the hand (dorsal venous network) and the palm (palmar venous plexus) and lead into the main superficial veins:

● basilic vein, seen on the back of the hand on the little finger side and up the centre of the forearm

● cephalic vein seen on the back of the hand around the thumb and up the forearm to the elbow

● median vein from the palm of the hand up the forearm where it joins the basilic vein.

Foot and lower leg

Foot and lower leg
Oxford Designers & Illustrators

Popliteal vein

Anterior tibial artery

Peroneal artery

Anterior tibial vein

Dorsal metatarsal veins

Dorsal digital veins

Long saphenous vien

Short saphenous vien

Posterior tibial vien

Dorsal pedis artery

Dorsal venous arch

Dorsal arterial arch

Metatarsal arch

Dorsal digital arteries

A large and important artery branches into each leg around the groin area: the **femoral artery**. It goes to behind the knee where it becomes the **popliteal artery** and branches into the main lower leg arteries:

● The anterior tibial artery passes between the bones of the lower leg towards the front of the leg to the ankle and from there to the top of the foot at the dorsal pedis artery. This branches to form the dorsal arterial arch and dorsal digital arteries. It then passes through the foot to form part of the plantar arch on the sole of the foot.

● The posterior tibial artery passes down the centre of the back of the leg, past the ankle to the inside of the sole. Here it branches to form the lateral and medial plantar arteries, which in turn supply the arteries to the toes. It also branches near the knee to form the peroneal artery running down the outside of the leg towards the heel.

Like the hand and arm, there are deep and superficial veins serving this area. The deep veins follow and have the same names as the main arteries. The two main superficial veins are the long **saphenous vein** which begins at the dorsal venous arch on the top of the foot and runs up the inside of the lower leg and thigh to join the femoral vein, and the short saphenous vein from the ankle up the back of the calf to the popliteal vein at the knee.

Obviously, there are many branches and smaller veins in the area that remove the deoxygenated the blood and take it on its journey back to the heart and there to the lungs.

Some common conditions involving the blood system

● Heart disease, even if it is minor, can cause a problem with circulation, leading to poor circulation at the extremities of the body. Weak nails and dry skin can result and nails can appear bluish in colour due to poor delivery of red, oxygenated blood.

● A lack of essential vitamins and minerals in the blood can affect the condition of skin and nails.

● **Anaemia**: this is a condition that results in a shortage of red blood cells, that is the cells that carry oxygen. This shortage affects the whole body. The most common symptoms are extreme tiredness and pale skin (and nail beds). In some instances, the body just needs extra iron. This condition is especially common in young girls who don't have a proper diet and women whose periods are heavy (for example during early stages of the menopause).

● **Varicose veins**: this is an impaired functioning of the valves in the veins. The veins can become swollen and tender and can result in ulcers in extreme cases. They should be avoided during a leg massage.

As with all conditions, a nail technician must never diagnose for their client. Understanding how the systems of the body work helps technicians to decide the best type of treatment for their client together with informed after care advice.

THE LYMPHATIC SYSTEM

The **lymphatic system** is a second system of circulation, closely associated with the blood circulation. It is just as complex and just as essential to the survival of the human body.

The system carries a fluid known as lymph. Lymph is a clear fluid that bathes every cell in the body and is the carrier of all the cellular requirements and waste products. Lymph carries white blood cells that are transported in and out of the blood stream as necessary. It is the main 'ingredient' of the human body's immune system. Like veins in the blood system, the vessels carrying the lymph do not have muscular walls and the pressure of a heart to act as a pump. The movement of the lymph relies on movement in nearby muscles and close arteries.

The main functions of the lymphatic system are to:

● drain the **intercellular fluid**; approximately 15 per cent of this fluid is not reabsorbed by the capillaries

● be responsible for the transportation and absorption of dietary fats

● initiates and regulates the immune responses.

The network of lymphatic vessels contains approximately 100 **lymph nodes** around the body and lymph fluid passes through at least one of these before eventually draining into venous blood. The nodes are small, kidney shaped structures and have two main functions:

1 They are filters of the fluid and will remove any unwanted micro-organisms and other foreign materials. The unwanted organisms are stored here and specialist cells (called **macrophages**) engulf and destroy the invaders.

2 They store several types of white blood cells needed for the fight and destruction of infections and release them as required.

When a harmful micro-organism enters the body, the lymph nodes usually become swollen with large amounts of the white blood cells (**lymphocytes**) that are ready to be released to destroy the invader.

If lymph nodes or vessels become blocked or the movement of lymph becomes sluggish for any reason (for example, lack of exercise, low metabolism, etc.) then local swelling may be noticed: known as **oedema**. Excess fluid is not being efficiently removed from the tissues and is very often experienced around the ankles. **Massage** techniques provided during a manicure and pedicure can encourage an efficient circulation of lymph and help to remove excess waste productions from the area.

All of the organs and systems of the human body are connected with and are influenced by each other. Some of the organs that are specifically associated with the lymphatic system are:

● The **spleen**, which is located in the abdomen. It filters the blood by breaking down old red blood cells and also manufacturers the lymphocytes essential to the immune system.

● The **tonsils** are patches of lymphatic tissue at the back of the throat. Their function is to help trap harmful materials trying to enter the body via breathing, eating and drinking.

● **Peyer's patches** – similar in function and structure to the tonsils – are located in the small intestine to destroy the bacteria that could thrive in that environment.

Some common conditions concerning the lymphatic system

- The condition that a technician is most likely to come across is dermatitis, where the immune system rushes to protect the body at one of its 'routes of entry' (see Chapter 4), that is absorption through the skin.
- Blisters are usually filled with a clear fluid; this is lymph where is collects to protect the skin.
- Oedema is a condition where fluid collects in certain areas. This is often seen in the feet and ankles as they are so far away from the heart. Exercise and stimulation by lymph drainage massage will help.
- **Lymphoedema** is similar to oedema but is due to an obstruction of the lymph vessels draining the area.

THE BONES OF THE HANDS AND FEET

The skeleton of the human body is a living structure and the framework that supports and protects the whole body. It functions in the following ways.

- Support: the skeleton creates the shape of the body allowing it to function, that is stand erect and move via the attachment of muscles. There are also other types of connections that provide support for the organs of the body.
- Protection: sections of the skeleton create cavities that encase and protect some essential structures of the body: the skull provides an exceptionally strong cavity for the brain; the spine provides a canal for the spinal cord that connects the brain to all other parts of the body; the rib cage provides a cavity and protective structure for some of the most important and delicate organs, e.g. the heart, lungs, spleen.
- Manufactures red blood cells. The central part of many bones is filled with a substance called bone marrow and is where red blood cells are manufactured.
- The skeleton also stores minerals.

The bones of a very young person are relatively soft and slightly bendy. As the body ages, the bones calcify and become harder and more brittle. Babies are born with 270 soft bones (64 more than an adult). Many of these will fuse together by their early twenties into the 206 hard, permanent bones.

All the bones articulate (move) against each other in order that the body can move. The areas where two or more bones come together are called joints. There are three types of joint:

1 Immoveable joints or **fibrous joints**. These are the skull and the pelvis. Each of these skeletal structures is created from several separate bones that are joined together with strong fibrous tissue. There are certain times when these need to have some movement. The skull needs to change shape during birth and a woman's pelvis can sometimes slightly enlarge during pregnancy and birth.

2 Slightly moveable joints or **cartilaginous joints**. These joints are found between the many bones in the spine where some movement is needed but is restricted.

3 Moveable joints or **synovial joints**. There are many more of these and they also fall into different categories depending on their range of movement:

- ball and socket joints allows circular movement, for example the shoulder and hip joints

- hinge joints allow a movement of approximately 90°, these are found in the elbows, knees and fingers

- gliding joints allow surfaces to glide over each other, for example the wrist and ankle joints

- pivot joints allow rotation around an axis, for example the movement allowed by the bones in the lower arm (radius and ulna) that gives the hand its circular movement when the palm is turned up and down.

For the purposes of hand and foot treatments, it is only the moveable (synovial) joins that are relevant.

The ends of the bones need protection from articulating against each other and there is a system in each joint that allows this movement and offers protection. The joint is surrounded by the synovial membrane that secretes synovial fluid and lubricates the joint to allow free movement. The bones are protected by **cartilage**, a gel-like substance, that also provides some cushioning.

There are several disorders and diseases that affect joints and therefore have implications during a hand or foot treatment. One of the most common is **arthritis** that can be caused by an illness or by wear and tear. Arthritis can cause the joints to become inflamed, painful and, in later stages, deformed.

For the purposes of massage, it is necessary to understand the positioning of the bones in the hands, lower arms, feet and lower legs and how they move against each other.

The forearm

The elbow joint is where the large upper arm bone, the **humerus**, articulates mainly with one of the two forearm bones, the **ulna**, creating a hinge joint. The other forearm bone is the **radius**, attached to the ulna at the elbow.

The presence and positioning of two bones in the forearm allows the hand to rotate, that is, the palm can be turned uppermost or it can rotate at the wrist so the back of the hand is uppermost. This is achieved by the articulation of the bone on the thumb side of the arm, the radius, rotation over the bone on the little finger side of the arm, the ulna (the radius rotates). This is a pivot joint.

The end of the radius articulates with the bones in the wrist, which, together, provide a wide range of movement for the hand.

The hand

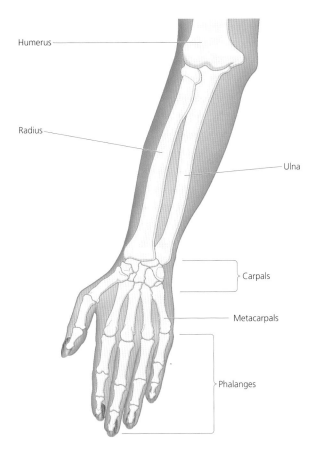

Humerus

Radius

Ulna

Carpals

Metacarpals

Phalanges

The hand
Oxford Designers & Illustrators

At the wrist there are several small bones, **carpals**, that glide over each other (gliding joint) allowing a great range of movement for the hand. There are eight carpals arranged in two rows of four. These bones fit closely together and are held in place by **ligaments**.

The palm of the hand has five bones, the **metacarpals**, which can be felt along the back of the hand and these articulate with the finger bones, the **phalanges**.

The hand has four fingers, each with three phalanges, and a thumb with two phalanges. Each bone of the fingers and thumb comes together in a hinge joint, which allows for the vast amount of dexterity a human hand can demonstrate. There is a certain amount of rotation at the joint between the metacarpals and the phalanges that allows further movement for the fingers and thumb. The hand has, in total 27 bones.

Our nearest relations in the animal kingdom, the apes, are very close to us in terms of anatomy and physiology. One of the main differences, which some evolutionists believe is the main reason humans evolved much further than the apes, is the movement we have in our thumb. A human thumb has a wide range of movement allowing us to become much more dextrous. An ape, an indeed a young baby learning to control their hands, can only move their thumb towards the hand and away in a pincer movement. The full movement of the human thumb allows for minute control and dextrousness.

The lower leg

The arrangement of bones in the lower leg is, in many ways, similar to the lower arm. The longest bone in the human body, the **femur**, or thighbone, extends from the hip to the knee. The femur articulates with one of the lower leg bones, the **tibia**, at a hinge joint, the knee. The knee has an extra bone that acts as a protective, the **patella**.

The lower leg, like the lower arm, has two bones that allow a certain amount of rotation of the foot. The larger one, the tibia, runs down the centre and the inside of the leg and is the one you can feel with a sharp edge as the shinbone. This articulates with the **talus** (one of the ankle bones) at the ankle. The smaller bone, the **fibula**, articulates with the tibia at the knee then runs down the outside of the leg to articulate, like the tibia, with the talus. It is the knobbly ends of these bones that stick out on either side of the ankle.

In the ankle, there are a collection of seven bones, the **tarsals**, that glide over each other to form the ankle. The largest of them, the **calcaneus**, forms the heel of the foot. On top of this is the second largest, the talus which articulates with both the tibia and fibula. There are then two rows of two and three bones, respectively.

The five bones that can be felt on the upper foot are the **metatarsals**. These articulate with the phalanges and, like those in the hand, there are three bones for the smaller toes and two for the big toe. Unlike the fingers, the movement in the toes is more restricted. Their main functions are concerned with grip and balance.

The foot

The foot   Oxford Designers & Illustrators

The foot is obviously essential to the balance and walking movement of the human body. Consider its shape as being similar to a tripod, with the points of contact being the heel, under the big toe and under the little toe. This structure is able to support the weight of the body when standing, walking, running, etc. and gives it balance when the body weight shifts to the various contact points. The arches in the middle of the foot, while being part of this structure, also allow for the free flow of blood to all parts of the foot without any pressure from contact with the surface.

Some common conditions concerning the bones

- Arthritis is a very common condition affecting the joints.

- Broken bones are relatively common and a technician is likely to come across this condition.

- Rheumatoid arthritis is an inflammation of the connective tissue in the joints similar to arthritis but often more aggressive.

MUSCLES

We have looked at the structure of skin, the blood and lymph circulation systems and the skeleton. Every system in the body relies on every other system to function. Think about how muscles affect the anatomical areas we have looked at so far.

The skin has muscles lying directly beneath it. These muscles in the face provide us with the wide range of facial expressions that is so important to human communication. The loss of muscle tone or substance creates visible signs of ageing and illness. This is especially visible on the face, the backs of the hands and the neck.

Muscles play a very important part in the circulation of blood and lymph. The heart is mainly comprised of a specialised muscle tissue that keeps it beating and pumping the blood around our body. It is muscle movements in associated areas that encourage the flow of lymph around the body. The skeleton can support and protect but it needs the vast array of muscles to allow it to move.

It would be impossible for a human body to do anything without muscles. Everything you conceive in your brain is expressed in muscular motion: talking, walking, drawing, reading, laughing, etc. Muscles turn energy from nutrition into movement. They are long lasting, self-healing, and are able to grow stronger with practice.

There are three different types of muscle in the human body:

1 **Skeletal muscle**. This is the type we can see and feel. We are usually aware that they are moving and that we are controlling them. They are attached to the skeleton and work in pairs, that is one muscle moves the joint one way and another moves it back. Muscles can pull but cannot push. The only times we do not control them voluntarily is when our nervous system sends an emergency message of self-protection, such as touching something hot, blinking if something approaches our eye. Skeletal muscles are the body's most abundant tissue and comprise approximately 23 per cent of a woman's body weight and 40 per cent of a man's.

2 Smooth muscle. This is the muscle associated with our organs and blood vessels. It is found in the digestive system (e.g. stomach and intestines for churning food and pushing it along) blood vessels (for pumping blood along the arteries), bladder, airways and uterus. The body is largely unaware of its control over this type of muscle; it is triggered automatically by signals from the brain.

3 Cardiac muscle. This is only found in the heart and is a specialised muscle where the fibres are connected together and are controlled by the brain.

For the purposes of treatments, only skeletal muscle is relevant, although an understanding of the basic systems of the body is important.

The basic action of a muscle is contracting. An example of this can be seen in lifting your lower arm. The muscle on the front of your upper arm, the bicep, contracts and lifts the lower arm, and can hold it there. When this action is no longer needed, the bicep relaxes, but the arm needs to be returned to its original position. This is when the tricep, on the back of your upper arm, contracts to bring the lower arm back. This example shows how skeletal muscles work in pairs because their basic action is to contract.

The order to a muscle to contract comes from the brain via the nervous system. The motor nerves situated in all muscle fibres initiate what is actually a chemical reaction that causes the minute fibres to contract and shorten. The chemical reaction needs specific nutrients and oxygen, which are carried to them via the blood system.

There are two types of contraction: isotonic and isometric contraction.

Isotonic contraction is where the length of the muscle shortens, as in the lifting of the forearm. **Isometric contraction** is where the muscle is put under tension but is not necessarily shortened. An example of this would be carrying a heavy bag. The force generated by the muscle allows the arm to do this. The toning of a muscle needs repetitive movements with little associated weight, while the building of muscle needs the tension and force required to move or support heavy weights.

Skeletal muscle is made up of bundles of fibres. It is also called **striated muscle** as stripes can be seen when viewed under a microscope. The fibres can be thought of as long cylinders and can vary in size from 10 per cent up to the full width of a hair. A muscle fibre contains many smaller, long cylinders called **myofibrils** (muscle protein) that surround **filaments**. It is the filaments that actually contract the myofibrils and therefore the fibres that are connected in parallel bundles.

Tired, overworked or slightly damaged muscles have myofibrils that are not fully relaxed and feel like knots in the muscle. Stress often causes a contraction that does not relax. A good massage, using techniques that stroke the fibres and encourage them to relax and return to their resting position, is very helpful and pleasant for the client. This is relatively easy to achieve on the lower arms, hands, lower legs and feet, as the muscles are not large and are close to the surface of the skin. On other parts of the body, such as the back and upper leg, the muscles are large and a much firmer pressure is needed to reach the deep muscles.

Associated with the muscles are two other types of tissue:

TIP

General terms relating to the action of a muscle:
Extensor: extends or straightens
Flexor: bends
Adductor: bring towards the body
Abductor: move away from the body
Supinator: turns palm of the hand up
Pronator: turns palm of hand down

1 **Ligament**. This is a short band of fibrous tissue that binds bones together.

2 **Tendon**. This fibrous tissue attaches the muscle to the bone. An example of this is found in the Achilles Heel, the tough ridge at the back of the heel that joins the heel to the calf muscle.

Both of the above can be damaged, usually by overstretching.

For massage purposes, it is necessary to know and have a basic understanding of how muscles work and their positions in the arm, hand, leg and foot.

The lower arm and hand

Flexor carpi radialis

Pronator teres

Supinator teres

Flexor carpi ulnaris

Thenar muscles

Flexor digitorum

The lower arm and hand
Oxford Designers & Illustrators

The muscles in the lower arm are concerned with the movements of the hand (the upper arm has the muscles that raise and lower this part of the arm). The muscles work in pairs, as explained above.

- One of the muscles that extends (or straightens) the wrist and helps to turn the hand is the extensor carpi ulnaris. Its name should suggest to you where it is and what it does. It starts at the humerus, runs down the ulna side of the arm to the little finger side of the carpals

- The opposing muscle to this, which bends the wrist and turns the hand in the other direction, is the flexor carpi ulnaris

- There is another muscle that extends the wrist and helps turn the hand that runs down the radius side of the arm: the extensor carpi radialis

- Its opposing muscle is the flexor carpi radialis

- The muscle that rotates the hand to bring the palm downwards starts at the humerus and extends down the top of the ulna to the base of the radius and is known as the pronator teres

- Its opposing muscle, the supinator teres, follows a similar route and connects with the other side of the radius.

Tendons from these muscles run down the hand to each finger:

- Extensor digitorum tendons run down the back of the hand, right along the fingers and allow the fingers to extend. These can be seen and felt as the fingers move and are particularly obvious in older hands as the skin loses its support.

- Flexor digitorum tendons are the opposing tendons that are in the palm of the hand and fingers and allow the fingers to bend.

The hand also has a group of muscles in the palm that gives the thumb and little finger their range of movement.

The wrist has four important ligaments that hold the carpals together, while allowing them to slide over each other during the movements of the wrist.

The lower leg and foot

The lower leg and foot
Oxford Designers & Illustrators

The muscle groups in the leg and foot have similarities to those in the arm and hand. However, in addition to the range of movements, these muscles are important for walking and balance.

- The large calf muscle, which starts at the femur behind the knee, runs down the lower leg to where it joins the heel (calcaneus) via the Achilles tendon and is known as the gastrocnemius. This muscle flexes the ankle to straighten the foot

- Its opposing muscle, the anterior tibialis, flexes the foot to bring it up towards the leg. It attaches at the upper tibia, runs down the front of the leg to join the metatarsals.

- The muscle that helps to stabilise the body when standing and flexes the foot inwards is the soleus. This starts with the upper tibia and fibula and joins the tendon of the gastrocnemius.

The muscles of the foot that lift the toes are the extensor digitorum brevis and they continue on to tendons for each toe: the extensor digitorum tendons. Under the foot is the flexor digitorum brevis leading to the flexor digitorum tendons.

Some common conditions concerning muscles

- Sprains and strains are a frequent problem with muscles. They mainly involve the ligaments, which can be overstretched and sometimes torn.

- A torn muscle, especially in the leg, is quite common, as are strained muscles that have been overworked.

THE NERVOUS SYSTEM

The organs and tissues that make up the nervous system are the brain, spinal cord, sense organs (eye, ear, skin, nose, tongue) and the nerves. The system can be differentiated into two main structural areas:

1 The **central nervous system** (CNS) comprising the brain and spinal cord

2 The **peripheral nervous system** (PNS) with all the sensory and motor neurones

The functions of the nervous system can also be differentiated into two categories:

1 The **voluntary nervous system**. These are movements under our conscious control, for example walking, speaking, etc.

2 The **autonomic nervous system**. These movements are out of our conscious control, for example blinking, breathing, and movements in the digestive organs. This system regulates the muscles in the skin (around the hair follicles and the smooth muscle of our internal structures), blood vessels, the iris of the eye and the cardiac muscle of the heart.

Messages to and from the brain and spinal cord use the peripheral nervous system and are transmitted along nerve fibres. Along these fibres are **neurones**. These are cells like tiny batteries that power the electrical circuits in the body (the method by which messages are transmitted). They transmit from cell to cell for communication, control and interpretation of the sensory input.

There are three main types of nerves:

1 **Sensory nerve** fibres that carry impulses from the nerve endings in the sensory organs (for example the skin) back to the brain via the spinal cord. This keeps the brain informed about our external environment.

2 **Motor nerve** fibres that relay messages from the brain and spinal cord to instruct relevant parts of the body to respond, for example bending an arm or jerking away from unexpected heat.

3 The **autonomic nerves** that are working all the time to control the subconscious workings of the body. This includes temperature control that affects the skin.

The skin is the largest sensory organ and responds to touch, pressure and heat. Receptors in the epidermis and dermis can detect pressure, vibration, mechanical stimulation, thermal and noxious (harmful) stimulation.

The hands have a plentiful supply of nerves, especially on the fingertips. Although all the skin is involved in the sense of touch, the fingers are especially sensitive.

There are some fairly common disorders, either permanent or temporary, that can affect the nervous system in the hands and feet. They can cause phenomena such as a loss of sensation in the skin and an inability to feel or quickly respond to extreme temperatures. This is why care must be taken when using heated products or equipment. Their temperature must be tested before the client uses them.

Nerves of the hand and lower arm   Oxford Designers & Illustrators

Nerves of the foot and lower leg
Oxford Designers & Illustrators

Some disorders involving the nervous system

- **Parkinson's Disease** affects more than 1 person in 1000 and 1 in 100 of those over 60. It results in shaking and tremors and muscular rigidity. It is a progressive disease.

- **Multiple sclerosis** affects the nerve fibres resulting in a progressive impairment of muscular control.

THE NAIL UNIT

A basic understanding of how the skin is structured and how it grows should help with understanding how finger and toenails are formed as a **nail unit**. Like the hair follicle, the area where the nail starts life is a fold of the epidermal layer where skin cells are instructed by their nucleus to make certain adaptations. In the skin, they become keratinised to form the flattened cells of the stratum corneum. In a hair, they are keratinised and adapted to create a hair shaft. In a nail, they are also keratinised and form flat layers that make up a hard nail plate. Like the upper layer of the epidermis (stratum corneum) and hair, the nail is non-living. Like hair it can be cut without any sensation.

Cross-section of the nail unit

The function of the nail

All species of primate have nails. They are linked to the evolution of using hands (and feet) to manipulate objects. Humans, however, are the only animals able to use the thumb and forefinger in a pincer movement. The higher primates, such as gorillas and chimpanzees, have hands that are very similar to ours with fingerprints and perfect nails, but they cannot manipulate their thumbs as we can. There is a theory that this arrangement of our thumbs gave our species the opportunity to evolve faster, as we were able to use a wider variety of tools.

The nail unit

Nails are on the ends of our fingers for several reasons and are not just there to paint or chew! They provide a rigid support for the end of the finger, allowing us to pick things up more easily, and they protect the end of the finger and the last bone from countless knocks.

Nails start to form in an unborn baby very early in the gestation period and by 17–20 weeks are fully formed. Nails will even grow for a short period after death, as the cycle of adaptation of the skin cells and keratinisation will continue, once it has started, without any nourishment from the blood supply.

The structure of the nail

Matrix

This is the most important area of the nail unit. It is directly under the **proximal nail fold** or **mantle** and it is where the skin cells are adapted to form the nail plate. As the skin cells become keratinised, they bond together and lose the other cell contents. Unlike in the epidermis, where the bonds break down and the cells are shed, the bonds in a newly-forming nail plate are much stronger and the **lipid** content is retained. The keratinised cells form layers, or lamellar, and several of these bond together to form the nail plate.

The shape and size of the matrix will determine the thickness and width of the nail. The matrix extends from the base of the nail down towards the first joint. The longer the matrix, the thicker the nail. Thin nails will tend to have a short matrix. The width of the nail will be determined by the width of the matrix. Naturally thin (or thick) nails are hereditary; however, a lot can happen to them once they are grown to change this characteristic.

The developing nail in the matrix is very soft until full keratinisation has taken place and damage to this area can result in a permanently deformed nail. Examples can be seen in a person who has shut their finger in a door, even as a child. If the area of the matrix is damaged, the base of the nail and the nail plate may have a permanent ridge. Another example would be if someone has had a serious infection in the area. If damage to the area is temporary and heals properly in the matrix, any deformity to the nail should grow out in approximately 6 months after the damage has healed.

Proximal nail fold or mantle

The epidermis of the skin on the finger, above the matrix, folds back on itself and underneath. As in the hair follicle, the deeper area of the fold forms part of the germinal matrix and helps protect the area.

This area of skin can often be quite large and unsightly, for example, when it is stuck to the cuticle, the nail grows and pulls the skin with it. When the skin is overstretched it splits, usually at the sides, and appears ragged. These splits can be quite sore and, if pulled, can become infected and inflamed. The split piece of skin can be very carefully removed with cuticle nippers. Proper care of the nails ensures that the nail fold does not stick to the nail plate as it is regularly lifted away. This area should not be pushed as this can cause damage to the underlying soft nail and matrix. The area also forms a seal around the proximal edge of the nail that prevents bacteria from entering. When the nails are soaked in water or softened with oils, the nail fold can be lifted with ease. It is not recommended that the lifted skin is cut on a regular basis. The body is expert at protecting itself and, if an area is removed, the body will often compensate and grow thicker skin. If the skin has been lifted for the first time and is unsightly, careful removal may be carried out with a hygienic pair of nippers, used correctly. The area should then be treated with oil or cream to keep the skin soft and prevent it from sticking to the cuticle.

Lateral nail fold or side wall

The skin of the finger folds down along the side of the nail and provides the nail plate with protection and a groove to guide the growth of the nail. A seal is formed here to prevent the invasion of unwanted substances or micro-organisms.

Eponychium

The **eponychium** is an area at the base of the nail plate where the proximal nail fold meets the nail plate. It acts as a seal for that area of the nail and guards against invasive bacteria. During a manicure, this area should be treated gently because, if the seal is broken, not only is it painful, but infection can occur.

The cuticle

The nail fold is often called the **cuticle**, but this is inaccurate. The underside of the proximal nail fold constantly sheds a layer of clear skin that sits on the nail plate and grows with it. This is the real cuticle and is not always visible until softened. This is the skin that should be removed during a manicure and always before the application of artificial nails to avoid any lifting problems,

TIP

A way to remember the difference between 'proximal' and 'distal' is to think of proximal as being 'in the proximity of', that is, close to. Distal is at a distance.

TIP

To help you remember 'lateral', think of 'lateral thinking', which can be described as sideways thinking.

as products do not bond with skin, only with the nail plate. This skin is sometimes called the pterygium. When using a cuticle knife, it is usually possible to feel the difference between skin and hard nail even if the skin is not visible. As the epidermis of the nail fold produces this layer continuously, there is always some to be found on the nail plate, however little.

The nail plate

As previously explained, keratinised skin cells form the nail plate. These flattened cells stick together and form layers. There are approximately 25 layers of keratinised skin cells. There is less concentration of lipids (fats) in the nail plate compared to the stratum corneum (1 per cent versus 20 per cent) and there are many air spaces; this allows ten times as much water to be absorbed by the nail than by the skin. This can be seen when the nails are soaked in water, e.g. in the bath they become very transparent and flexible.

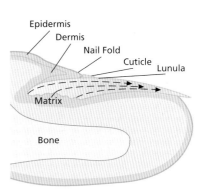

The bonds holding the cells together are tougher in the nail plate than in the stratum corneum, as the skin cells are designed to be shed, whereas the nail plate needs to be kept together.

Evaporation of water soaked up by the nails can be quite damaging as it breaks down the bonds that hold the cells together and causes weak and peeling nails. In fact, water is one of the most damaging substances for nails.

Growth of the nail plate from the matrix

The uppermost layer of nail is formed in the deepest part of the matrix, while the lower layers are formed nearer the cuticle. This results in a very hard surface and much softer lower layer of the nail plate.

The layers of keratinised cells form themselves into three main layers of nail plate. The upper and lower layers are the thinnest with the middle layer making up approximately 75 per cent of the nail plate. The upper layer is dense and hard, but thin. This is the layer that often peels, due to the damage caused to the bonds between it and the middle layer, exposing the slightly softer but thicker middle layer. The break in these bonds allows more water to seep between the layers and causes further peeling. The lower layer of the nail plate is very thin and contains some soft keratin. This layer bonds strongly to the **nail bed**.

When nails become too dry and peel, not only are they thinner, but also the hard upper layer has been lost, leaving the pliable and weaker lower layers. Nails must be protected from this condition and that is why wearing gloves for washing up, etc. is always recommended. Nail varnish can also help protect the nails, as can massaging oils or cream into the cuticle area.

As the nail plate leaves the end of the finger, it forms a projection called the **free edge**. This appears whiter than the main body of the nail as it is not attached to the nail bed.

The nail plate has a proximal and distal area and the free edge could be described as the distal edge.

Lunula

The **lunula** is also known as the half moon, an area of the nail by or under the proximal nail fold, and the front end of the matrix.

It appears whiter because the cells are not yet completely keratinised and not totally transparent. Not every person has an exposed lunula and it is a misconception that the lunula (or half moon) should be visible. The nail is still slightly soft in this area and easily damaged so, if anything, it is better that the lunula is protected by the nail fold. People who have a large exposed lunula usually have very ridged nails which is often more noticeable on the thumbs. This is due to continual trauma to the soft nail from everyday living. During a manicure or any work done in the cuticle area, care must be taken not to press too hard on the lunula, as it will cause a ridge in the nail that will need to grow up and off the end before it disappears.

The nail bed

This lies directly under the nail plate. It is skin just like on the rest of the body, but it has a very rich supply of blood and lymph vessels to keep the nail healthy. It also has a series of ridges and grooves that fit into ridges and grooves on the underside of the nail plate. These are what hold the nail onto the nail bed. If the ridges are disturbed or if the nail plate becomes too thin and flexible, this 'hold' is broken and causes the nail plate to separate from the nail bed. This is a dangerous situation as it allows bacteria in under the nail that could cause severe problems. Nail technicians must take extreme care not to over-buff the nail, as this will cause the nail to become too thin. If this thinning occurs anywhere on the nail, it will eventually grow up to the end of the nail bed where it is most likely to result in separation. The nail plate appears pink in this area, owing to the colour of the underlying skin.

The hyponychium

This is the area of skin at the very end of the nail bed under the beginning of the free edge. It forms a very tight seal that prevents bacteria entering. There are many nerve endings in this area that act as a warning to this seal being broken. Sometimes, this area grows under the free edge, especially on those people with almond shaped nails, and forms an area that can be painful if pushed. It is thought to be a form of support to the free edge and care must be taken not to disturb it. It is sometimes called the **solehorn**.

Like all areas of skin, the epidermis sheds dead skin cells continuously. These cells can often be found under the free edge, especially of the toenails, where they get trapped.

The onychodermal band

Thinned (over-buffed) nail plate showing ridges on nail bed. Seen as red stripes on the nail bed near the free edge.

This is the area of the hyponychium where a slight change of colour in the skin can be seen. When applying a **French manicure** or artificial nails using a **white-tip powder** or **gel**, it is referred to as the '**smile line**' and its ideal shape should mirror the shape at the base of the nail to create a symmetrical 'top and bottom'.

THE PROCESS OF NAIL GROWTH

Rates of growth

Like hair, nails grow at different rates in individuals and at different times of the year but, unlike hair, grow continually. Fingernails grow faster than toenails. As an average guide, nails grow at the rate of between 3mm per month and it takes approximately 5–6 months for a fingernail to grow from the matrix to the free edge and up to a year for a toe nail. The growth rate is faster in the summer and during pregnancy and usually slows down with age. It can be speeded up or slowed down by illness. This slow growth rate complicates the treatment of nail conditions as damage caused to the nail plate takes a long time to grow out.

The speed or strength of nail growth is not linked specifically to diet, vitamin or mineral intake but can be improved, along with the condition of skin and hair, if a well-balanced diet is followed.

It is quite common to be able to see the effects of systemic trauma on the nails. For example, a general anaesthetic, bereavement, illness, etc. will often show up as a line or ridge on the nail plate where the growth has been affected.

Technicians and their clients will often notice an increased growth rate immediately after artificial nails have been applied. This is due to the stimulation produced by buffing during application. The nail matrix and nail bed have a concentrated supply of blood and lymph vessels that supply the area with nutrients and remove waste products. Stimulation of the circulation in this area will improve this function and assist growth.

Buffing the natural nail during a manicure is a valuable treatment, but care must be taken not to thin the nail or create too much heat through friction, as this can cause splitting.

The effect of stimulation to the circulation can be seen in the general growth of nails: nails on the dominant hand grow faster, as does the forefinger. Nail biters have faster growing nails owing to the continual nibbling.

As a technician, the growth rate of an individual's nails will affect maintenance treatments (see Chapter 5). Artificial nails must be maintained to compensate for this growth. The majority of clients will need to return every 2–3 weeks, but some clients need to return only every 4–5 weeks, as their growth rate is slower.

Nail composition and strength

Keratin and amino acids

The skin cells that are formed in the matrix have, in their nucleus, the 'instructions' needed to keratinise but, unlike the keratinised skin cells of the stratum corneum that form a barrier and then are lost, these cells form together to create the hard nail plate layers.

Keratin is a type of **protein** that is made in the body and the body has many different proteins that are essential to its functioning. Proteins are made up of certain sequences of **amino acids**. Amino acids are chemicals created by the body that, when linked together in various specific sequences, make the necessary proteins. The linked amino acids form long 'strands' and these strands are then linked together at intervals with another amino acid, bonding the strands together and creating a strong structure. The keratin of the nail has many more of these bonds than that of the skin and hair.

Hard and soft nails

The progression of cells from the matrix to the nail plate is very similar to those making the journey in the epidermis of the skin. The cells are created

> **TIP**
>
> An excellent stimulation for nails to encourage faster and healthier growth is to place the hands together, like praying, then curl the fingers in so the nails touch each other. Then rub them back and forward to produce a clicking sound.

> **TIP**
>
> Nails that are naturally thick or thin are hereditary. A longer matrix will produce a thicker nail. Conversely, a short matrix can produce only a thinner nail.

by cell division deep in the matrix and, as they are pushed forward, lose the cellular fluid and become flatter. The lunular is thought to be an area where this process has not quite finished, hence its whiter appearance. As the cells are pushed forward by the reproducing cells behind, they become completely keratinised, flat and hard. Therefore the nail plate nearest to the nail fold is softer than the distal edge, and can be easily damaged.

- A strong nail is one that can withstand breakage. This does not necessarily mean hard as 'hard' could suggest **brittleness** and the nail could easily snap. Many products on the market are nail 'strengtheners', and that can mean nail 'hardeners'. If a weak nail is hardened too much, it will become brittle. If a hard or brittle nail becomes too soft and flexible, it will tear. The spaces between ketatinised cells are full of moisture from the nail bed beneath and from external sources. The right amount of moisture will keep the nail flexible and help absorb shocks. Too much, and the nail bends, too little and the nail becomes dry and brittle.
- The nail plate is very absorbent and too much water can cause splitting and peeling. Excessive water can cause the nail plate to soften and swell. Repeated softening and swelling can cause surface peeling.
- The only truly effective moisturiser for skin and nails is water (and natural lipids), but in the right amount. Using creams and oils is beneficial as they can seal natural moisture in and keep too much out. Solvents, such as acetone and nail varnish removers, can remove natural oils and water and can be the cause of dryness if overused.
- The perfect nail is a combination of strength and **flexibility**.

A nail specialist should be able to diagnose the exact condition of a client's nails and be able to recommend the ideal treatment and products. It may be that a weak nail needs a hardening treatment for a period of time followed by a moisturising treatment. A brittle nail may need moisturising then hardening. An understanding of nail growth and structure brings with it the ability to correctly diagnose conditions.

Protein, calcium and nails

As mentioned before, nails are keratinised skin cells. Keratin is a protein composed of amino acids formed together in long chains and linked by an amino acid bond. The vast number of these strong bonds is specific to nails and is what makes them so much harder than skin and hair. The protein, keratin, is mostly composed of carbon, oxygen, nitrogen, sulphur and hydrogen. The nail plate also has traces of many other chemicals, e.g. iron, zinc, sodium, calcium, titanium, even aluminium, copper, gold and silver.

There are many myths about calcium and nails. The body's intake and absorption of calcium is essential for teeth and bones, but as calcium is only 0.07 per cent of the nail, it does not play a large part. The body needs vitamin D in order to absorb calcium and that is obtained from the sun and diet. If this vitamin is lacking, conditions such as rickets can occur. White spots on the nail are often blamed on a lack of calcium, but this is usually incorrect (see Chapter 9). They are usually caused by trauma to the nail plate causing minor separation of the layers. In rare instances, the spots may be caused by lack of the trace element, zinc, in the body, but a reasonable diet and good health does not cause this condition.

The artificial nail and the natural nail

The strength of the nail can be influenced, even during the wearing of artificial nails or varnish. The nail plate is at its softest in the area of the cuticle and there should be a narrow margin of nail that is not covered. A nourishing oil massaged into this area daily will affect the new nail growing, so weak or brittle nails can be improved while artificial nails are worn. The massaging will stimulate the area and the oil will help to reduce the moisture loss from the new nail. If the artificial nails are correctly maintained, the natural nails should be stronger when they are removed.

Can artificial nails damage natural nails? They certainly can if they are incorrectly applied or the wearer does not understand how to look after them properly. It is usually an inexperienced or unprofessional technician or an uneducated client who causes damage to natural nails. It is really important that technicians explain what the wearer needs to do (or not do) in between treatments.

SUMMARY

This chapter has explained the basic anatomy and physiology of skin, muscles, bones, blood circulation, the lymphatic system, the nervous system and nails, nail structure and growth and the potential problems a technician may encounter in treating a client if nail trauma or past illness has occurred.

Assessment of knowledge and understanding

1 Explain eight functions of the skin.
2 Name the layers found in the epidermis.
3 What are the main structures found in the skin?
4 Describe four functions of blood.
5 Explain how blood is circulated around the body.
6 What are the main purposes of the lymphatic system?
7 Name the bones of the hand and foot.
8 What are the three different types of muscle and where are they in the body?
9 How do muscles work in pairs and what are the terms used the describe the groups?
10 Describe the nervous system in general terms.
11 What part does the matrix play in the process of nail growth?
12 Why is it important to understand the process of nail growth and factors that affect it?
13 Why should special care be taken when working in the area of the lunula?

chapter 3

PREPARING THE WORK AREA

Learning objectives

In this chapter you will learn about:

- **the equipment and furniture required by a nail technician**
- **how to create a comfortable and safe working environment**
- **how to work with potentially hazardous chemicals**
- **how to protect yourself, your clients and colleagues**
- **hygiene procedures**
- **the legislation affecting technicians and salons**
- **the information and correct usage of all tools and equipment**
- **pricing treatments and services**

INTRODUCTION

The only way to provide professional nail treatments is in a suitable, comfortable and safe environment with the right tools, correctly used. This chapter will show how to create that environment, make it safe for both technician and client and how to keep it that way while abiding by the relevant legislation.

Starting with the general environment, we need to think about what sort of area is needed for a nail technician to work in, what is required within the salon and what problems need addressing that are specific to artificial nails.

EQUIPMENT

Whether the technician is working in a nail salon, a beauty salon or a hair salon, a minimum amount of space is needed. In comparison to the other services, however, the space needed is very small. This industry has a great many mobile technicians, but virtually all of the requirements that make a salon a safe, hygienic and comfortable place also apply to working as a mobile technician. The only difference is that tools, equipment and products need to be portable for a mobile technician. As clients are always central to the work, all the safety rules must still apply.

The desk

When thinking about the minimum space required for a nail technician, a desk is the first consideration. There are many nail desks available from wholesalers that have been specifically designed for the job. If space is at a premium, the minimum worktop would need to be approximately 75 cm wide and approximately 35 cm deep. Ideally, the desk should have a couple of drawers, and be very stable in construction. The width of the desk should be not so wide that the technician needs to stretch to reach the client's hands if the client is sitting back in the chair, nor should it be so narrow that it causes the technician to bend their neck down too far. Before buying a ready-made desk, make sure the measurements are right for the space in the salon; sit in the chairs that are going to be used for both the technician and the client. Think about storage of all the equipment needed and, if necessary, the space required for any additional storage needs. Most ready-made desks usually have a suitable worktop that can easily be kept clean, but remember to take that into consideration.

Many salons have their desks made specially to match the image of the salon. It is possible to make a functional desk fit in with any décor, but remember that the suitability and safety of the desk and chairs must take priority over image. Think of the essential requirements first and design the desk around them, rather than thinking of the design first and trying to make it work.

The technician's chair

There should be sufficient space around the desk for a comfortable seat for both technician and client. Care should be taken when choosing the technician's chair, as there are several factors to take into account:

- A busy technician can be sitting in the same place for, sometimes, up to 12 hours a day with very few breaks. This is far from an ideal situation, but most salons have at least one late night.

- As with any work equipment, safety must come first. A chair must have the correct support for the user. The seat should be padded and of a depth that supports the legs. The tilt of the seat also affects how we sit. The backrest should give support to the back and the combination of the

Portable manicure and pedicure stool   Courtesy of Beauty Express

Nail desk with space for a UV lamp and dust extraction
Courtesy of Beauty Express

Nail desk with dust extraction and integrated desk lamp
Courtesy of Beauty Express

Technician's chair   Courtesy of
Beauty Express

Oxford Designers & Illustrators

back and seat should encourage the user to sit upright with a slight hollow in the lower back. Technicians are forced to work in a very unnatural position, leaning forward and with the head looking down. This puts great strain on the back and neck. Every technician should be aware that this position causes stress in the neck and shoulders and could lead to severe problems in later years.

- Many technicians work by leaning one elbow on the desk and having their body twisted. This is obviously very dangerous. The upper body needs to be square to the desk with the back straight and only a slight tilt forward. The shoulders should be kept relaxed and the neck should not be held bent too much. There are 'posture' chairs available, on wheels and incorporating a rocking motion, that are designed to help those working at a desk. These chairs have a tilted seat and a padded support for the knees to rest on. They are ideal for the person who sits upright all the time, such as a typist, or a person who needs to lean forward slightly, as they will keep the curvature of the back in the correct position. However, owing to the nature of the technician's work, a lot of pressure is put on the knees in this position, which can be quite painful by the end of a day and may cause problems later.

- There are several exercises that a technician can do at various times throughout the day, but, at all times sitting in the safest position and staying relaxed is essential advice.

Exercises

1 Sit comfortably, relax shoulders and breathe in. While breathing out, drop chin onto chest. Relax. Breathe in again and, while breathing out, drop head to one side. Relax. Repeat for the other side then drop head back. Drop chin back to chest while breathing normally.

2 Breathe in and lift shoulders towards ears, breathe out and let shoulders drop. Relax. Repeat several times. Rotate one shoulder several times, then the other while breathing normally.

3 Interlace your fingers and stretch your arms out in front of you with palms facing out. Feel the stretch in your upper arms and upper back.

4 Move your arms up above your head with fingers still interlaced and push up. Feel the stretch on the outer edge of your arms and ribs.

5 With your arms still extended, lean from the waist, first one side then the other.

6 Clasp your hands behind your head, push your elbows back and pull your shoulder blades together.

7 Put one arm over the opposite shoulder, hold just above the elbow and push elbow towards the shoulder while looking the other way. Repeat with the other arm.

The client's chair

The chair for the client is almost as important as the one for the technician.

- The client must feel comfortable, but must also be in the right position for the technician. A client could spend up to 2 hours in the same chair, so comfort is important. A fabric-covered chair with a soft seat is preferable (plastic can get uncomfortable). The height of the seat should be such that the client can rest their arms on the desk easily while keeping them and their shoulders in a relaxed position. They should also be able to get close enough to the desk so that their arm is still supported if they lean back into the chair.

- When seating a client, and during the whole treatment, make sure they are sitting straight in front of the desk. This is important for the treatment because if a client is sitting sideways, their hand will not be in the centre and not held straight to the technician. This could result in artificial nails being applied unevenly on the finger.

It is worth acquiring the very best furniture that you can afford at the time. It is often a false economy to buy things cheaply thinking that they can be replaced soon. What usually happens is that the cheap items wear out and start looking shabby very quickly, but there is always some other priority that requires the money. If space in the salon is not at a premium, it is often worth having a much larger desk than necessary (as long as it is not used as extra room to make untidy!) as small displays can be put on the extra top space. There are many inventive technicians who have designed wonderful desks with display areas, built-in waste disposal and multiple desks.

> **TIP**
>
> Make sure there is plenty for the client to look at, especially retail lines. It will be something interesting for them and should encourage questions that could lead to sales.

The desk lamp

Desk lamps play a very important part in the work of the technician and their desk set-up. It is essential to have excellent light when providing any nail treatment, so a lamp of the right design is important. Good light will help prevent eye strain while carrying out close work; direct light, which casts no shadows, is needed to examine artificial nails for imperfections; applying varnish and nail art needs bright light to ensure accuracy and neatness.

Lamps are visually very obvious on a desk, so they must look pleasing and fit in with the décor of the salon. More importantly, there a number of factors that need to be taken into account when choosing a lamp.

Heat

One of the most important factors is heat. Commonly used tungsten bulbs give off a great deal of heat. 'Daylight' bulbs, useful for keeping colours looking true, also get very hot. This is far from ideal for the technician. The lamp needs to be quite close for the best effect, but the working temperature for the technician can get very uncomfortable. The heat will also affect many artificial nail products and make working with them difficult, for example volatile products, such as nail varnish remover and liquid monomers will evaporate faster, creating a potentially high concentration of vapour in the air space around the technician and client. Halogen or low energy bulbs do not get too hot and are a good choice.

Shape

The shape of the lamp needs to be such that the light does not glare into the eyes of the technician or the client; it must be close enough to be effective but not in the way; it also needs to be stable on the desk.

Electricity supply

Thought must be given to the electricity supply for the lamp. Trailing wires in a workplace are a safety hazard and should be avoided. A socket close enough to avoid trailing wires is the most suitable, but there are many alternatives. Some manicure tables have a plug socket attached to them for electrical equipment. This, of course, needs to be connected to an electricity supply and, again, wires across the floor must be avoided. If there is no alternative to a wire on the floor by a desk or any area where people could walk, then it must be covered with a rubber conduit that draws attention to it and has sloping sides to prevent tripping while protecting the cable from damage. There should be no wires on the floor under the desk as the wheels of the chair could run over them, damage them or pull the equipment off the table. Wherever possible, wires and cables should be attached to the desk, floor or wall using special clips designed for the job that are readily available from any DIY shop.

Remember, 'nails' are part of the image industries, so make sure you always present the right image to your clients.

Good working practices

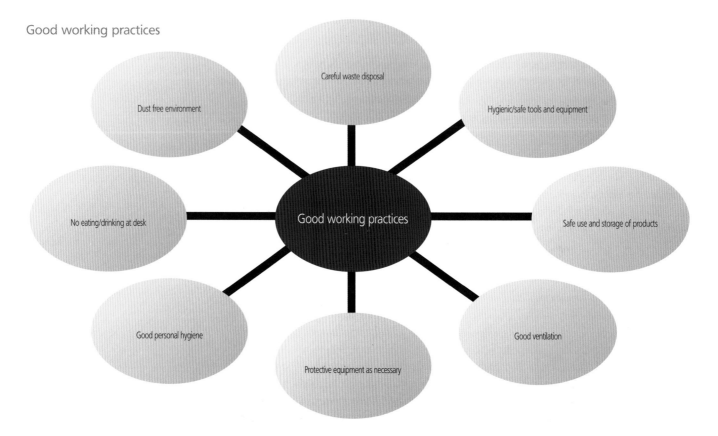

USING NAIL PRODUCTS SAFELY

Problems with irritants and corrosive materials

The majority of nail products come under the category of **hazardous** chemicals and many of them are classed as **irritants**. Care must be taken when using these types of products. There are some irritants that are also classified as **corrosive** and these will cause a bad reaction with everyone. A day-to-day example of this is household bleach that stings and itches when in contact with skin.

- A common example of this type of chemical in the nail industry is an acid-based primer. This is a product commonly used in artificial nail systems and, as the name suggests, is an acid that will sting and itch on contact with skin. Washing in running water will remove the chemical, but it is likely that the skin will be temporarily damaged.

- Many other commonly used products are irritants – for example, nail adhesive is an irritant, and every bottle and tube should carry a warning. Obviously the adhesive will bond to skin very easily, but a drop of it spilled onto skin can also cause a chemical burn. (Water will stop the burning and acetone will debond the skin.) If adhesive is spilt onto clothing and penetrates through to the skin, very severe burns can be caused. The chemicals in the adhesive react with man-made fibres in the clothing and burns requiring cosmetic surgery have been known as a result of this accident.

- It is a legal requirement for there to be warnings on many labels, but the absence of a warning does not necessarily mean a product is safe. All products should be treated with respect and all potentially hazardous products should have a document called the Material Safety Data Sheet (MSDS) available from the supplier (see p.85).

> **TIP** ✔
>
> Make sure adhesive container lids are on securely and that there are no air pockets in the application nozzle that could cause the adhesive to spurt out. Clean the nozzle with remover before replacing the lid.

Allergies and sensitivity

All chemicals are potentially harmful but the dividing line between a safe and harmful chemical is often the *quantity* of it. This dividing line varies from person to person. When a harmful chemical touches the body in any way, the body reacts to it. This reaction can take many different forms, but the most common is an allergic reaction.

- People develop an allergy or sensitivity to a substance by coming into contact with too much of it. It is this level of 'too much' that is so variable. One individual may become sensitive to a particular ingredient in a hand cream after two uses; another may take years before a reaction occurs, if one occurs at all.

- As many nail products are classed as irritants, it is very likely that most individuals will develop a sensitivity to them at some time. As no one can tell how long this will take or how much of a specific product needs to come into contact with a person, it is important to take measures to avoid the possibility of a sensitivity building up. It is also just as important to be able to recognise the first signs of this in both the technician and their clients (see Chapter 4).

ABSORPTION, INGESTION AND

INHALATION

There are three ways that potentially harmful chemicals can enter the body and if each of these 'routes of entry' is prevented as far as possible, all hazards are avoided. The 'routes' are:

1 **Inhalation**: that is, *breathing in* vapours or dusts. This one is not so easy to control, but by following strict working practices and hygiene rules, the problem can be solved.

2 **Ingestion**: that is, *through the mouth*. Avoidance of this is even easier! Wash hands frequently, especially before eating; do not eat or drink at a desk; and follow reasonable salon hygiene rules.

3 **Absorption**: that is, chemicals can enter *through the skin*. This is probably the most common cause of problems for technicians and their clients and can be easily avoided.

We will look at all three in more detail.

Inhalation

If you think about the salon environment and what type of salon it is, you will realise there are certain requirements to ensure the safety and comfort of staff and clients.

Vapours

- Many nail products involve *volatile chemicals* and even the tidiest technician cannot totally prevent some of the **vapours** escaping into the air. Adequate ventilation is therefore essential. In a very busy nail salon a sophisticated **ventilation** system is ideal, but this can be costly and is not always necessary for smaller establishments with a few nail desks. If a larger salon decides that suitable ventilation is needed, expert advice should be sought as there are complicated calculations involved in determining the type of ventilation equipment required to change the air in the salon several times an hour.

- Chapter 7, will discuss this in more detail, but vapours are **molecules** of actual chemicals *in the air* and, although most nail products have strong odours, if there is no obvious smell it does not mean the vapour is not there. Not all hazardous chemicals have odours that can be detected. A fan in a salon is no substitute for a ventilator, all it does is move the air around. The salon needs the air to be changed regularly, and this can only be achieved by proper ventilation. Extractor fans can assist in removing vapours and are relatively inexpensive, but there must be enough of them of the right size and they must be in the right position to be effective.

- The vapours that need to be eliminated are always *heavier than air* so the molecules will collect nearer the floor. High-level extractors, if of a sufficient size for the room, will in theory lift the vapours up and expel them. However, in doing that, the air is brought up past the breathing spaces of those in the salon so some of the vapours will be inhaled. Some vapours will also be left at the lower levels. Extractors that are set lower down will remove the vapours without having to lift them up.

- Some nail products are used as a *spray*. This is an obvious potential hazard as the chemical vapour is actually being put into the air. Pump sprays are less harmful than atomisers or aerosols as they produce larger droplets rather than a fine **mist**. Keep the use of sprays to a minimum, but if they are used, good ventilation is essential.

- Wearing a disposable dust mask will not protect anyone from vapours. Chemical molecules that are present in the air are much smaller than dust particles and the mask is not a barrier to them. There are vapour masks available, but these are much larger pieces of equipment and are costly to buy. They are also very off-putting to clients!

- Safe, hygienic and correct working procedures will avoid almost all vapours escaping in to the air and, in a small to medium salon, this, together with adequate ventilation from an open window or door, should be sufficient to ensure safety.

Vapours and eyes

- *Contact lenses*: Never wear contact lenses when working with nail products. It is possible that vapours can be absorbed by soft lenses and seriously affect the eye. Safety glasses worn with lenses will not protect your eyes from vapours when wearing contact lenses.

- *Safety glasses*: Wearing plain safety glasses is highly recommended. It is a practice with some technicians to nip off old overlay, a practice that is very strongly discouraged as it severely damages the nail plate; however chips from this can fly and enter the eye. But eye accidents can also happen to the most careful technician, by clipping a plastic tip or nail, or opening a bottle of adhesive that has an air bubble in the nozzle, for example. A busy technician spends many hours very close to a number of hazards and eyes are very precious!

Keeping vapours to a minimum

There are a few simple rules that can be followed to keep vapours to a minimum:

- Keep all bottles and jars closed

- Keep any dishes covered

- Have a metal waste bin with a lid at every nail desk

HEALTH AND SAFETY ✚

If you cannot smell a chemical in the atmosphere it does not mean it is not there! Good working practices are the best safeguard.

HEALTH AND SAFETY ✚

Always have an eye bath with several small bottles of distilled water available in case of accidents involving eyes.

ANECDOTE

A client of mine always kept small bottle of nail adhesive in her bag in case of accidents. One night she was on her way to dinner with her husband; they were in the car, it was dark and she was in the passenger seat. She felt a bit tired and her eyes were 'gritty'. She knew she had some eye drops with her, so rummaged in her bag to find the bottle. She opened it and tipped her head back to use the eye drops. Out came a drop but… she had mistaken the eye drop bottle for the nail adhesive bottle. She didn't go to dinner, but spent the night in casualty! Luckily although her eye was sore for a few days, there was no permanent damage done.

- Put all nail wipes/cotton wool straight into the bin after use

- Change the paper towel under client's hands after each stage and put into the bin

- Wipe up spills immediately with absorbent paper and put paper in an outside waste bin

- When using a solvent to remove artificial nails, keep the bowl covered with a towel and remove directly after use

- Keep the use of sprays to a minimum

- Discard all unwanted solvents and nail monomers immediately by soaking in absorbent paper and placing in a covered waste bin; larger quantities should be placed in a safe place in the open and allowed to evaporate – do not pour down sinks or lavatories

- Store brushes in covered containers, not open on the desk

- Maintain adequate ventilation at all times, and make sure the salon is not too hot.

> **TIP** ✔
>
> In larger salons it may be worth having a large glass jar with wire mesh across the top. This can be placed in the open air but not anywhere near a designated smoking area. Volatile liquids can be put in the jar to evaporate safely. This is only suitable for small quantities as larger amounts need specialist disposal.

Dust

Dust is another major problem in the salon. Although the amount of dust can be minimised by correct working procedures, it is impossible to avoid the production of quantities of dust.

- Dust falls into two categories: the dust you can see and the dust you cannot see. All dust is potentially harmful, but the dust you can see is slightly less harmful than the dust you cannot see. Larger dust particles will settle on surfaces and not float around in the air to be breathed in. The body has some very clever mechanisms to prevent unwanted 'foreign matter' entering it. Our respiratory system is designed to take air in through the nose and out through the mouth. The nose has thousands of hairs inside it and is lined with a mucous membrane, which act together to trap particles that must not be breathed into the lungs.

- This safety mechanism is very efficient in catching the dust particles that can be seen. It is not as efficient at catching the particles that cannot be seen, as they can be so small that they can be inhaled right into the lungs. There are more mucous membranes in the lungs that will catch a great deal of the inhaled dust but it is an irritant and excess dust can cause respiratory problems.

An extraction system integrated into the salon décor   Marco Benito

Avoiding excess dust

Like any potential risk situation, it is far better to try to avoid it than correct or treat any problems that arise. There are a number of ways that excess dust can be avoided.

- The ideal arrangement is to have a dust extractor fitted into the desk. These units, like extractor fans, create a light suction that draws the dust being generated from filing through a grille in the desk top and into a collection bag or unit, rather like a vacuum bag. The collected dust can then be regularly disposed of; an efficient unit can remove almost all the dust before it disperses in the air. The grille need only be exposed during the stages that generate dust; otherwise it can be covered with a manicure mat and towels for the comfort of the client and hygiene of the salon.

- If this type of extractor is not possible, the following suggestions should help to cut down on dust:

  – Lay several sheets of disposable towels over a terry towel before each client arrives. After each stage of treatment that generates any dust, fold the top layer and discard. This ensures that dust is not left lying under your hands and being continually disturbed.

  – Wipe the desk surface after each client with a damp cloth to collect any dust. This is also the ideal time to use a hard-surface disinfectant to dampen the cloth.

  – Wipe all surfaces in the salon with a damp cloth every day. Dusting with a dry cloth will just 'rearrange' the dust.

  – Keep air moving with adequate ventilation via windows and doors, which will help remove fine airborne dust.

  – Brushing reusable files and buffers to remove dust will lengthen their life. Brush them under running water before disinfecting them.

  – Buffers and files should not be used for more than one client without disinfecting. Put used files in a covered box until the cleaning process as they will 'shed' dust wherever they are put down.

Dust masks

For those technicians who feel susceptible to dust, a *disposable mask* can be worn. They are comfortable to wear and should be changed every few days. It is unlikely that a client would need to wear a mask, as they are exposed to the dust for a much shorter length of time. A technician, however, is working in the same environment all day. A technician who wears a mask should explain this to all clients in case they feel at risk.

Disposable dust mask   Courtesy of Beauty Express

Drills

The use of drills is not recommended in this book. Modern products and techniques do not require the use of drills, unlike the old, thick and brittle dental acrylics that took hours to buff. Good application techniques should negate the effectiveness of drills. If a technician chooses to use a drill, a course of practical tuition must be undertaken to fully understand the correct use of the equipment. It should also be understood that drills create huge quantities of very fine dust. Anyone using a drill must wear a dust mask for their own safety and follow stringent rules for the management of the dust.

Ingestion

Obviously, technicians do not make a habit of eating or drinking any of their nail products! It is, however, exactly what does happen in a great number of salons by hundreds of technicians. Every time there is a coffee cup on the desk, every time a technician grabs a quick bite of their lunchtime sandwich or the sandwich is left open in the salon, small amounts of dust and vapours are getting into the food and are being ingested.

It is unlikely that this will affect a client as they will drink a coffee or eat a sandwich in the salon so infrequently. A technician, however, could be doing this every day and several times a day. The levels will soon build up.

Simple rules to follow would be:

- Do not drink hot liquids at the desk; it is possible for them to absorb vapours from the air

- Avoid placing any drinks on the desk, as the container could collect dust

- It is possible for uncovered food to absorb vapours or dust; keep all food away from the salon

- Wash your hands before eating anything, even a small piece of chocolate.

Absorption

Every time a chemical, even water, touches the skin or nails, some of it will be absorbed into the skin. The body is quite happy to have thousands of different chemicals enter the upper levels of the skin. Specific cells within the blood maintain total vigilance and investigate anything 'foreign'; most of these 'foreigners' are recognised as being friends and are left alone. However, there will also be many 'foreigners' that are not recognised as friends, and they will be removed and destroyed. These cells will recognise any non-friendly chemicals if they appear again and may just remove and destroy them without any fuss. However, if these foes continue to appear, the blood will develop a substance that will fight them and this is when a reaction is noticed.

- The most obvious reaction is irritated skin in the area of absorption. If the irritant is not immediately removed, this can develop into a very painful skin condition that will take a very long time to clear up.

- Local irritation is not always the first sign of an allergic reaction. Puffy or itchy eyes could be a reaction to a product on the nails. Headaches, tiredness, mood swings, nosebleeds, dizziness, coughs, or a sore throat can also be signs of a reaction to chemicals via any of the routes of entry.

- If the irritating chemical is removed, the symptoms should also disappear. They will, however, reappear if the chemical is reintroduced, as once the body is sensitised it will always be sensitised to that substance. From the point of view of a technician, if this sort of sensitivity is created to a commonly used product it may be difficult to find an alternative. This could mean that the technician can no longer work, which is a very drastic result of what amounts to laziness or lack of understanding. For a client, it can be very distressing and they may be lost as a client or, worse, take legal action against the salon or technician.

As these potential problems can all be avoided with a little extra care and a real understanding of the work, it is not worth taking any risks.

STERILISATION, DISINFECTION AND SANITISATION

Hygiene in the salon can be divided into three categories:

1 **Sterilisation**: this process kills all living organisms and needs to be used on metal tools as they may have come into contact with body fluids.

2 **Disinfection**: this will kill some living organisms and inhibit the growth of others and must be used on hard surfaces and tools and equipment that do not come into contact with body fluids.

3 **Sanitisation**: this will inhibit the growth of certain living organisms and must be used to clean hands and prepare nails for treatment.

We will look at each of these in more detail.

Sterilisation

There are only a few items used in the process of applying artificial nails that need to be treated with sterilisation methods but they do, however, need careful treatment. It is a legal requirement for salons to have suitable sterilisation methods in place and local Environment Health Departments can have differing requirements. Before choosing a system for the salon it is worth checking the local requirements.

The reason for such stringent requirements is that the risk of the spread of disease must be minimised. Body fluids, such as blood and lymph, could carry viral infections such as hepatitis or HIV.

Tools to be sterilised

The commonly used tools that will need to be sterilised are cuticle nippers, nail clippers and cuticle knives – that is, anything with a sharp edge or blade. These are easily sterilised.

Tools that are not so easily sterilised and can sometimes carry the same risk are files and buffers. Occasionally, a technician may break the skin with a file or buffer around the nail plate or sometimes clients have very delicate skin at the side of the nail or a hangnail so that rough handling breaks the skin. If this happens the only safe procedure is to discard any file and buffer that has been used. Wood, paper and sponge cannot be satisfactorily sterilised.

Sterilisation methods

There are many sterilisation methods available on the market.

A very large salon may benefit from some of the larger and more costly equipment, such as an autoclave, that uses extreme heat to destroy bacteria. There are some systems that seal the tools into a bag that then goes into a unit to sterilise them. The tools are removed from the bag only when needed. As tools are sterile and germ-free until they come into contact with air, this method keeps them as hygienic as possible until required.

Another method that is probably more suitable for smaller salons is chemical sterilisation, where the tools are immersed into a solution for a minimum period of time. Checking with the local environmental health department is recommended, as some brands are not recognised in certain areas. Care should be taken when using the chemicals as they are very powerful irritants and should never come into contact with skin. The directions should also be carefully followed as they usually need diluting with water and only specific dilutions are effective over certain time periods.

In preparation for sterilisation, tools should be scrubbed with soapy water or a solvent to remove any grease or debris and then carefully dried with disposable towels.

Ideally, all metal tools should be sterilised after every client; however, in the 'real' salon environment, this is rarely practised. If there is any possibility at all of a break in the skin or contact with a skin or nail condition, the process must be rigorously followed. If the skin and nails are healthy, however, then metal tools can be wiped with a solvent to remove grease and debris and immersed in a **disinfectant** solution for the recommended time.

Disinfection

Work surfaces

There are many areas that require regular disinfection. This process will destroy many bacteria, **viruses** and fungal spores and is essential for general salon hygiene.

All hard surfaces should be cleaned on a regular basis with a disinfectant solution. For example, desks should be wiped over after every client, preferably with a weak disinfectant; they should have a thorough clean at the end of every day. Floors, light switches, sinks and basins should all be cleaned with disinfectant on a regular basis.

Towels

Terry towels used during treatments and those used to dry hands should be washed with the addition of a suitable disinfectant solution. Commercial disinfectants are often available at beauty wholesalers or cleaning-product wholesalers that are suitable for all these jobs. Some beauty and nail product companies also supply products designed for this use.

Tools

All tools need some form of disinfectant and there are branded products available for this, together with suitable equipment to carry out the process easily and efficiently. All reusable tools must be disinfected after every use and, like the sterilisation solutions, the manufacturer's instructions should be followed carefully. The only acceptable exceptions to this rule are the brushes used to apply acrylic overlays. Disinfecting these brushes would destroy them; they are used with solvents so are unlikely to be a health risk, and they do not touch any soft tissue (see separate instructions for cleaning).

Files and buffers

Files and buffers should either be disposable, personal to specific clients only, or be of a quality that can be submersed in water.

A recommendation for every nail desk would be to have a disinfectant solution in a suitable container where all metal tools are stored waiting to be used. When they are needed, they are removed and dried with a paper towel. After they have been used and if do not yet need sterilising, they should be wiped with a solvent and returned to the disinfectant, care being taken not to remove them before the recommended time period (usually around 15 minutes).

Used files and buffers should be stored in a covered container until they can be cleaned of dust and then placed in the disinfecting solution. After the minimum time period, they can be removed, rinsed to remove the solution and left on paper towels to dry.

Sanitisation

This is a process that is essential for the cleansing of hands and the preparation of nails. Skin cannot be sterilised or disinfected as the chemicals that can do this are irritants and sometimes corrosive. Sanitisation is the lowest level of **decontamination**, but it is necessary to avoid the spread of diseases and, in the case of nail preparation, is essential to maintain healthy nails.

Technicians

Technicians' hands should be washed before and after every treatment for the safety of themselves and their clients. It not only limits the spread of bacteria and viruses, it also removes traces of artificial nail products and dust.

Washing the hands in soap and water is not always enough. Ideally, an antibacterial soap should be used that contains moisturisers to prevent the skin becoming dry. Hands should be dried with paper towels, as terry towels can become an efficient breeding ground for bacteria and there is some proof that hot air driers can also cause problems with bacteria.

> **TIP** ✔
>
> If an antibacterial wash is used, there could be a build up of some of the ingredients on the skin. Thorough rinsing is needed to prevent this and this regular immersion in water must be counteracted with the regular application of moisturisers.

Clients

Clients should also have clean hands, but nails are ten times more absorbent than skin. Once a client has washed their hands with soap and water it is possible that the nails have absorbed quantities of water and there could be soap traces left on the nail plate. If washing with water is preferred by the salon and client, ask the client to avoid the area of the nails.

There is an alternative that has many advantages over soap and water. There are many hand sanitisers available on the market that have the ability to cleanse skin more efficiently without the use of water or drying the skin. The advantages are that the technician and client can cleanse their hands at the desk so both can be confident that this procedure has been carried out; a good-quality product will be more efficient that an antibacterial soap and water: there is no water absorbed into the nails that may carry bacteria and will then be trapped there with the application of an overlay. The sanitiser should be applied liberally to the hands then rubbed together and wiped dry with paper towels to remove any debris. The technician should make a point of washing their hands regularly with moisturising soap and water to avoid a build up of the sanitising product.

LEGISLATION FOR SALONS AND EQUIPMENT

There are many acts of parliament and other pieces of local and national legislation that refer to salons with five or more employees. However, every technician should be aware of all of these. All the necessary information and ready made forms are available in the HABIA Health & Safety Implementation Pack that is strongly recommended for all salons. Use of this pack also provides valuable evidence in the gaining of qualifications. There is additional useful information on the HABIA website: www.habia.org

There are actually eighteen acts and regulations that affect salons:

- The Health and Safety at Work Act 1974
- The Workplace (Health, Safety and Welfare) Regulations 1992
- The Working Time Regulations 1998
- The Management of Health & Safety at Work Regulations 1992
- Control of Substances Hazardous to Health Regulations 1998 (COSHH)
- Health and Safety (Training for Employment) Regulations 1990
- Employers' Liability (Compulsory Insurance) Act 1969
- Electricity at Work Regulations 1989
- Health and Safety (First Aid) Regulations 1981
- The Reporting of Injuries, Diseases and Dangerous Occurrences Regulations 1995
- Health and Safety (Information for Employees) Regulations 1989
- The Fire Precautions Act 1971
- The Environmental Protection Act 1990
- Offices, Shops and Railway Premises Act 1963
- The Provisions and Use of Work Equipment Regulations 1992
- Personal Protective Equipment at Work Regulations 1992
- The Health and Safety (Display Screen Equipment) Regulations 1992
- Manual Handling Operations Regulations 1992.

Fortunately, not all of these need be fully understood in order to gain a relevant qualification! Some of them, however, are essential and they are

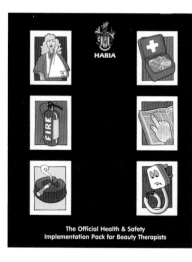

HABIA Health & Safety Implementation Pack
Courtesy of HABIA

covered in some detail in this chapter. Others apply to employers but employees need to know they exist so a brief explanation is included. The rest are listed for information but must be dealt with by employers.

The Health and Safety at Work Act 1974 (HASAWA)

This act relates to an employer but its requirements make for good working practices. Also, employees have a duty to work following these rules to ensure their safety, that of their colleagues and clients. The act requires that an employer must:

- Provide safe equipment and safe systems of work
- Ensure that all substances are handled safely, stored and transported correctly
- Provide a safe place of work with safe access and exit routes
- Provide a workplace that is safe with regard to fire, first aid and the recording of accidents
- Provide all the necessary information, instruction, training and supervision and ensure that all staff are aware of all the relevant safety issues, for example of where fire fighting equipment is and its correct use
- Supply all necessary personal protective equipment free of charge.

Every establishment of five or more employees must have a written Health and Safety Policy. Employees include part-timers, trainees and those working in different locations. All salons should have a written list of Good Housekeeping Rules. The Policy, the Housekeeping Rules and any amendments must be brought to the attention of all employees.

There must be a person who has designated responsibility for:

- overall health and safety
- health and safety on a day-to-day basis, plus a deputy
- healthy and safety training
- general housekeeping
- fire safety
- first aid
- keeping the accident book up to date and reporting accidents
- carrying out, updating and monitoring COSHH assessments
- inspecting electrical equipment and arrange for annual checking.

An employer must ensure all these requirements are met and every employee must be aware of them and work in such a way that they ensure their own safety and that of their colleagues and clients.

HEALTH AND SAFETY

What are the Housekeeping Rules in your establishment?

TIP

Your 'establishment' refers to your place of work, your training establishment or your place of assessment.

HEALTH AND SAFETY

Do you know who is responsible for each of these items in your salon or training establishment?

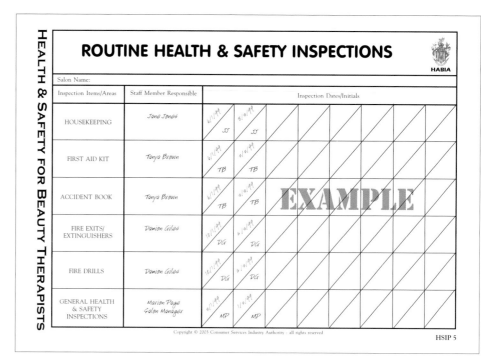

Courtesy of HABIA

What ventilation system is being used in your establishment?

The Workplace (Health, Safety and Welfare) Regulations 1992

This addresses specific areas within the workplace, such as ventilation and temperature, sanitary and washing facilities, eating and changing facilities.

The Working Time Regulations 1998

This covers obligations relating to working hours, rest periods and holidays.

The Management of Health and Safety at Work Regulations 1999

Who is responsible for risk assessments in your establishment?

This is legislation that requires employers to appoint a person or persons to make regular assessments of the risks to health and safety to employees, clients and any other visitor. This means regular risk assessments must be carried out on the entire salon. (A young person, aged under 18, has special requirements in terms of risk assessments.)

There are steps that need to be followed and records to be kept concerning these assessments. See the HABIA Health and Safety Implementation Pack. An employer must follow these steps and an employee must be aware of who is appointed to be responsible for the various issues.

Control of Substances Hazardous to Health 1999 (COSHH)

This set of regulations is particularly relevant to all nail technicians. Many of the products used in nail treatments fall into the category of hazardous substances and every technician must be aware of these hazards, how to manage them and how to protect themselves and their clients from being harmed by them.

Employers have very specific obligations under the regulations. Hazardous substances must be identified and the risk to health from exposure to these must be assessed. Different people will pose different levels of risk (for example, a receptionist is at less risk of skin contact with acrylic liquid than a technician; a person who suffers from asthma is more at risk from dust irritation than someone who does not have the condition). When a complete assessment has been made, substitutes of less hazardous products made where possible, precautions must be taken to prevent or control the exposure to any potential risks.

> **NOTE**
>
> Personal protective equipment should always be the last resort. COSHH assessments must be carried out, precautions taken, all information recorded and the situation reviewed on a regular basis.

Product companies are obliged to supply a product data sheet for each product that details any risk associated with using an individual product and precautions that should be taken for its safe use.

Steps for a COSHH assessment

1 Read the manufacturer's instructions and data sheet for every product

2 If the product is potentially hazardous, record it on an assessment form (see example)

3 Decide what the risk is, the degree of that risk and who is at risk

4 Decide how that risk is going to be minimised and controlled

5 If further action needs to be taken, such as replacing a product with a safer version, or finding and providing protective equipment, a COSHH Action Plan should be made and carried out

6 All details of the COSHH assessment, results and action plan must be made very clear to all members of staff and any relevant training provided and recorded

7 The assessment should be regularly reviewed and any new products added.

These steps do not just apply to salons. A mobile technician is well advised to carry out this procedure to protect themselves, their clients and their clients' homes.

A general list of the products likely to fall into the 'hazardous' category will include:

- cleaning materials (e.g. bleach)
- sterilising and disinfecting solutions
- detergents
- solvents
- cuticle removers
- nail varnishes

HEALTH & SAFETY FOR BEAUTY THERAPISTS

COSHH RISK ASSESSMENT

HABIA

Staff Member Responsible: Date: Review Dates:

Hazard	What is the risk?	Who is at risk?	Degree of risk High/Med/Low	Action to be taken to reduce/control risk
Aerosols (list aerosols used in your salon)	These can contain flammable gases and irritant chemicals. There is a risk of fire, explosion and intoxication.	Everyone in the salon, but in particular the user of the aerosol and the client.	Low	Look for aerosols with non-flammable gases if possible. Do not expose to temperatures above 50 C. Do not pierce or burn containers. Do not inhale.
Nail polish remover (list products used in your salon)	Irritant to the skin and eyes. Moderately toxic if swallowed or inhaled.	Beauty therapists, juniors, trainees and clients.	Medium	Store in a cool place. Reseal after use. Do not use on damaged or sensitive skin. Avoid breathing in. Never place in an unlabelled container.

EXAMPLE

Courtesy of HABIA

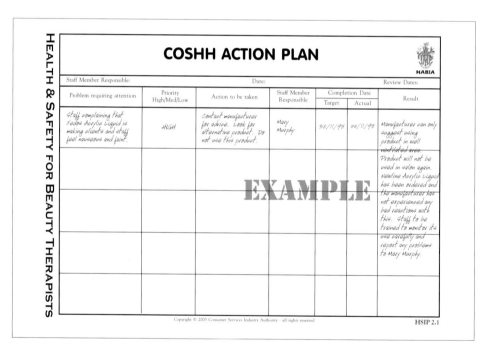

HEALTH & SAFETY FOR BEAUTY THERAPISTS

COSHH ACTION PLAN

HABIA

Staff Member Responsible: Date: Review Dates:

Problem requiring attention	Priority High/Med/Low	Action to be taken	Staff Member Responsible	Completion Date Target	Completion Date Actual	Result
Staff complaining that Xedos Acrylic Liquid is making clients and staff feel nauseous and faint.	HIGH	Contact manufacturer for advice. Look for alternative product. Do not use this product.	Mary Murphy	30/11/98	22/11/98	Manufacturer can only suggest using product in well ventilated area. Product will not be used in salon again. Newline Acrylic Liquid has been ordered and the manufacturer has not experienced any bad reactions with this. Staff to be trained to monitor its use carefully and report any problems to Mary Murphy.

EXAMPLE

HSIP 2.1

Courtesy of HABIA

- nail treatments
- hand creams
- adhesives
- acrylic liquids
- accelerators
- nail primers
- nail preparation products.

HEALTH AND SAFETY ✚

Carry out a risk assessment on all your personal products.

Employers' Liability (Compulsory Insurance) Regulations 1998

Every employer must insure all their employees against any injury sustained or disease developed during the course of their employment. This insurance certificate must be displayed for the information of all employees.

HEALTH AND SAFETY ➕

Where is the certificate displayed in your establishment?

Electricity at Work Regulations 1989

Every piece of electrical equipment used is covered by these Regulations. There must be a person responsible for ensuring that all electrical equipment, including wall plugs, light switches, fuse boxes, etc. is safe and regularly inspected. All equipment must be tested by a certified electrician each year and all records kept. See the Electrical Equipment Register and Electrical Test Records.

The Health and Safety (First Aid) Regulations 1981

This regulation requires that every employer provides adequate supplies of first aid equipment and products. First aid boxes can be easily purchased from high street chemists and beauty wholesalers and the size will depend on the number of employees. This information is given on the boxes. An eye wash bottle should also be provided in a salon, preferably with a bottle of distilled water for washing the eye if necessary. No medication of any kind (e.g. aspirin) should be kept in a first aid box and should never be given to staff or clients.

HEALTH AND SAFETY ➕

Where is the First Aid box in your establishment?

HEALTH & SAFETY FOR BEAUTY THERAPISTS

ELECTRICAL TEST RECORDS
HABIA

Salon Name:

Names and Addresses	Phone Number	TARGET	ACTUAL	TARGET	ACTUAL	TARGET	ACTUAL	TARGET	ACTUAL
ELECTRICAL CONTRACTOR									
Goldman Bros. 22 Cantley Terrace Smithton GG1 1PY	32 6690	6/3/98	10/3/98	6/9/98	22/10/98	6/3/99			
		EXAMPLE							

Copyright © 2003 Consumer Services Industry Authority - all rights reserved   HSIP 6

Courtesy of HABIA

HEALTH & SAFETY FOR BEAUTY THERAPISTS

ELECTRICAL EQUIPMENT REGISTER

HABIA

Salon Name:

No.	DESCRIPTION	SERIAL NUMBER	DATE OF PURCHASE	DATE OF DISPOSAL
1	Warm Wax Pot	GN0002756753	20/1/91	26/2/98
2	Cash Register	XXM-666X-3A	2/3/93	
3	Microwave	ZNAOO98235561	3/9/91	
4				
5				
6				
7				
8				
9				
10				

EXAMPLE

HSIP 7

Courtesy of HABIA

The Reporting of Injuries, Diseases and Dangerous Occurrences Regulations 1995 (RIDDOR)

Salon Name: TOP TO TOE

Accident Report Form   **Number** 4

Details of the person who had the accident

Name JULIE HARPEN

Address 2 MILES WALK, GUILDFORD, SURREY

Postcode GU16 1BZ

Job Title BEAUTY THERAPIST

Details of the person who filled in this accident form

Name MARY MURPHY

Address HILLTOP, WEST LANE, FARNHAM, SURREY

Postcode FN12 7QR

Job Title SALON MANAGER

Details of any witnesses

Name NONE

Address

Postcode

Job Title

Accident Details

Date of accident 27/08/03 Time 10.30 Place STAFF ROOM

How did the accident happen:

Hot water splashed out of kettle when making client a cup of tea

Details of any injuries (be specific e.g. cut little finger on right hand above first joint):

Slight scald on back of left hand below middle finger.
Did not form blister

Details of any treatment given:

Rinsed in cold water for five minutes

Is the accident reportable under RIDDOR?   Yes ☐   No ☑
If yes, how was it reported (by phone, by fax etc)
Who reported it

Signature of person who had the accident: Julie Harpen   Date: 27/08/03

Signature of person completing the form: Mary Murphy   Date: 27/08/03

EXAMPLE

Courtesy of HABIA

Again, this applies to employers, but all employees should be aware of the requirements and who is responsible for them.

This act requires that any personal injury suffered at work is recorded in the Accident Book that all salons should have, even if the injury is very minor. A more serious injury must be recorded and reported to the Incident Contact Centre (for example an injury that results in incapacity for more that three calendar days). Also, if any client is injured and taken to hospital, a report must be made to the Incident Contact Centre.

Certain diseases are reportable. Two that are especially relevant in a salon are occupational asthma and dermatitis.

HEALTH AND SAFETY ✚

Where is the Accident Book in your establishment?

The Fire Precautions (Workplace) Regulations 1999

Every employer must carry out a fire risk assessment (see the Checklist in the HABIA Health and Safety Implementation Pack). This exercise will ensure that the premises are as safe as possible for staff and clients or visitors should there be a fire. They must also ensure that every employee has received sufficient training in fire drills and the correct use of extinguishers. All fire fighting equipment must be checked annually and records kept.

Classes of fire and types of extinguisher

There are four classes of fire:

A: Fire involving solids such as paper, wood, etc.

B: Fire involving liquids such as petrol

HEALTH AND SAFETY ✚

Where are the extinguishers in your establishment?

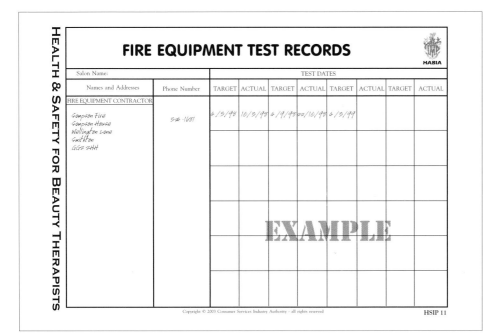

Courtesy of HABIA

C: Fire involving gasses such as propane or butane

D: Fire involving metals

There are five main types of extinguisher:

1 Water
These are red and are only appropriate for Class A fires. They must NEVER be used on electrical fires.

2 Foam
These are cream/buff and used for Class B and small Class A fires.

3 Carbon dioxide (CO_2)
These are black and appropriate for all classes of fire

4 Dry powder
These are blue and suitable for all fires

5 Vaporising liquids
These are green and are suitable for all fires

The Environmental Protection Act 1990

Under this act, every technician has a duty to dispose of waste safely (see earlier in this chapter).

The Provisions and Use of Work Equipment Regulations 1992

All equipment used must be suitable for the purpose it is being used for, properly maintained and all relevant staff trained in its correct use. There are several pieces of equipment that fall into this category. For example:

● UV lamps

● heated mitts and bootees

● foot spas

● airbrushing equipment

● paraffin wax baths.

As with most of the regulations, written records of this equipment should be kept, who is trained to use its and its safety check record.

General guidelines for safe working practices

In general, every employee has legal duties under all the health and safety legislations:

● Take reasonable care of your own health and safety and that of colleagues and clients.

● Co-operate with your employer on all health and safety issues.

- Use all equipment correctly, including personal protective equipment, by following your training instructions.

- Never interfere or misuse anything provided for health and safety purposes.

- Be aware of what your employer is required to do or provide with regards to your health and safety and that of others.

Safety

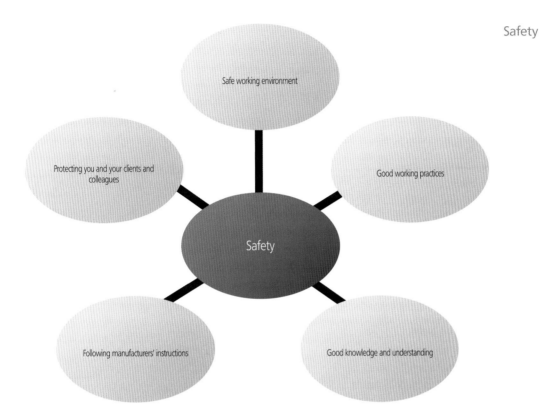

TOOLS OF THE TRADE:

THEIR CORRECT USE AND CLEANING

The following section lists and explains the correct use of the various tools used during nail treatments and the methods for keeping them hygienic.

Files and buffers

There are many, many files and buffers available. In some cases their use is specific and, in other cases, personal choice is relevant. In general a file is used to shape natural and artificial nails, remove length from a natural or artificial nail and remove and shape product on an artificial overlay. A buffer, on the other hand is used to refine, smooth and polish natural and artificial nails. Files are usually long and flat with an abrasive on both sides and buffers are usually chunkier, cushioned and can be either long and thin or in a block form.

Before understanding the various uses of files and buffers, it is important to understand their abrasive qualities. An abrasive is able to grind down by rubbing and it is measured by the amount of **grit**, that makes the abrasive, on an area of 1 sq inch. Therefore, low numbers describe an abrasive that has fewer, larger pieces of grit per sq inch. This makes it harsher. The higher numbers have more, smaller pieces of grit, so the abrasive is finer. The most common grit sizes used in the nail industry are:

- 80 grit: very coarse. Only used for hard, old fashioned powder/liquid overlays or those using MMA as the liquid (see Chapter 7). Unnecessarily harsh for any modern artificial product.

- 100 grit: coarse. Can be used for removing old and bulky overlays.

- 180 grit: medium. Can be used for shaping or removing overlays and length of artificial nails.

- 240 grit: fine. This is the lowest grit that should be used on the natural nail, either the free edge or nail plate. Any lower number grit size will cause damage that is easily avoidable.

- 360 grit: very fine. Used as a natural nail file for delicate nails but excellent as a general file for manicure treatments.

- 400–900 grit. This is usually the grit used in block buffers that are designed to refine the shape and smooth the surface of artificial nails prior to shining. Can be used gently on a ridged big toe nail before buffing.

- 900–12000 grit. Usually used on a three-way buffer where the roughest side is used first to smooth, then the next to refine and remove any scratches followed by the smooth side to bring surface to a high shine. Used on natural and artificial nails.

When carrying out manicures, it is unnecessary to have files harsher than a 240 grit. Pedicures may need a file of 180 grit, as the big toe nail can be quite tough.

A good file to use for all artificial nails is a combination of 180/240. this means that when the natural nail is touched (free edge or nail plate during blending the tip or during maintenance) the finer side can be used. The slightly rougher side can be used for all artificial products, such as the tip and overlay.

When choosing a file there are several things to take into account. Can it be washed? Can it be immersed in water? How long will it last? What is the price? As with most tools, the longer lasting files are usually more expensive. It is worth having a basic understanding of the components of a file in order to help you decide which ones to use.

There are three parts to a file: the core, the backing and the abrasive, all of which can be made from a number of different materials.

1 The core.

   (a) Wood – the old traditional method of making a file. It is inexpensive but cannot even be washed. It is also very brittle and prone to breaking.

(b) Plastic – usually a polystyrene that is slightly flexible. This type of core reduces the vibration felt during filing. A good plastic core has a balance of rigidity and flexibility so pressure can be exerted without it snapping or bending.

(c) Foam – cushions the file and increases its efficiency. The foam could be an open celled foam that is soft but porous so cannot be put into water or a closed cell foam that is waterproof.

(d) Many files have a combination of a plastic core for strength covered by foam for efficiency.

2 The backing. This is the material that the abrasive is put onto.

(a) Paper – has a short life and cannot be made wet.

(b) Waterproof paper – has an oil-based resin coating that lengthens its life and allows it to be immersed for short periods, but it will soon break down.

(c) Mylar – a trade name for a specific polyester material. It is washable, can be immersed and is durable.

(d) Cloth – usually cotton, this has a cost implication but is long lasting.

(e) Foam – quite expensive but durable and immersible. The abrasive is sprayed directly on to the foam.

3 The abrasive. This comprises the particles that are glued to the backing.

(a) Garnet – a common gemstone that is inexpensive and long lasting. The old, traditional files, still available today, are made from wood, paper and garnet but are very harsh and should not be used on a natural nail.

(b) Silicon carbide – the black grit file in common use today. It is a synthetic crystal composition. It is very hard and very jagged. It also has the characteristic of losing little bits that leave behind a fresh jagged edge. This is annoying for the user but does prolong its life and efficiency.

(c) Silicon carbide with zinc stearate coating – the coating acts as a lubricant to make filing smoother and quicker. It also prevents dust from building up between the particles and blunting the file.

(d) Aluminium oxide – this abrasive can be coloured. It is less jagged so therefore less harsh.

The ability of a file to be immersed in water is not only dependent on the materials used in its construction, but also on the glue used to assemble it. Files are usually labelled as washable or submersible. Washable files cannot be submersed in water so cannot be disinfected, they can only be sanitised with an antiseptic spray. If there is no labelling, they cannot be washed.

Ideally, a file should be used on one customer only and then either thrown away (or kept for their exclusive use) or disinfected. The cleaning method for files that can be immersed in water is:

● Using a stiff brush, clean away all dust from the file under running water. This will avoid the spread of dust.

- Rinse the file and place it in disinfectant for the manufacturer's recommended time.

- Remove the file, rinse, blot dry, and place between paper towels to dry thoroughly.

- When dry, keep in a closed container ready for use.

A tip when using a new file is to remove the sharp edges with another file. It is very easy to cut the soft tissue around the nail with a brand new file.

When using a file on a natural nail it is important to file in one direction only (see Chapter 5). When using a file on top of the nail during artificial nail treatments, the whole length of the file should be used without too much pressure. Although everyone has their own way of holding a file when more practised, a good way to start, that will ensure efficient filing without causing too much damage to the nail plate, is the following:

The correct way to hold a file

- Place the end of the file between the forefinger and middle finger with most of the file pointing towards the thumb.

- Place the thumb near the other end of the file.

- By holding the file in this way, the whole length can be used during use, the wrist can be kept flexible so the curve of the nail can be followed and it is difficult to exert too much pressure on the surface of the nail.

Cuticle knife

For an experienced technician, a correctly used cuticle knife is the most efficient method of removing softened cuticle. There are many shapes and sizes available and personal preference plays a large part in choosing the right one. It is a metal tool and, as such, can be easily cleaned and sterilised. It is also capable of causing damage with incorrect use.

Examples of cuticle tools   Courtesy of Beauty Express

General guidelines:

- Cuticle should be softened before removal otherwise the nail plate can be damaged

- Whatever the shape of the tool, it should be used quite flat against the nail plate to avoid damaging the nail

- Cuticle cannot always be seen and can have grown quite far up the nail plate. With experience, cuticle can be distinguished from nail by the feel of the surface when using the cuticle knife

- Care must be taken not to mistake nail for cuticle. A sharp knife is quite capable of scraping off a layer of nail

- Force should never be used. If the cuticle does not come away easily it must be softened more or left until the next treatment when home care by the client has helped

Remove cuticle, keeping flat against the nail plate to avoid damaging nail

- A cuticle knife is not to be used for pushing back the proximal nail fold. This can be gently lifted off the nail plate but not forced.

After use, the knife should be wiped with a solvent or antiseptic solution using a disposable wipe to remove any debris and product, then immersed in a disinfecting solution for the appropriate length of time. If the tool is double ended, remember to turn it around to disinfect both ends.

If the knife has been used near any broken skin, nail or skin disorders, the procedure for sterilisation must be followed.

Cuticle nippers

It is important, when buying nippers, that a good quality pair is chosen. It is worth paying a little extra to get better quality. The blades of nippers need to be very sharp as otherwise they can tear the skin. It is worth finding a supplier that has a sharpening service as a good pair of nippers will last a very long time and can be sharpened periodically as they become blunt.

Nippers that have become blunt or where the ends of the blades have become bent must never be used.

Cuticle nippers are not to be used to cut away the lifted skin of the nail fold. They are for removing cuticle that has been lifted by a cuticle knife and is still attached to the nail plate. They are also used for removing hangnails.

The correct use is by closing the blades over the skin to be removed, squeezing and releasing the blades. The tool should never pull the skin as this will tear it. A good, sharp pair of nippers will efficiently remove the unwanted skin without causing damage.

After use, the blades should be wiped with a solvent or antiseptic solution on a disposable wipe, then immersed in a disinfectant solution for the appropriate length of time. If they have been used near broken skin, nail or skin disorders, the procedure for sterilisation must be followed.

Correct use of cuticle nippers

TIP

If small glass disinfecting jars are being used for this tool, place a disc of cotton wool in the bottom to prevent damage to the tip of the nippers. Replace the cotton wool each time a new solution is made.

Nail clippers

Clippers, as opposed to scissors, are tools that have blades that meet together in a pincer movement. The blades are usually curved but the cutting edge is flat (see picture). They are used for removing the excess length of a nail, either a finger or toe nail.

As with all blades, they must be very sharp so the nail is efficiently and cleanly cut through. Blunt blades will cause trauma to the nail and cause splitting and splintering. This will lead to peeling.

When cutting a nail, several cuts must be made following the curve of the nail. The nail must never be cut in one movement. As the cutting edge is flat, the blade would flatten the nail and pressure would be put on the sides. This could not only cause some damage, it is also uncomfortable for the client.

Clipping nails leaves a rough edge. Always file the nail after cutting to smooth and seal the edge and therefore prevent peeling.

When cutting toenails, always use the larger, heavy-duty clippers as toenails can be very hard. Never make one cut on a nail for the reasons given above and also to prevent the nail flying up into your eyes.

When using clippers, several cuts must be made following the curve of the nail

Clippers can also be used to remove the length of a plastic tip once it has been applied to the nail. As with natural nail cutting, make several small cuts following the curve and never one big cut.

After use, follow the cleaning procedure for all metal tools.

Hoof stick

These are usually made from plastic with a rubber end. They are not designed to remove cuticle but are used to make the skin of the nail fold neat following treatment. The rubber end is used to gently ease the skin into a neat oval at the base of the nail as it can be left untidy after the cuticle treatment.

The other end is often pointed and is for cleaning under the free edge. It can be used for this purpose, but disposable orange sticks are more hygienic.

After use, wipe with solvent or antiseptic solution and immerse in a sterilising solution.

Orange sticks   Courtesy of Beauty Express

Orange sticks

These are inexpensive wooden sticks that can be used in a variety of ways. Some manicurists use them in place of a cuticle knife but, not being a blade, they are not very efficient for this use.

They usually have an angled shape at one end and a point at the other. They also come in different lengths. The longer length is probably more useful to a technician but the shorter ones can easily be used. They have a number of uses and should be discarded after each use:

- Use the pointed end to clean under the free edge towards the end of any treatment. They can then be discarded to avoid any contamination

- The angled end can be used instead of a hoof stick to neaten the cuticle

- They can be used to clean up the skin if it is touched with polish. Use dry if the polish is still wet and dipped in remover if dry

- When practising overlay applications, stick a plastic tip on the end with either Blu-Tack or adhesive, then hold the stick while applying the overlay to the tip

- Use in the same way when creating or practising nail art designs

- When applying polish secures, dip the pointed end into water and pick up the polish secure. It can then be accurately placed on the nail. Alternatively, mould a small piece of Blu-Tack on the end to form a point. This will easily pick up polish secures

- In an emergency, a stick can be used to apply adhesive to a tip. When the nozzle comes off with the lid or becomes too blocked to use and there is no other bottle to hand, dip the stick into the bottle and apply the adhesive onto the tip. Discard the stick safely.

TIP

Wrap a little cotton wool around the angled end of an orange stick, wet with remover and use to clean up around the edge of the nail after painting. Or saturate cotton wool with cuticle oil and sweep it around the cuticle area for an instant tidy.

Skin abrasives (foot files, pumice)

During a pedicure treatment, the hard skin is removed using an abrasive. Its method of use will depend on the type being used. Following the treatment it needs to be dealt with in much the same way as files and buffers. It should be washed under running water using a stiff brush to dislodge any debris, then with soapy water in case there are any creams or oils remaining and then immersed in a sterilising solution.

Remove hard skin with an abrasive

Scissors

There are many different types of scissors. They are not necessarily the best tool for cutting natural nails. The action of scissors can traumatise the nail plate and cause peeling unless they are very, very sharp and large enough to cut through thick nails easily. However the various types of scissors have many other uses.

- Cutting fabric: scissors with long thin blades are ideal for cutting the fabric used in some overlay systems. The fabric is very thin and delicate and needs very sharp blades. The long thin blades are also good if the fabric needs trimming after it has been applied to the nail.

- Pre-tailoring tips: very often the contact area of a tip needs removing or shortening before application and occasionally the sides of a tip need removing. A curved blade is useful for this.

- Nail art: there are many, many uses for small sharp scissors when creating images using various materials.

Variety of scissors used for cuticle removal, cutting nails and fibre   Courtesy of Beauty Express

As the above uses of scissors do not bring them into contact with skin they do not need sterilising, but must be kept clean and free from any products. If they are used for cutting nails, the usual procedure for metal tools must be followed.

Tip cutters

When applying artificial tips, it is very useful to have tools designed for specific jobs. Clippers can easily be used for cutting tips but a 'one cut' tip cutter is especially useful. They are designed like the clippers vets use for claws and have a guillotine action. They efficiently cut the tip without putting any stress or pressure on the nail bed (see Chapter 8 on ways of cutting tips).

Wiping them with a solvent is sufficient cleaning. Occasionally the spring mechanism will need some oil to keep it working smoothly.

Brushes

There are several different types of brushes for the wide variety of nail treatments. This section will deal with them generally in specific groups, but there are many available on the market.

- Liquid and powder brushes. These are almost always made from natural hairs of varying quality. Personal preference and budget are the main factors when choosing a brush for this purpose. They do need careful treatment if they are to work efficiently and last a long time. General guidelines for care include:

  - Only use the liquid monomer on them. Do not clean them with anything else as some of the chemical you use will remain in the brush and contaminate your monomer.

  - When using a new brush for the first time, the 'dressing' in the hairs must be thoroughly removed. Pour a little monomer into a clean dappen dish. Dislodge the dressing by rubbing the brush between your fingers then dip the brush into the monomer. Lift the brush out and wipe on a disposable towel. Do this several times until the brush is completely clean. Discard the remaining monomer and wipe out the dish. Shape the brush while wet into a point.

  - Store brushes flat in a covered container. Do not store upright in a pot as monomer will run down the brush into the ferrule (metal collar) where it will stay until the brush is dipped in fresh monomer. The old monomer will then contaminate the dish and cause discolouration in the overlay.

  - Never put the brush down during or after use without cleaning it on a disposable towel and shaping it to a point. If this is not done cured acrylic will stay in the brush and the brush will be clogged and unusable.

  - Never shape the brush with your fingers as the monomer should not touch your skin.

  - If the brush does get clogged with acrylic, soak it in a little monomer. The acrylic may soften enough to remove. Discard the monomer.

  - The brush should never touch any skin and the monomer is strong enough to prevent any bacteria from growing on the hairs. No additional cleaning is required.

- Gel brush. These are usually, but not always, made from synthetic hairs. These must be cleaned after every use. Use a specific brush cleaner as recommended by the Gel manufacturer or use acetone on a disposable wipe. Wipe the brush thoroughly with the wet wipe and store in a covered container.

- Nail art brushes. There are many shapes and sizes of brushes used in nail art. All of them can be cleaned in water if water based paints are being used or remover if oil based or varnish is being used. They should be stored in a covered container with their bristles protected from damage.

Shaping a powder/liquid brush to a point

Dappen dishes

There are several types of containers available for the liquid and powder system as small amounts of each need to be decanted for use with each treatment. They should all have lids fitted to prevent contamination and evaporation. Only the amount you expect to use for each treatment should be placed in the dishes as product must not be returned to the bottle of monomer or container of powder. The monomer is contaminated with powder every time a brush is dipped in to it, so larger quantities of monomer just get more contaminated as the day goes on. Keep the lids closed when not in use.

When the treatment is completed, discard unused monomer into a disposable towel and put that into the covered waste bin. Throw any remaining powder into the bin. Then wipe out each dish with a clean disposable towel. Wash occasionally with soapy water, but make sure all the soap is rinsed away and the dishes are left to dry thoroughly overnight.

PRICING STRUCTURES IN THE SALON

One of the most difficult challenges when first starting out, either as a mobile technician, working freelance in a salon or opening a salon, is deciding a pricing structure. A good way to start is to research the local area to see what other salons are charging for specific services. Also look through the local paper, especially if you are planning to work as a mobile technician.

When you have a good idea on the level of prices in the area, you need to decide whether you want to be cheaper or more expensive than your competitors. There are benefits to both ways: lower prices may attract some of their clients who want to try a less expensive service, it may also attract new clients who call several salons to compare prices; higher prices may encourage potential clients to try your services in the belief that more expensive should mean better. Most technicians opt for the safer, cheaper route but, if you truly believe the service you are offering is the best, then charge a little bit more and make local standards higher rather than lower.

After you have done your research and decided where you want to price yourself, you must do your sums to make sure you will be covering all your costs and make a profit. This is difficult when opening a salon, as definite costs are not known until it has been open for a few months. However, if you want to succeed in your new venture or career, planning is very important. It is not sufficient to base your prices entirely on someone else's. What makes a good enough profit for them may not work at all for you.

Most product suppliers will be able to give you a rough idea of the cost of products used in specific treatments, particularly if you are using a complete branded range. If you buy your supplies from a wholesaler, this information is not always available so you will have to work it out yourself by estimating how many treatments can be given using each item. For example:

- A tub of hand cream @ £10 (incl VAT) will be sufficient for 20 manicures (or similar), therefore each manicure will cost 50p in hand cream.

Complete this exercise for each product you are going to use. Then make a list of all the products you use for each treatment, including all disposable items. This will give you a cost per treatment.

When you are still learning and need plenty of practice, it is a good idea to work out these costs to you and then offer to give treatments to all your friends and family. Ask them to pay for the products used, which will be a very small amount, and you will give your time for free. In this way everyone wins: they receive a treatment that is enjoyable and, hopefully, has good results, you get some practice at estimating quantities of products used and giving treatments without it costing you in products.

There are many other costs or overheads you need to take into account and these will depend on how you are planning to work. If you work as a mobile technician, then the cost of your car (petrol, tax, special insurance, servicing, wear and tear), professional insurance, wear and tear on your equipment, promotional material, etc. must be covered by the income you make. These costs would be similar if you work freelance from a salon without the travelling costs, but with the additional costs of rent (or equivalent) paid to the salon.

To make sure you have everything covered, add up all your costs or overheads for a year, then divide this figure by 12 to bring the overall costs down to an amount for each month. Divide this figure by the number of days you intend to work each month. This will give you a figure that you need to earn each day before you make any profit. If this is added to the approximate cost of products you can expect to use in a day, you will have a good idea of the total overheads you will incur by working.

If you are opening a salon, seeking professional advice to create a proper business plan is really essential. The principles are the same as above, but many more things need to be taken into account.

After you have carefully worked out your cost and pricing structure in this way, you will have a good idea of the cost of products plus the additional costs that need to be met and how they relate to your income from charges. It does seem an awful lot of work but it will be worth it, as it will ensure that you will earn a living from the skills you have worked to acquire.

> **TIP** ✔
>
> Remember that as a self-employed person, you are responsible for your own tax and National Insurance. This means that any profit you make will immediately be decreased by at least 30 per cent.

SUMMARY

This chapter has demonstrated how a safe and comfortable environment may be created and maintained by the technician to comply with all local and national legislative provisions on workplace health and safety in self- or salon employment. It has provided the necessary information on the use of tools and equipment and guided a technician towards appropriate service pricing structures.

Assessment of knowledge and understanding

1 Why is it important to have suitable desks and chairs for treatments?

2 How do the Health and Safety at Work Act and the Control of Substances Hazardous to Health Regulations relate to the products being used?

3 What are the main 'routes of entry' of a chemical into the body?

4 How can potentially harmful chemicals be prevented from entering the body?

5 What are the three levels of decontamination?

6 Why is effective decontamination essential before, during and after each treatment?

7 Give one example of the type of products that could be used for each of the levels of decontamination.

8 How should solvents be disposed of?

9 What is an allergic reaction?

10 How are metal tools effectively cleaned?

11 What are good working practices?

12 What is the purpose of an Accident Book?

13 What is the Health and Safety Policy that relates to you?

chapter 4

PREPARING YOU AND YOUR CLIENT

Learning objectives

In this chapter you will learn:

- **how to prepare a safe working environment for you and your client**

- **how to recognise the skin and nail conditions that could restrict treatments**

- **how to recognise the skin and nail conditions that could prevent treatment**

- **the importance of a good client consultation**

- **how to provide suitable treatment advice**

- **what after care advice should be given**

INTRODUCTION

As discussed in Chapter 3, the preparation of the working area is very important for the comfort and safety of both the technician and their clients and in order to comply with the legal requirements that ensure the working environment is a safe place for all. From a technician's point of view, it is important that every client is safe, but clients are in the environment for only a short period of time while technicians are exposed to many hazards during all their working hours, and this chapter builds on Chapter 3 to detail how correct client preparation can be a crucial factor in workplace hygiene and sanitisation. A thorough client consultation will also help you to provide the best possible service for your client.

'Making a remedy into a poison'

There are two quotations from a very useful textbook that are relevant to this issue and are always worth remembering:

● 'The Overexposure Principle'. This rule says, 'Every chemical substance has a safe and unsafe level of exposure. Simply touching, inhaling or smelling a potentially hazardous substance can't harm you. Exceeding the safe level of exposure is the danger you must learn to avoid.'

● 'Paracelus, a famous 14th-century physician, was the first to study and understand toxic substances. He said, "All substances are poisons; there is none which is not a poison. Only the right dose differentiates a poison from a remedy." Over the last 500 years, the public has forgotten what Paracelus discovered. The Overexposure Principle is the modern day interpretation of what he learned.' (Douglas D. Schoon, *Milady's Nail Structure and Product Chemistry*, Delmar Learning (Milady), 1996)

> **HEALTH AND SAFETY** ✚
>
> Water is essential to life but exceed the safety limit or be exposed to incorrect use and you can drown in it!

Paracelus is correct; everything is potentially a poison, therefore we must avoid the dose that makes the remedy into a poison. All products should have a Material Safety Data Sheet (MSDS), available from the manufacturer or distributor. An **MSDS** provides the information on things such as how to store the product, any specific hazardous ingredients, emergency first aid advice, possible routes of entry, how to deal with large spills, and similar advice. It is obvious that the chemicals that are considered a potential hazard on any MSDS, or those that require a warning on their labels, are more likely to have a much lower 'poison' dose than any others. But technicians are not in the position to know what the 'poison' dose for each individual is for each of the chemicals. It is therefore far safer to assume that any dose is a potential 'poison' dose to prevent any problems.

Following all the simple rules for safety in Chapter 3 will ensure maximum protection. Further protection will be gained by following correct working practices, as described in this book, and also following the manufacturer's instructions on the use of the various products.

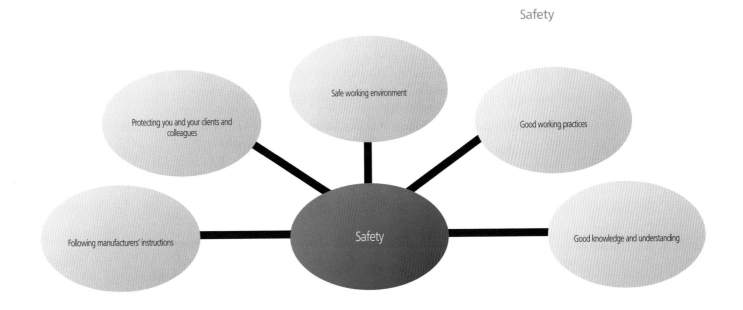

Safety

ALLERGIES AND OVEREXPOSURE

There are two frequent queries or worries that tend to be expressed by both experienced and new nail technicians. One of them concerns allergic reactions and the other is health and safety in the salon. There are some general rules that should be followed.

Allergies

Allergic reactions and sensitivities can occur to anyone at any time. Unfortunately, this is a very common problem in an industry that uses a variety of chemicals every day. However, it need not be such a problem if good working practices are adhered to, such as practising strict hygiene and not letting artificial nail products touch any soft tissue.

- Any individual, at any time, can become allergic to a particular product or food. It may be something that has been used for years or a few days but there is usually a warning that an allergy has developed, e.g. itchy skin, rash, headaches, etc. This happens when an individual has been exposed to too much of the product but every person's level of 'overexposure' is different.

- If a technician or client develops an unusual symptom, the most common one being an itchy rash on the hands or fingers, there is a likelihood that an allergy is starting. In the case of a technician, they must stop using the product or start wearing gloves and, in the case of a client all the products must be removed immediately. Do not wait to see if it gets worse: it will!

- If these actions are taken quickly enough, the symptoms may go fairly rapidly. If not, the condition will worsen and the hands could become swollen and bleed, with the nail plate lifted and distorted. Obviously, the chance of infection at this stage is very high and will make the whole condition even worse. It is really not worth taking the chance of reaching this stage.

- Once the product has been removed, the condition may go. If the client is willing, a different system could be tried which may be successful. If the initial reaction is severe, however, it would be a good idea to do a patch test in the same way as for lash tinting. There are a few products that are the most likely to cause an adverse reaction in any system. Top of the list is the liquid monomer in any acrylic system (or unreacted monomer that may be found as a sticky layer in a UV cured system); an acid-based primer is corrosive so that could be the culprit if it has touched the skin; or sometimes it could be the nail adhesive. It is unlikely (but not impossible) that the dust from a cured acrylic will have any effect nor will the dust from a light-cured material as long as there is no trace of the 'sticky layer'. (Excess dust, however, can cause other problems, so it should not be considered safe.)

- If the condition does not go within a few days or if it should seem worse after the removal of all products, the client or technician should get medical advice. It is important to remember that technicians are not medically qualified and should never diagnose any condition. Instant removal of products as soon as any reaction is noticed is the only safe course of action; leaving it to see if it gets better is unacceptable and could result in legal action being taken against the technician and salon for negligence. To leave a product on a client knowing that it could be the cause of a reaction is negligent.

- There is little point in blaming the manufacturer or seeking recourse if things go wrong. Correct labelling should have all necessary warnings and a professional technician should be aware of how to use all products correctly and safely. We all know household bleach is corrosive and will burn skin and bleach clothes; whose fault is it when this happens with correctly labelled bottles?

'Safe' levels of exposure

A little story that should raise a smile: it is not always easy to explain to some people about safe levels of exposure and how everyone is different. Some just cannot grasp such intangible concepts. I heard a comment recently, about a trainer who was running a course for beginners learning acrylic who, while struggling to explain this to one particular blankly-faced student, used an analogy of how products with peanuts seem to have been in the news in recent years as some people have developed an allergy to them. The light suddenly came on behind the student's eyes and a delighted voice said: 'Oh right, I see now. So which of these products have peanuts in them?'

TIP

If a technician develops a rash on the fingers of the hand using the file and the palm of the other hand it usually means that there is an amount of unreacted monomer on the surface of the overlay that is buffed off during the refining stage. The monomer is touching the fingers holding the file and dropping into the palm of the other hand. If this is happening often, an allergic reaction starts. More care at the removal of the sticky layer is needed or a longer cure time if the product is a light cured liquid and powder system.

TREATABLE CONDITIONS AND

UNTREATABLE CONDITIONS

As nail specialists, it is important to be able to recognise various nail and skin conditions. There are many common conditions that do not prevent manicures or application of artificial nails, others which need special care and, less commonly, some which prevent any treatment altogether.

Two key rules

Always remember the two key rules:

1   Professional technicians are not doctors or dermatologists and therefore should not diagnose a medical condition.

2   If there is any doubt about a condition, do not continue, but refer the client to a specialist.

It is worth pointing out that if a client has an obvious medical condition of the skin or nails and is treated by a technician without an agreement from their GP or specialist, the technician's insurance can be void and he or she would be directly responsible for any claim against them should problems arise.

Splinter haemorrhage

Beau's lines

Lamellar dystrophy

Severe nail biter   Courtesy of
Marco Benito

Onychorrhexis

Treatable conditions

These are conditions of the hands, feet and nails that do not prevent treatment, but an understanding of the condition is important as suitable care needs to be taken.

1   **Leukonychia**: white spots on the nail plate. Some people are more prone to these than others and it can depend on the client's occupation. If white spots are prevalent on most nails, there may be a systemic cause but, more commonly they are caused by minor trauma injuries to the nail plate such as knocking. The spot is where the nail plate layers have separated in a small area. The spot will grow out but is likely to be a slight problem when it reaches the end of the nail, as it may peel.

2   **Splinter haemorrhage**: tiny black streaks under the nail. Usually due to minor trauma and occasionally due to illness. They will grow out.

3   **Beau's lines**: horizontal ridges across the nail plate. Mechanical trauma, e.g. overbuffing of artificial nails or systemic causes, for example, illness, drugs, skin disorders around the cuticle area. They will grow out.

4   **Lamellar dystrophy**: peeling or flaking nails. Usually caused by dryness. Use gentle filing with a very fine emery board, moisturise nails and cuticles and advise client to avoid too much water, detergents, etc.

5   **Onychophagy**: nail biting. Frequent manicures will help stop this problem, as the cuticle can be treated immediately to improve appearance and condition and that is often enough encouragement to stop the habit. Artificial nails can be applied but must be kept very short (to the end of the finger) and the client must return weekly until the natural nail has grown enough to support the artificial one.

6   **Furrows**: longitudinal lines from matrix to free edge. A single furrow may be congenital or caused by injury to the matrix. Multiple furrows are usually caused systemically. Treat with care, as the furrow may be very thin. Do not overbuff to try to smooth the ridge as this will cause splitting.

7   **Onychorrhexis**: longitudinal splitting associated with furrows. As above, but the thinned nail may split along the ridge. Treat with great care, as the nail is delicate. If there is no inflammation or infection, an overlay could be applied to repair the split and prevent further splitting. As the fault is in the matrix, the condition is usually permanent. Strong, healthy nails can be encouraged by careful treatment that will help avoid splitting or a permanent overlay will solve the symptom, not the cause.

8   **Blue nails**: nails with a bluish tinge. Usually due to poor circulation or sometimes illness. The nails are often weak and thin. Hand massage and careful buffing will stimulate the circulation in the area. Artificial nails are not recommended if the nails are very thin, as the treatment will cause too much trauma to the nail.

9   **Hangnail**: small tear in the cuticle or sharp point on the side of the nail, usually due to neglect of cuticles or dryness. The nail fold, if neglected, will often stick to the nail plate and, as the nail grows, is pulled with it. If this happens and the skin is overstretched, it will split at the sides leaving a ragged corner. The lateral folds (side walls) can often produce sharp points of skin. Both of these may be carefully removed with a

clean pair of nippers. This condition can be prevented by gently lifting the nail fold, when softened, from the nail bed and keeping it moisturised.

10 **Bruised nails**: dark spots of blood under the nail plate. Avoid the area if painful, if there is pressure under the nail or the bruise covers more than a quarter of the nail. Otherwise treat gently. The blood will eventually grow out.

11 **Eggshell nails**: thin, pale and fragile nails, usually curving under. Often a sign of chronic illness. Treat very gently.

Eggshell nails

12 **Habit tic**: a series of horizontal ridges down the centre of the nail. Caused by picking at the nail fold. Usually associated with a very large and exposed lunula. Advise the client of the damage being done, but do not try to buff out.

13 **Koilonychia**: flat or spoon-shaped nails, which are thin and soft. Can be caused by an iron deficiency or excessive exposure to oils or soaps. Treat gently.

Habit tic

14 **Pitting**: small pits over the surface of the nail, usually due to psoriasis or dermatitis. Can also be caused by applying a cortisone cream to another area of the body. Treat gently.

15 **Hyperidrosis**: this is over-activity of the sweat glands on the feet. If the condition is severe, then the client should be referred to a GP or chiropodist. It can be quite mild and is sometimes detected by the very soft skin and even 'pulpy' skin between the toes (not to be confused with athlete's foot). The client should keep the feet clean and dry at all times and the use of a fungicidal foot powder may be helpful.

Koilonychia

16 **Corns**: this is a patch of hard skin often found on the side or top of the toes and usually caused by pressure from ill-fitting shoes. The surface of this can be removed during the hard skin removal stage but, if the corn is big, the client should be referred to a chiropodist.

17 **Callus**: similar to a corn, but over a larger area such as the heel or under the foot.

18 **Bunion**: a misaligned toe joint. This can be very painful so care must be taken when working in the area.

Untreatable conditions

These are conditions where the technician must not give any treatment. If you are unsure whether you may treat, refer your client to their GP for permission.

1 **Infections/inflammation**: if there is any noticeable infection or inflammation, treatment should be avoided. Not only is there the possibility of aggravating the condition, there is also, in the case of infection, a risk of the technician becoming infected. Examples of this are:

- infected hangnail

- **whitlow** – localised painful, swollen area at the side or base of the nail plate

- **paronychia** – inflammation of the soft tissue surrounding the nail

- **warts** – raised lumps of horny tissue, caused by a contagious viral infection

- **verruca** – found on the foot. This is similar to a wart but is ingrowing. It can often be identified by a black spot in the centre. A chiropodist should treat this.

2 **Onychocryptosis**: ingrown nail. More often seen on toes but can occur on the fingers. Sometimes associated with inflammation and pain. Suggest that the client sees a chiropodist.

3 **Onycholysis**: separation of the nail plate from nail bed. Seen as a white area. This can be an allergic reaction and is often associated with a fungal or bacterial infection. If a narrow white area is noticed on several nails, it is usually the beginning of an allergic reaction. All products, including nail varnish must be removed from the nails. If the condition does not improve quickly, the client should see their GP. If the seal is broken under the free edge, fungal or bacterial infections can enter and grow on the nail bed. A GP's or pharmacist's advice should be sought. Sometimes, psoriasis can cause separation, but this is usually associated with pitting or other evidence of the disorder.

4 **Onychomadesis**: the nail becomes loose at the cuticle and the new nail pushes the old one off. This is usually caused by trauma in the cuticle area. It should not be treated, in case infection develops under loose nail.

5 **Onychomycosis**: lifting, discoloration or rotting of the nail plate. A fungal or bacterial infection. Some fungi feed on the non-living keratin of the nail, others on living tissue. Any infection must be avoided and the client referred to a GP.

6 **Fungal infections of the skin or nails**. This is sometimes noticed as white areas under the nail plate. An example of a fungal infection of the skin of the feet is athlete's foot. This is usually noticed between the toes as flaky, cracking skin that can look quite wet. This is contagious and should be treated by the client before any pedicure can take place.

THE PROFESSIONAL TECHNICIAN AND

COMMUNICATION

When meeting someone for the first time, a person has only one chance to make a 'first impression', but this impression can have enormous implications for the future of the relationship. As a professional person, the first, second and every impression the technician has on the client is important.

A technician can be an amazingly good practitioner when it comes to applying nails or providing manicures, but will not be taken seriously if their appearance and manner towards their client is inappropriate.

When dealing with the public, personal hygiene and dress requires certain standards. Just think how you would expect a professional person to be when you are paying for their services and hoping to be confident in their advice and skills. You would expect them to be clean, neat and tidy and following an acceptable dress code for the environment in which they work.

There is a large aspect of 'nails' that is connected with image and a professional working within that type of industry should promote a good image. It is not always necessary for a technician to wear a clinical white uniform, unless the establishment has such a dress code, but a technician should be suitably dressed in clean and pressed clothes that are of a style that cannot cause any offence to anyone. A technician's nails should be well cared for and immaculate. Jewellery on the hands should be kept to a minimum for the safety of the technician (products could get trapped under jewellery and cause a skin reaction) and hair should be worn in a way that does not impede working.

> **TIP** ✔
>
> Hair that is continually being tucked behind the ears could create an allergic reaction on the face.

A professional approach in manner is also very important. Clients should not be kept waiting but, as this is sometimes unavoidable, it helps if it is dealt with rather than ignored. If a technician is running late with a previous client, acknowledgement of the situation must be made with apologies. The waiting client must be comfortable and made to feel that they are important, their custom is valued and their patience in waiting appreciated. If waiting is unacceptable to a client who has arrived on time for an appointment, remember it is not their fault and they may be pressed for time. Everything must be done for that client's convenience; for example, another technician (or junior) could start to prepare the client for their treatment or someone else might finish the late running client.

Those dealing with the public, especially in the service industries, must have good communication skills. Their approach, while professional, should also be friendly and interested. They should make the client feel at ease and comfortable, and genuinely important.

A common mistake of those working in this type of industry, and one often parodied, is the technician who continually talks about themselves, their relationships, their social life, their clothes, etc. More often than not, clients are not actually interested in their technician but are much more interested in themselves, their nails and what their technician is doing in the treatment. Use the time during a treatment usefully and educate your client in understanding what they need to do with their nails, hands and feet.

CLIENT CONSULTATION AND ASSESSMENT

Initial information

Assessing the client for treatment is a very important part of every client's appointment. It is a requirement of the National Occupational Standard and the keeping of records is a requirement for insurance purposes. It is widely accepted that the first appointment with a new client warrants a client consultation; what is very often missed is the importance of a consultation before every treatment. A full client consultation should provide a great deal of important information:

- **Name, address and telephone number**: this is obvious, but it is a very useful tool for the professional technician. The address can allow you to do mail shots, send invitations to special events, greetings cards, etc. A record of a daytime and evening telephone number can also be essential if a problem arises with an appointment, such as a technician who is unwell. A timely call to the client can avoid unnecessary travel or upset schedules.

- **Date of birth**: this is a recognised part of an individual's identification, although it is not necessary information for a nail technician. Some clients are not forthcoming with their date of birth and it can be an optional element. One use would be to send a regular client a birthday card as a good PR exercise. If a technician suspects a client is under 16 years, then the question of age must be asked, as it is necessary for under 16s to have a letter of consent for any treatment from a parent or guardian.

- **Name of GP**: this is another piece of information that could be considered to be intrusive. There are not many circumstances when a technician would need to contact a client's GP. If medical assistance is sought or approval is needed from a GP, it is the responsibility of the client to get it and the technician to keep that approval on record in case of later problems. There are some advanced beauty treatments where a GP's information would be useful, but there is no reason why this should apply to nail treatments.

- **Occupation**: a useful piece of information, not only for conversational reasons but also to give an idea of the type of nails a client could cope with. It could also offer clues to any nail and skin problems.

- **Medical history**: with nail treatments, it is unnecessary to go into any medical history in any depth. A client may be quite willing to tell their technician all manner of medical details but what, as a technician, can be done with that information? Without medical training, the implications of the many illnesses and conditions cannot be known. There are some that are relevant in a general way and the main questions that should be asked are:

  - **Allergies**: If a client is prone to allergies, there is a good chance that they may be allergic to some of the products that will be used. If this is the case, it would be a good idea to carry out a skin test on a test nail.

  - **Diabetes**: if a client suffers from this condition great care must be taken with all treatments. Circulation is often poor and consequently diabetics are slow to heal. Any injury sustained during a treatment could therefore result in a problem. Diabetics who do not have their condition under control and are unwell should really have approval from their doctor before embarking on any course of treatment.

  - **Other**: a general enquiry of the client should be made to ascertain whether there is any other condition that may be relevant to nail treatment, for example any loss of sensation in the hands or fingers, past nail or skin conditions that may reoccur and heart conditions that may affect circulation in the extremities.

- **Previous nail treatments**: it is worth finding out if the client has received nail treatments in the past. Results from these treatments would be useful to know, as a sensitivity to products may have occurred or the client may be unable to keep on artificial nails owing to lifestyle or habits (like nail biting or picking).

- **The condition of the skin and nails**: this should be noted on the client's record card at this early stage. If everything looks healthy and in good condition, it should be noted in case something changes at a later stage. If there is any indication of a skin or nail condition, whether it restricts treatment or not, *it must be noted*. Obviously any condition that prevents treatment should be noted, together with the recommendations made by the technician. On occasions when medical approval is necessary, the letter should be attached to the card. Sometimes doctors are not prepared to give a letter. If this is the case, but the client has seen a doctor who has verbally agreed to the treatment, this should be noted on the card and the client sign to say that this is true. The technician has then done everything possible to safeguard both the client and themselves.

If there is any condition, however minor, that is noticed on hands, fingers or nails, it should be noted with a full description. The reason for this is to make sure that the condition does not get worse. Examples could be minor nail separation or a minor skin condition on the hands. This is an area where great care must be taken. The technician must be confident that any treatment will be safe. If there is any doubt all treatments should be avoided especially where irritating chemicals are involved.

Treatment advice

The initial information-gathering part of the consultation should provide the technician with lots of preliminary ideas as to potential treatments. This information should be gathered in an area of the salon where other clients and technicians cannot overhear, as some people do not want others to know their personal details. The client can be asked to complete a questionnaire on their own.

The next questions that need to be asked concern the treatment that the client expects during the appointment. An important piece of information would be to find out exactly what the client *expects from the treatment*. It can often be the case that, owing to lack of knowledge or understanding, the client may expect the most amazing results. A common expectation is for the client to think that a set of artificial nails will stay on forever and never need any maintenance. Another commonly held belief is that artificial nails damage natural nails. This could mean that the client thinks that they can never have artificial nails as they are not prepared to accept the damage or it could mean that they are ready to accept the damage for the sake of beautiful nails. Obviously this is wrong and the technician needs to thoroughly explain that damage will not occur if the nails are correctly applied and maintained and if homecare advice is followed.

> **IMPORTANT**
>
> At the end of the consultation and discussion on treatments, the information should be recorded in writing on the client's record card. This should include all the information about the client and the condition of their nails and skin, their expectations of the treatment, the recommendations of the technician and the treatment that has been agreed. The client should then sign this and a note made of which technician carried out the treatment.

The treatment booked is not always the best one for the client and another treatment may be more appropriate. The reasons for this are varied but two common situations are when:

- the client has reasonably long nails but they are in poor condition or a bad shape. The client may be unaware that natural nails can be overlayed to strengthen them and correct the shape and has assumed that artificial nails are the only option.

- the client does not realise that a full set of artificial nails requires a commitment of both time and finances. They may be prepared to wait a little longer for long nails and start a course of manicures that still involves time but does not cost as much. If they are not prepared to commit to either the time or the financial aspects, it may be better to suggest that they should not have artificial nails as neglecting them will result in damage.

Once this discussion has taken place it is worth reminding the client of all the options available in order that both parties are sure the correct choice is being made. The technician should note down on the record card what the treatment is and what the client's expectations are. This can be referred to later to see if the expectations were fulfilled and it is also useful if another technician treats the client.

Data Protection Act 1998

This Act affects any establishment or person that processes personal data and a client record card is classed as personal data. The previous Act was concerned with data that was to be stored electronically, that is on a computer and therefore only affected salons that used an automated record and booking system. The Act has been updated to include any relevant filing system or accessible system.

The general principles of the Act are:

- Personal information is fairly and lawfully processed. It is reasonable to assume that a certain amount of information about clients must be collected and stored.

- The information is processed for the relevant purpose and will not be processed for any other reason. For example, it will not be passed on to any third party or used for any purpose other than efficient and effective salon business.

- Personal data shall be adequate, relevant and not excessive in relation to the purpose. Therefore, there is no need to go into in-depth medical history that cannot be used by a technician. This may be appropriate for more advanced beauty treatments but not nail treatments.

- The information will be accurate and kept up-to-date.

- The record will not be kept longer than necessary. So if a client has not returned for a considerable time, their record is destroyed.

- Data subjects have rights and these must be observed.

- All reasonable measures will be taken to avoid unauthorised or unlawful processing or accidental loss or destruction. Client records should be kept in a safe and secure place and should not be removed from the salon.

There is a new category that involves 'sensitive' personal data and this has additional safeguards. There is no reason why any data of this nature would be kept on a record card. It involves areas such as racial or ethnic origin (skin type is relevant, but this has no real bearing on ethnic origin), political opinions or religious beliefs, physical or mental health.

The additional safeguards require the person to give their explicit consent to this data being processed. This means that if any reference to racial origin or physical health is made, the client must read it, understand and sign to say that this has been read and is approved. Therefore a signature will cover this requirement.

There is no need to be overly concerned by this Act, if reasonable and professional procedures are followed with regard to record cards.

Products and after care

Details of products used should be noted, if there are options, and some technicians, especially during training, like to make a note of the size of tips used. The importance of **after care** or homecare advice cannot be stressed enough. The easiest way of ensuring this happens is to provide every client with a pre-typed list of after care points with space to add any extra ones. If this list is given to the client, it should be noted on the record card. Then, if a client returns with a problem and insists that they were not told what to do, there is a record that this is not the case.

All of this information forms the full treatment plan for the individual client and it should be kept in the salon in a secure place. On subsequent appointments, the record card should be available and read through before any treatment begins (see Chapter 9).

CLIENT PREPARATION

After the client consultation has finished, the technician and the client must be prepared.

Cleansing the hands

The first step is to ensure that the hands of both the technician and client are clean and that any protective equipment required is in place (such as a mask or a plaster for cuts on the client's or technician's hands).

- The most common form of hand cleaning is soap, preferably antibacterial, and water. If this method is used, great care must be taken to dry the nails and surrounding area. It is better if disposable towels are used for this to avoid the spread of any bacteria from unclean terry towels or hot air dryers.

- If artificial nails are to be applied, ideally, the client should avoid washing the nail area and concentrate more on the hands. The nail plate is many times more absorbent than skin and will retain a small amount of the water and possibly soap. This extra moisture and other chemicals could be trapped in the nail plate and there is a chance that it may cause lifting at a later date. Careful nail plate preparation by the technician should minimise these problems if the technician is aware of the risk.

- There are many sanitising gels and sprays available on the market today that can make the use of water unnecessary. These can be used by both the technician and the client at the desk and can often be a much more efficient method of decontaminating the hands. Some branded products will state which bacteria and viruses will be eliminated and many will be much more effective than antibacterial soap and water. There is also the additional benefit of not having to leave the desk.

- Another very important benefit of using sanitisers is the avoidance of water. With this method, there is no possibility of excess water being absorbed into the nail plate. There are some manufacturers who recommend that nails should not be overlayed for at least 30 minutes after hand washing with water to give time for the water to evaporate.

- The technician should be aware that hand washes and antibacterial soaps can build up on the skin if not thoroughly rinsed and frequent hand washing will dry out the hands. Regular applications of a moisturising hand cream or barrier cream will benefit the hands of the technician.

The technician and the client are now ready to begin the agreed treatment.

SUMMARY

This chapter has explained how to conduct a good client consultation while being able to recognise treatable and non-treatable nail and skin conditions. It has showed how to create a safe and comfortable environment for both technician and client and has provided the necessary information for suitable treatment and homecare advice.

Assessment of knowledge and understanding

1 What is 'overexposure'?

2 How can overexposure be avoided?

3 Why is effective communication with clients so important at the consultation stage?

4 What treatment alternatives should clients be aware of?

5 Why is it important that clients understand all aspects of the treatment, homecare and subsequent treatment requirements?

6 Why are client record cards necessary?

7 How does the Data Protection Act affect you?

8 How are the correct methods of correct product usage discovered?

9 Name four treatable conditions of the nails.

10 Name four untreatable conditions of the nails.

11 Name four treatable conditions of the skin.

12 Name four untreatable conditions of the skin.

13 Why should a technician be able to recognise nail and skin conditions?

14 How would you avoid an allergic reaction?

chapter 5

PROVIDING A MANICURE TREATMENT

Learning objectives

In this chapter you will learn:

- what a manicure is
- all the techniques used in a treatment and their purpose
- painting techniques
- the purpose of products used
- additional treatments, their procedure and purpose
- various treatment alternatives and their timings
- after care advice

INTRODUCTION

There are many variations to treatments that improve the hands and natural nails. This chapter explains in detail the various techniques that may be used during these treatments, their purpose and value and procedural steps for a variety of treatments.

Why a manicure?

Our hands are obviously very important parts of our body and should be kept in good condition. For centuries, both men and women have decorated their hands to make them more interesting and attractive or to demonstrate their class or standing in society. Today the reason for looking after your hands is probably a little simpler: appearance is important to most people and good looking hands and nails are a part of good grooming, plus the decoration of the hands with jewellery and paint on the nails is very much part of today's fashion culture.

A **manicure** is becoming a more commonplace treatment for both sexes. The importance of appearance continues to grow and the availability of disposable income increases with every generation. Another reason for the importance of this treatment is the fact that their owner sees the hands all the time! A 'bad hair day' or a blemish on the face can usually be forgotten until someone looks in a mirror. Dry skin on the hands, short or broken nails, chipped or old polish usually makes a person want to hide their hands and not use them where they will become too noticeable. However, good looking hands and nails can be displayed and used more in emphasising speech, holding a glass or pointing to an object. In fact, they can make the person feel better and more confident and are in evidence to their owner every moment of the day.

HAND AND NAIL TREATMENTS

There are several levels of treatment that are relevant to the hands and nails. The manicurist can carry out some of them and others will require a medical practitioner.

- The simplest treatment (other than good homecare) would be a short manicure that temporarily improved the appearance of the hands and/or nails. This would be appropriate for a client whose hands and nails are in excellent condition and wants this to be maintained with perhaps the addition of having the nails painted. Alternatively, it would suit a client who has time or financial restrictions and needs a fast or inexpensive treatment maybe in the form of an application of hand cream or a reshape of the nails plus paint or it might concentrate on improving the nails.

- The next level would be a manicure that was part of a treatment plan that improved the condition of the skin and nails suffering from common conditions such as dry, rough skin or weak, peeling, dry, brittle or bitten nails. The condition of the hands and nails cannot be dramatically improved immediately, so this type of treatment would be part of a plan for the client that was working towards permanently improving these type of conditions. It could also be a one-off treat for a client who wanted a bit of pampering.

- A manicurist cannot diagnose or treat more serious hand or nail conditions and the client should, initially, see their GP who may be able to recommend and prescribe a course of treatment. A pharmacist can treat some conditions, such as minor eczema or dermatitis and minor fungal or bacterial infections.

- If a condition is difficult to diagnose or treat by a GP then referral will be made to a dermatologist who may recognise the condition or conduct various tests in order to accurately diagnose and treat the condition.

The following section takes each stage of a manicure treatment, explains its purpose and benefits and how the procedure is carried out. Although the stages are in a logical order they do not necessarily relate to a complete treatment.

> **NOTE**
>
> A manicurist must never diagnose a skin or nail condition that has a medical or systemic basis. Simple environmental damage, such as dry skin or peeling nails, are part of the manicurist's remit, together with individual characteristics that result in similar, common conditions such as weak, thin nails or delicate skin. The manicurist will come across many different conditions on many different clients and must be able to recognise all the more common ones and know when a manicure can continue and improve the condition (e.g. peeling nails, dehydrated skin), when a manicure can continue but with certain restrictions (e.g. when bruising or minor eczema are present) or when a manicure treatment cannot be carried out and a client should be referred to a pharmacist or GP (e.g. severe eczema, fungal or bacterial infections).

Manicure treatments

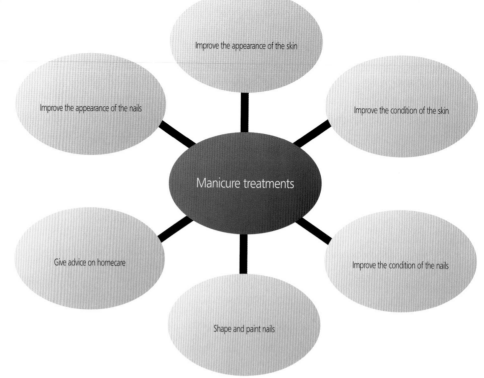

The next section discusses the various manicure options and lists the stages in the order they should be carried out.

MANICURE TECHNIQUES

Filing

It is easier to file a nail into a good shape when it is at it hardest (that is before it is put into water or soaked with oils). This is because an over-hydrated nail will have a tendency to bend and it will be difficult to achieve a smooth and even edge. Also, the moisture may disturb the natural bonds between the nail plate layers and filing could cause the layers to separate.

For all natural nails, a very fine file or emery board must be used. The edge of the nail is easily damaged by causing trauma to the layers and a harsh **abrasive** will splinter the layers and cause them to part.

If you imagine the nail plate as being similar to a piece of plywood, layers of the wood can be seen when looking at the edge. This is how the nail plate layers are at the free edge. Now imagine using a heavy rasp on that edge; the thin wood layers would splinter leaving a ragged edge, especially if the rasp were used in a backwards and forwards motion. Think of using sandpaper on the edge of the plywood; the edge would be smooth and not splintered and the glue between the layers would still be intact holding them tightly together to form a solid piece of wood. This is exactly what happens to the nail plate when a rough file is used in comparison to a very fine file.

Thinking of the same piece of wood, again, imagine a large pair of pincers cutting into the extreme edge to make the piece of wood shorter. The layers would be squashed between the blades and the thin layers would splinter. Now imagine the wood being cut with very fine and very sharp blades that slice through the wood with very little pressure, leaving behind only minimal damage and splintering, which a fine sandpaper could smooth away. This is what happens when any tool other than one with extremely sharp blades is used to cut nails.

If nails need to be severely shortened, cutting with a sharp pair of scissors of clippers followed by filing with a fine emery board is safe. For minor length reduction, a file is all that is needed.

When removing length, it is important to file from the side of the nail into the middle and then from the other side into the middle. Again, reference can be made to our piece of plywood: working against the grain of the wood or against a curve causes trauma and more splintering, whereas filing with the grain or in the direction of the curve is smooth. Filing downwards towards the side of the nail can not only damage the layers, but also feels most uncomfortable for the client.

Filing from sides to middle

When shortening the nail, the file should be held at right angles to the edge of the nail as this will efficiently remove the edge. When the right length has been achieved, first of all bevel the top of the nail to help 'seal' the nail plate against water invasion, then angle the file slightly under the edge to refine the shape and help to seal the edge of the layers.

The top layer of nail is slightly harder than lower layers so, by making this slightly longer it will help to protect the end-on layers from the trauma of knocks (e.g. typing, tapping nails on a hard surface), which can cause the layers to peel.

It is very important to the condition of the nail that the layers are kept sealed. The slightest break in the bonds between the layers allows water to seep between them and cause more bonds to break down. This is the main cause of peeling nails and therefore weak nails. Day-to-day living causes trauma to the nail plate and the bonds between the layers. Knocking the nails, using the ends of the fingers, washing the hands, putting hands in cleaning chemicals, etc. are likely to cause minor (or major) layer separation. Without attention, this situation can become a vicious circle with water seepage, layer separation, top layer peeling so the seal cannot be repaired and therefore more water seepage.

Bevelling the nail

A client, following the manicurist's advice, should remove the extreme edge of the nail at least once a week either during a regular manicure or once a week following a weekly home maintenance routine. The ends of hair become dry and split with day to day living and these are removed during a trim in order to keep the hair healthy looking and prevent the hair breaking off. This is exactly the same as nails but the 'trim' needs to be more frequent as nails suffer more abuse.

The shape of the filed nail should be to the preference of the client who may follow the current fashion or have a personal preference. If client has no real preference and leaves the decision to the manicurist, the shape that best suits the finger is the one that mirrors the shape of the cuticle.

Other shape options would be **oval**, **square**, '**squoval**', or **tapered**. It is important with all shapes to maintain the strength of the nail. The weakest

Finishing with the file – file is angled slightly under the edge

part of the nail is on the sides where it leaves the protection of the lateral nail folds. This is one of the most common places for breakages to occur. The edge of the nail plate where it leaves this part of the finger is quite thick but if it is filed away a thinner, weaker nail plate is exposed. This part of the nail must be allowed to grow straight before any curve is created. Even on an oval or tapered shape, the edge of the nail plate must not be filed for the first 1–2mm.

The nail shape should be even and not longer one side and all the fingers should be the same shape. A client comes to a manicurist because this may be a difficult effect to achieve on themselves and they expect the manicurist to be experienced and skilled at creating the finished results. However, not everyone has a natural eye for form, shape and balance and many less experienced manicurists and technicians file a shape that leans to one side. This is not acceptable and there are ways of checking that the shape is even and in line with the finger.

File down finger for even free edge

Take an emery board (not a buffer or thick file) and place it, upright down the centre of the finger and nail. Few fingers are straight so an overall middle line should be found. Then look at the shape of the free edge, first one side of the file and then the other. They should match each other and be perfectly even. The most common fault, and one to look out for, is the shape of the free edge on either side of the file. One side can be very different from the other but, without the help of the file, they can look the same.

This technique can also be very helpful when creating a perfect free edge shape.

● For an oval or tapered shape, place the file along the centre line of the finger. Look at the placement of the file on the extreme edge of the nail. This is where the centre of the oval should be: central to the finger. Sometimes the shape of the **hyponychium**, that may be uneven on the finger, disguises the centre of the finger. This is not so important if the nails remain unpainted, but if the nails are painted, free edge will look uneven. When the 'middle' has been clearly identified, the nail can be shaped using the sides-to-middle movement.

Oval nail   Tapered nail

● For square or 'squoval' shapes, the 'squareness' of the nail needs to be at right angles to the finger. Place the file as before and look at the free edge. The extreme edge of the nail on one side of the file should be at right angles to the file. If necessary, place another file on top of the first and at right angles to it to see where the straight edge of the nail needs to be.

Square nail

Squoval nail

For an extreme square, file this straight edge and leave the sharp corners of the nail intact or, for a less extreme square, create this straight edge and then slightly angle the file under the free edge to remove the sharpness of the corners. For 'squoval', create the straight edge first and then round it off to make a slight curve on the extreme edge.

Obviously the length of the nail is another element of the shape to take into account. This should be dictated by either the preference of the client or the condition of the nails.

A longer nail is weaker than a short one and it would be difficult to grow a long nail if the condition is very weak or peeling. Although client preference is important, as a general rule a natural nail is reasonably strong and looks very good if the free edge is no longer than 1/3 of the length of the nail bed. This can be thought of as the 'pink and white' parts. If the white is too long the nail is weaker and does not look naturally attractive. However, if a client likes a longer white and is prepared to look after a weaker nail, that is their prerogative.

Cuticle removal

This is often an area of some confusion for manicurists and consumers and it is very important that a good manicurist fully understands this area and how to deal with it.

Return to the section of the book that describes this area of the nail unit (see pp. 43–4) and make sure you have a good understanding of the difference between the **lateral nail fold** and the **true cuticle**.

Where the skin of the finger folds back to create a seal with the nail plate (eponychium), it is the extreme upper layers of the epidermis that forms the frame in this area of the nail plate. There are no dermal layers on the edge of this fold and no supply of nerves and blood capillaries. It is literally a fold in the epidermis and appears as a pale, almost clear, margin around the nail. This is not the cuticle and should not be removed.

The cuticle (as its name implies: a thin layer on the surface) is a layer of epidermal skin that grows from under the nail fold and sticks to the nail plate. It is this that can be removed but not as far back as the seal of the eponychium.

The effects of not removing cuticle are:

Remove cuticles of first hand

- The skin of the nail fold sticks to the cuticle and the cuticle sticks to the nail plate. The nail grows and so does the cuticle. The nail fold gets pulled along with this growth and the depth of the fold of the epidermis increases as it is pulled up the nail. This results in an unsightly margin of skin around the nail that, when pulled beyond its elasticity will split at the sides. This split can be sore and become infected. It always becomes dry and annoying.

- Nail polish does not bond with skin; it peels off. If the cuticle is left on the nail plate then any polish applied will probably peel off in this area.

When the cuticle is softened with water, oil or proprietary removers, it is very easy to remove it from the surface of the nail. Usually, the correct use of a good cuticle knife will make an efficient job of this with the very occasional use of a pair of clean, sharp cuticle nippers.

When the cuticle is removed in this way, the nail fold has nothing to stick to and is therefore lifted from the surface of the nail. This lifted area of skin should not be cut off! Cutting it may result in a very neat frame to the nail but this is living skin and part of the skin of the finger. The body has excellent mechanisms to protect itself and cutting living skin stimulates the body to grow stronger skin in that area. Hence, continual cutting in this area results in thick, rough skin that grows back quicker and quicker.

The nail fold only grows in depth because it is being pulled by nail growth. If the cuticle is removed and the lifted nail fold kept moisturised and healthy, it will shrink back to a small neat margin around the base of the nail.

Therefore, cuticle nippers may be used to remove cuticle *not* the skin of the nail fold. They may also be used to nip off spikes of nail or skin (hangnails) that sometimes appear tucked inside the lateral nail folds. These can sometimes become very hard and dry and annoying. Pulling at them or biting them can sometimes break the skin and a painful infection can result.

Good client education and homecare advice is necessary during this part of the treatment. Clients should be encouraged not to request excessive nipping and, if the process is explained to them, should understand the reasons and outcomes. If the nail fold is very overgrown, it will not look very neat after the first treatment and it is essential that the client understands why this is. It is also essential that the client understands that this area must be kept moisturised several times a day as it will become dehydrated very quickly and become annoying and hard. The skin will quickly shrink and, with continued care, will stop being a problem.

Some clients may insist that the skin is cut off. This is really not recommended and it becomes even more important to make sure the client understands what the results will be. However, it may, on occasion, be unreasonable to refuse, for example, if this is a first treatment on a severely overgrown area of skin, it will look extremely unsightly when lifted from the nail plate and it will be almost impossible to prevent it dehydrating. Alternatively, it may be that the client is having the treatment for a special occasion and wants their hands and nails to look their best. When this happens, the emphasis must be placed on subsequent manicures that must *not* include removal of this skin.

The actual procedure of cuticle removal requires that the cuticle is softened. This may be achieved in four ways.

1 Soaking the client's nails in softened warm water placed in a manicure bowl (most brands have a softening product for this purpose, otherwise use a small drop of fabric softener). There are many ingredients included in brand-name hand/cuticle soaks. Sometimes there will be an ingredient that will help to remove staining on nails; this may be lemon or a very mild bleach (for example 20 per cent volume hydrogen peroxide) or even oxygen bubbles. This process needs only a couple of minutes as the cuticle softens very quickly. A long soak in water is not good for the nail, as it soaks up a great deal of water that will eventually evaporate taking with it some of the natural oils and moisture. After a couple of minutes in the water, ask the client to remove their fingers from the bowl and place into a clean dry towel you have waiting. Thoroughly dry the fingers, nails and around the edges of the nails.

Soaking the client's nail in softened warm water

2 A branded product to remove cuticles. These are usually alkaline based (for example potassium hydroxide) and often have moisturisers in them too. Alpha hydroxy acids (AHAs) are a popular ingredient, as they soften the layer of skin, help exfoliate and aid cell renewal. The manufacturer's instructions must be followed, but the usual procedure is to apply a small amount to the cuticle area and leave for 2 minutes before washing off. This can easily be done during a manicure and the product washed off in a bowl of water and dried as above, or it could be removed using a disposable wet towel.

3 Nail oil. An application of nail oil to the cuticle area will soften the cuticle sufficiently to remove. This does not need removing, as it is nourishing for the area.

4 Following a hot oil treatment, or heated mitts treatment when the area has had a good application of creams. As before, the cream or oil does not need removing before cuticle work can begin.

The methods used during any kind of manicure will depend on salon procedure or the brand of manicure products being used. It is always advisable to closely follow manufacturer's instructions.

Once the cuticle is soft, a clean cuticle knife can be used (see Chapter 3 p.76). to remove the cuticle on the nail plate. The nail fold will be gently lifted during this process. An orange stick covered in cotton wool or a hoof stick can be used to neaten the nail fold after this process, but these tools are not sharp enough to remove all the cuticle. Explain to your client what you are doing and advise against them using a cuticle knife of any kind at home. They can use a covered orange stick dipped in oil to moisturise and neaten the area between visits.

When this has been completed, check the sides of the nails for hang nails and nip these off.

Buffing

This is a useful procedure for several reasons:

- the stimulation to the nail plate increases blood circulation in the area
- it can remove superficial staining caused by polish
- it produces a very healthy looking shine that will last several weeks

A buffed and unbuffed nail

- it will minimise ridges
- it helps to make the nail plate less porous
- polish bonds better and is therefore less prone to chipping
- when used on the free edge, it will help to seal the layers and make the edge smooth and rounded.

An old fashioned way of buffing the nails for stimulation and some shine involved a chamois leather buffer and buffing cream that had a slightly abrasive quality. This can be used if preferred, but the easier method by far is to use a three-way buffer, a tool that has progressively finer abrasives on its three surfaces. Usually they are coloured black for the first and most abrasive side, then white for a finer abrasive, and finally grey for a smooth surface.

The abrasives must be used in the correct sequence. The first side must be used gently to buff over the surface of each nail and then on the free edge. Only a few buffs are necessary to just remove the natural shine on the nail plate. The finer abrasive follows this and slightly more buffing can be used, including on the free edge. Finally, buff each nail with the smooth side. It is not necessary to build up any heat while buffing, in fact excess heat can have an adverse affect on the nail plate and cause the layers to part.

Care must be taken not to over-buff as this can thin the nail, particularly over ridges. The full three-side buffing should only be done about once a month as any more could thin the nail. The last two sides can be done more often to bring up the shine.

Massage

Clients often say that the massage is the best part of the manicure as it so relaxing. It is also definitely the only stage that they cannot carry out effectively at home and it can turn a manicure into a real treat and luxury treatment.

Apart from keeping the client happy, there are many reasons why a massage of the hand or, time allowing, hand and lower arm is beneficial. The hands and feet are the extremities of the body and are often the first to feel the cold or suffer from sluggish or poor circulation.

Benefits

- Blood circulation is stimulated and, therefore, during the period of the increase, becomes more efficient at delivering nutrients and oxygen to the cells of the area and removing cellular waste
- The improved circulation will also help with muscle tone, skin tone and colour
- Lymphatic drainage is improved by the manual friction, so waste from the tissues is removed and the body's mechanism for dealing with infection has a period of increased efficiency
- Absorption of the nourishing cream used during the massage is improved so its nutrients reach deeper tissues
- A good massage can relieve tension in the muscles and joints
- It is relaxing and soothing for the client.

Restrictions

Avoid massage entirely:

- over open cuts or wounds as cross infection could occur or bacteria could be introduced to the open skin
- over recent scars as they could be stretched
- in any inflamed or infected areas
- over areas of bruising.

Restrict massage:

- over painful, inflamed joints, for example in clients with arthritis whose joints should be avoided during the massage
- at any joint that is painful.

Movements

There are four main massage movements but only three of them are relevant to hand and lower arm massage. Once you understand the effects of the movements it is best to create a routine of your own.

1 **Effleurage**. This is the movement that usually starts and finishes a massage sequence, as it is used to spread the massage medium, prepares the client and then, at the end of the sequence, slows down to physically show the client that the massage is coming to an end.

   It is a stroking movement, either lightly or with deeper pressure, applied by the flat of a relaxed hand. The pressure should be slightly increased in the direction of the circulation towards the heart and pressure lifted on the return stroke while keeping contact with the skin.

   Quick movements in this way will stimulate the circulation while long, slow movements aid lymphatic flow and also relax the client.

2 **Petrissage**. This is a more active movement that has a stronger effect on the blood circulation, often resulting in a reddening of the area. Work is concentrated on the muscles in a rhythmic way that is both soothing and stimulating for the client. The hands pick up the skin and underlying muscle in a kneading motion. Absorption is increased from the tissues and the skin as the lymphatic vessels are squeezed and released.

3 **Frictions**. For this movement the thumb is used to massage tissue below the skin in small areas. This is excellent for releasing tension in muscles. Small circular movements are made by the thumb, reaching down under the skin to underlying areas of muscle.

4 **Tapotement**. This movement is not appropriate during a hand and arm massage. It is suitable for the larger muscle areas of the body where maximum stimulation is needed, or for certain areas of the face to encourage drainage. As the name suggests, it involves tapping.

A massage routine

- Make sure you have sufficient massage medium in your hands for the complete massage of one hand and arm. Knowing how much to use will only come from experience with the specific product and your client's skin. As a general guide, pour the medium into your palm – about the size of a ten-pence piece – and rub your palms together to spread the medium and warm it.

- Make sure both you and your client are in the most comfortable position and the hand and arm can be manoeuvred without knocking anything over.

- Have a clean, soft pad covered with a disposable towel under your client's arm for comfort and support.

- Once you have started the massage, do not take both hands away from the area at the same time. This can be disconcerting for the client. One hand may be removed to move position but never both.

- When the massage is coming to an end, slow the movements down and finish by placing the client's hand down on the desk. Make the final stroke down the hand and off at the fingers.

- The client will need to roll up her sleeves and remove any jewellery. If necessary, tuck a tissue around the edge of the sleeve to protect it from the cream.

- Encourage the client to keep her hands very relaxed and remind her if the hand starts to tense.

Step-by-step massage routine

Effleurage by medium

Squeeze muscles on either side of arm

Effleurage with thumbs on back of hand

1 With the chosen massage medium on both hands, take your client's hand with one of yours to support the hand and arm and, with the other, spread the massage medium up the arm to the elbow. Repeat with the other hand so the area to be massaged has been spread with sufficient medium for the treatment. Repeat these actions 2 or 3 times as a relaxing start to the massage.

2 Continuing to support the hand and arm with one hand, and using the fingers and thumb of the other, gently squeeze and release the muscle near the wrist on one side and repeat this up the arm to just below the elbow (petrissage). Slide your hand back down to the wrist. Repeat this once or twice more then repeat with the other side of the arm.

3 Holding the client's hand, palm down, in both your hands, use your thumbs to apply effleurage movements over the back of the hand in a rhythmic movement. Apply more pressure on the stroke towards the wrist.

Frictions on back of hand

4 Supporting the client's hand in one of yours, use your thumb to apply small friction movements between each metacarpal on the back of the hand from the fingers to the wrist.

Drainage movements on back of hand

5 Repeat but use a deep sliding movement with firm pressure on the upward stroke. This is a lymph drainage movement.

Rotate fingers

6 Still supporting the hand, start at the little finger and with your free hand, grasp and gently rotate the finger once or twice in each direction and finish off with a gentle pull, sliding up the length of the finger. Repeat for the other fingers and thumb.

Frictions on palm

7 Turn the client's hand over and use your thumbs to apply deep friction movements all over the palm of the hand. Pay special attention to the pad at the base of the thumb as this can often release tension in the area.

Spread hand

8 With both your hands, spread the client's palm by hooking your little fingers between her little and ring fingers and forefinger and thumb and smoothing the palm with your thumbs.

Rotate hand

9 Grasp the client's wrist, palm down with one of your hands and interlock the fingers of your other hand with those of your clients. Rotate the hand from the wrist a few times in each direction. Finish with a gentle pull to stretch the wrist joint.

Effleurage hand

10 Apply a few gentle effleurage
movements to the hand and arm
becoming slower, and finish off
with the last down stroke coming
off at the fingers as you place
your client's hand down on the
pad. Repeat for the other hand
and arm.

The best response a manicurist can get is a client who is very relaxed and
truly thinks that the massage is the best part of the manicure. Ideally, the
skin will have absorbed the massage medium by the end of the treatment. If
not, use a clean towel or soft disposable towel to remove any excess cream.
At the completion of this stage, ask your client to replace her jewellery.

Hand creams

If a manicure system is being used, there will be specific creams for different
skin conditions. Hands usually need a heavy duty moisturising cream as they
are so abused and least protected. Detergents and soaps destroy the natural
moisture, even deep in the skin.

Ideally a moisturiser (or emollient) that has skin softening properties but
does not leave the skin too greasy should be used. They all have quite a high
water content with emollient and fragrance.

Another type of treatment for hands is a barrier cream. This is not
necessarily used in salon treatments, but it is a useful homecare product as
application of this cream will help protect damage to skin from detergents
and soaps. It works by leaving a layer of a type of wax on the skin that
prevents the absorption of chemicals and the loss of natural moisture.

Painting

Nail varnishes (or nail enamels) are clear or pigmented layers. They all have
basically a similar formulation in that they are a film-forming plastic in a
solvent. The solvent evaporates leaving behind a film of clear glossy plastic,
with or without pigment (colour).

The plastic is usually a nitrocellulose with a plastic resin for the gloss, a plasticiser for flexibility, a solvent for quicker drying and pigments. Nitrocellulose and solvents are highly flammable, so bottles must be kept away from flames or heat (e.g. a window in the sun).

There has been a great deal of debate in recent years about some of the ingredients in varnish, mainly centred on formaldehyde and toluene. Formaldehyde has now been banned in the United States and many varnishes sold in Europe no longer have it in their formulations. Formaldehyde in its natural state is harmful to the body, but it was used in varnishes in the form of a resin with other chemicals to give a good, hard wearing gloss. Some people are allergic to this but a good alternative has been found. Toluene is another debated ingredient. It is commonly used as a solvent in varnishes, but some people may be allergic to it.

Not every client will want painted nails, but those who do should be delighted with the result and the colour or effect achieved. A beautiful, professionally painted set of nails should be better than most clients can do for themselves. The paint should last longer and the finish should be perfect.

Clients can see the result of your painting skills long after they have forgotten the lovely massage or the comfort of the salon and their beautiful nails are what they will show their friends and, hopefully, receive plenty of compliments.

Colour collection for 'grooming'

Some clients know exactly what colour or effect they want. This may be because they have a favourite or because they want it to match a specific outfit or lipstick. Many clients, however, like a bit of help and guidance in choosing a colour as too much choice can often be confusing.

It can sometimes be difficult to help a client choose a colour that they will like during the manicure and then continue to like for the next few days. I believe that there is an easy way to help you decide where to start with your recommendations. All clients who want their nails painted fall into one of three categories:

Colour collection for 'fashion'

1 This group of clients likes their nails to be part of good *grooming* in the same way as they like a good hair style, clean, neat clothes and nice make-up. They do not necessarily want their nails to be dictated by fashion trends, but are looking to complement their general style with a colour that they can wear for several days without it clashing. These clients will like a colour that is from a range that will complement all of the colours in their wardrobe. They may like a 'French' as it looks clean and healthy and will not clash with anything or they may like a colour that is very neutral and complements their skin tone. It is unlikely that they will be happy with a strong colour in any colour range (unless they have one predominant strong colour in their wardrobe).

2 For these clients, their nails are a *fashion* accessory. They will like the seasonal trend colours that perfectly complement or match their clothes or make-up. They will also like the current thinking on length and shape and will be happy with any bold colour (as long as it is 'in'), or 'French', or pale or neutral. In fact any colour or effect that gives them more opportunities (i.e. their nails) to accessorise their current 'look'.

3 The third group of clients like to make a *statement* with their image. This usually accompanies a total image, i.e. hair, clothes and make-up, but can also include clients who may be conservative in their appearance yet like to make a bold statement with their nails whether it be their colour,

Colour collection for 'statement'

decoration or extreme length. This client may choose nail art but will certainly like the more unusual colours from the range!

When helping your client to choose the colour they would like, pay attention to your initial consultation and any conversation during the treatment for clues to the three categories of *grooming*, *fashion* or *statement*.

This will give you a starting point to suggest some colours or effects.

Skilful painting, like all other skills, needs plenty of practice. An excellent manicure can so often be let down by bad painting and the client takes away the proof of that lack of skill to look at many times a day.

The results of good painting are:

- colour that stays on for more than five days; it should stay on for seven or more (this can depend on the condition of the natural nail as it is difficult to stop paint chipping from a peeling nail, for example) and good homecare advice can extend the life of the paint
- a smooth and even surface
- a neat, even edge that neither touches surrounding tissue nor shows any unpainted nail
- a layer that is not so thick that it takes an unreasonable time to dry.

Nail varnish is actually quite a difficult medium to work with. It dries too quickly to give the user time to paint neatly and repair mistakes but it dries too slowly to allow the hands to be used for quite some time after. It is affected by air so if you leave bottles open the varnish will get thicker over time and can become unusable long before it is used up.

Several coats of varnish actually take over two days to totally harden. The surface will dry quickly, but deeper varnish will stay soft for a long time, hence the dented surface when thick polish has been touched many hours later. As a rule, thicker varnish will take longer as will those with a denser pigment. Therefore a thin, sheer varnish will dry much faster than a thick dark red. The reason for this is the ease with which the solvents contained in the varnish can evaporate. Dense pigments prevent solvents at the lower levels from escaping easily.

The fast dryers available on the market will certainly dry the surface very quickly to make the varnish dry to the touch but not to any pressure. Some paint-on fast dryers will form a hard layer very quickly to help prevent damage from pressure but few, if any, can harden a thick layer of pigmented varnish so it cannot be damaged easily in a short space of time.

Therefore avoid thickened varnish. Even very deep colours will dry quickly if two (or more) thin coats are applied as the solvent evaporates from each layer before the next is applied. It is not necessary – and it is impractical in a salon environment – to wait for each coat to dry before applying the next. A thin coat will have dried sufficiently after painting 10 nails and the next application with its solvents will wet it again anyway.

A thick bottle of varnish can be thinned by using proprietary thinners, but this can be done only once or twice to the same bottle. Any more often will change the formula of the varnish and alter its efficiency.

Some general tips about varnish:

- Make sure lids are tight
- Wipe the neck of the bottle before replacing the lid if any varnish has spilled down the outside
- Keep out of sunlight and away from heat (bottles can explode!)
- Throw away any bottle where the varnish has become thick; it is not worth the effort of trying to use it
- If you find a bottle that has a perfect brush, when the varnish is finished, clean the brush and keep it; sometimes you will come across a very poor brush that makes painting very difficult and you can substitute the clean one
- It is permissible to mix varnishes. If you have a bottle where the level of varnish is too low for the brush and it is still thin in consistency, mix it with another either to make a new colour or to consolidate several opened bottles of the same colour. Make sure the bottle is shaken well to mix the varnish.

There are no magic tips about painting. There are no foolproof steps to follow to produce a perfect result. Each varnish will be different to use depending on the brand, the colour, the brush and the temperature. There are, however, some guidelines that may help, but practice is what really counts – and then more practice.

General guidelines:

- Practise holding the bottle in the palm of the hand that is holding the client's finger. This is also safer than using the bottle on the desk top where it can get knocked over by your brush. It is quicker to reload the brush and it is useful to be able to do this comfortably as sometimes there are situations when you will not be working on or near a desk.
- Hold the client's finger either side of the nail pulling back the skin to expose the side of the nail plate. This will make painting much easier.
- When removing the brush from the bottle, lift it out in a spiral motion, wiping the shaft of the brush on the neck of the bottle. This will prevent varnish on the shaft running down and flooding the brush or dripping off.
- Wipe the brush away from you on the neck of the bottle. This will leave the brush with sufficient varnish loaded on the side you are going to place onto the nail.
- Try to load the brush with sufficient varnish to cover the nail and so avoid the need to go back in the bottle for more. Varnish is drying while you are painting, so you want a good coverage quickly. Remember to be aware the size of the nail being painted, i.e. a small nail will need much less varnish than a long nail or the thumb.
- A good brush will fan out when slight pressure is applied to it on the nail. This will greatly assist a neat and even edge at the cuticle area. The way to do this is to load the brush and place it in the centre of the nail plate first. This will avoid flooding the cuticle area with too much varnish. Then ease the brush towards the cuticle putting a slight pressure on it by holding it fairly upright (see picture) and allowing the straight edge of the fanned brush to create the edge of the varnish, then pull the brush down the length of the nail to the free edge. For a wide nail, repeat this either side of the first paint stroke. Otherwise, sweep the brush around each side and make sure that the sides of the nail are painted and have a neat edge also.

Holding the polish bottle

Painting at the cuticle (note: most of the varnish is under the brush)

- Avoid over-working the varnish on the nail. Use the minimum number of strokes, as over-working will start to drag the varnish off and make it bumpy.

- Whatever the colour, don't worry if the coverage is uneven after the first coat. Keep the layers thin and, if necessary, apply a third coat of the colour to get a good, even coverage.

- Always use a base coat. These products are formulated differently from coloured varnish. They are developed to create a stronger bond with the natural nail than coloured varnish and help to form a barrier between the nail and the varnish. Deep pigments can stain the natural nail but pale colours can also have this effect, especially when worn in sunlight or on a sunbed. The barrier of the base coat may not prevent this, but it will certainly minimise it.

- Special base coats are also available and can be used if appropriate. Ridge fillers can be useful, but remember that the thicker the layers, the longer the varnish will take to dry. Ridge fillers work by being slightly thicker and smoothing the ridges. This should not be a problem with a thin varnish, but it will create a very thick layer with a thick, densely pigmented varnish. There are also many base coats that are an important part of a branded manicure system and are developed to help improve various nail conditions. These should be used as the manufacturer's instructions suggest.

- A top coat should also be used. Like the base coats they have a different formulation as their job is to create a good shine and be hard wearing. In addition they are often quick drying. After painting the nail plate, run the side of the brush around the edge of the nail. This will seal the nail plate and also the layer of varnish to help protect the nail and avoid chipping. It is very good homecare advice to recommend that the client reapply a top coat every other day and reseal the edge. This will refresh the varnish, help to avoid chipping and protect the edge of the nail.

- Painting is the last stage of the manicure treatment and the client will need to wait for a while before collecting their belongings, putting their coat on, etc. Without offending, it is good practice to suggest that the client may like to settle her bill and book her next appointment before this stage. This will help to avoid damaging the wet varnish by diving into handbags and purses. Some clients even like to put their coat on and get their car keys out so they are ready to leave as soon as practicable. (There is a key ring attachment available that helps to open car doors to avoid smudging varnish or breaking long nails.)

- There are many quick drying top coats available. Some of them use heat or UV light. It is worth trying a selection of them to decide which is best.

- This is the final stage of the manicure and it is essential that there is no trace of any oil or moisture on the surface of the nail plate, as it would cause the varnish to peel off the nail very quickly. Thoroughly wipe the nail with varnish remover from the free edge towards the cuticle (this direction will avoid any moisture from the skin being wiped onto the nail plate) to ensure it is clean and dry. Some removers have oily conditioners in them and these can leave a film on the nail plate and cause a problem with the varnish. It could peel off very quickly or sometimes bubble. This is when small imperfections in the surface of a newly painted nail can appear.

Sealing the edge with top coat

- If the varnish does not look good or if you make a mistake, it is far better to remove the varnish and reapply (even if the next client is waiting). The client must leave with proof of a first class manicure that took a little longer rather than a second rate one that was rushed.

- It is a good practice to apply a small drop of oil after painting to the cuticle area with the nail angled down to allow it to run over the surface of the nail. This will ensure maximum hydration of the skin, and the coat of oil on the surface will stop the varnish being tacky and attracting fluff or hairs, etc.

Dropping oil on the cuticle

Procedure for painting

1 Wipe over the nail to remove any trace of moisture
2 Apply a thin layer of base coat or appropriate treatment base
3 Apply two thin coats of the chosen colour
4 Assess the coverage of the varnish and apply a third coat if necessary
5 Apply a top coat and seal the edge
6 Apply a drop of oil to the cuticle and let it run down the nail
7 If appropriate, escort your client to an area where she can wait for a while until her nails are dry enough to leave. Carry her belongings for her to avoid damage to the wet varnish and make sure she is comfortable.

French manicure

This is a term used to describe varnish effect that is close to nail art, but is a very popular service for clients. Once again, it needs plenty of practice and only perfect results are acceptable.

A French manicure is the use of two colours of varnish to create an effect that:

a. makes the nail look natural, clean and healthy, or

b. has a stronger looking effect but with similar colours.

Sometimes the term French manicure is used to describe the method but performed using different or unusual colour combinations. It always applies to the effect where the free edge of the nail is painted a different colour from the rest of the nail.

In a traditional French manicure, the free edge, or tip, is a variation of white while the rest of the nail is a sheer neutral colour. However, there are many variations of this in addition to the most well-known version of a white tip with a sheer pink top coat.

1 The natural versions use many variations of white on the tip. The range can be from an opaque off-white or cream to a semi-opaque white or even one with a shimmer. The top coats can be sheer pinks of various shades, sheer beiges or slightly more milky versions. The 'smile line' (the boundary between the free edge and the nail bed either genuine or created by varnish) has a more indistinct and therefore more natural appearance. When deciding which of the many combinations is right for the client there are a number of things to take into account:

A short and unattractive nail
Marco Benito

After painting with French!
Marco Benito

- Client preference i.e. what type of effect she likes.

- Her skin tone, i.e. does it suit a pink or beige and does she want it to tone with her skin or not?

- Does the free edge need to be made to look longer than it is by painting a deeper tip? This will require the more opaque white.

- Is a cream or white based tip colour most suitable for the top coat?

- Are there any imperfections on the nail plate that need disguising? If there are, then a milky top coat will be more effective than a sheer one.

- What will the colour of the nail bed do to the colour of the top coat? It is worth trying it out on one nail to see the effect.

2 The stronger looking French manicure uses a very opaque bright white or cream that produces a very sharp edge at the 'smile line'. The top coat can be sheer, so the nail bed can be seen clearly or a milky version so the nail bed is less obvious but the white tip is still strong.

3 The more unusual variations involve any combinations of colour, e.g. black tip with white nail, silver tip with red nail.

Variations 2 and 3 are the most difficult to paint perfectly, so should be practised the most. It is also worth practising the various combinations of tip and top colour to discover the effects.

General guidelines

- As with all painting use a base coat

- Decide if the nail colour is being painted under or over the tip colour. The effect is different for each method

- Do not paint the tip colour straight across. This looks ugly and is not what this effect should be

- When painting the tip colour, create an even curve around the 'smile line' taking great care to take the colour to the edge of the nail in a sharp point and not a rounded finish. (This shape is sometimes called 'dog ears' and they should be pointed not rounded!)

- Try to paint the tip from one side of the nail to the other in one brush stroke and, if the nail is long, blend the varnish up over the whole free edge. This can be tricky but it is worth practising until it is perfect. Opaque white is very thick and too many brush strokes make it lumpy and uneven

- Don't paint the white too thickly, as it will chip off very quickly

- When painting the nail colour over the white tip, use a few light strokes as the still-wet white can get picked up by the brush and streaked over the nail plate

- Even when using a sheer pale colour, pay attention to a neat edge in the cuticle area and side walls

- Always finish with a top coat.

Some people refer to an 'American manicure'. This usually means an opaque cream tip and a deep but totally sheer pink/red.

3 versions of French: different, bold, natural   Tracey Stephenson

---

TIP ✔

White varnish needs to be a thin consistency. Thick varnish is difficult to paint and chips very quickly. Discard a bottle if varnish is thick.

Paraffin wax treatment

This is an additional treatment that is offered in many salons either as part of a luxury manicure or as a specific treatment for conditions such as dry or rough skin. It can be very soothing for arthritis sufferers. It has many benefits:

- it is very relaxing and soothing
- it will soften dry, rough or calloused skin
- it temporarily gives the skin a younger-looking appearance
- it improves blood circulation during the treatment
- it softens cuticles ready for removal
- it soothes aching joints and tired muscles.

It is not advisable to paint the nails after a paraffin wax treatment as the nail will have absorbed oils and the paint will probably peel off very quickly.

Although this treatment is called paraffin wax, as well as paraffin wax obtained from the petrochemical industry, beeswax from beehives can also be used. Some salons and clients are unhappy using petrochemical derivatives, so this should be taken into account when choosing the wax.

There are many waxes available on the market and some have other beneficial additives, for example tea tree oil, which is soothing, slightly antiseptic and with certain healing properties. Some have aromatherapy oils added for a range of additional benefits. All wax is solid at room temperature and is supplied in either a solid block, smaller bricks or pellets.

This is a relatively inexpensive treatment from the salon's point of view. Set-up costs consist primarily of a heater for the wax, but the wax itself is a reasonable price and the only other necessity is a disposable method of wrapping the hands after application.

The specialised heaters available for this treatment heat the wax to approximately 53°C (but the manicurist must always check the temperature before using on a client) and can be used for immersing both hands and feet.

A less expensive version of these heaters can be used if cost is an issue or, due to their smaller size, by a mobile manicurist. These heaters are not big enough to immerse a hand or foot, but the melted wax can be painted on with a wide brush. *All* used wax must be discarded and not returned to the heater.

Procedure for a paraffin wax treatment

1 Make sure the heater is on for sufficient time before it is needed
2 Have a disposable wrap ready (this could be plastic gloves, cling film or foil) together with clean towels. (This treatment can be used with heated mitts, in which case have them ready to use with relevant accessories)
3 Make sure client's hands are clean by wiping them over with a damp disposable towel (this will prevent the wax from being contaminated)
4 Check the temperature of the wax
5 Hold the client's arm just above the wrist and dip the hand in the wax and remove, keeping the hand over the heater. Repeat this several times until a thick coat of wax is covering the hand
6 Wrap the hand in the prepared disposable wrap and then a towel or place in the heated mitts

A hand and foot wax paraffin bath

Dipping a hand in the bath

Peeling after the wax hand treatment   *Courtesy Amanda Craven*

7 Repeat with the other hand

8 Leave wax in place for approximately 10 minutes

9 Remove one hand from wraps and peel away wax. Discard used wax and disposable wrap. Repeat with other hand

10 Continue with manicure treatment.

Masks

In luxury and treatment manicures it is now usual to treat the hands just like the face and a beneficial treatment is to apply a mask to the hands. This is not necessarily used in addition to the other treatment possibilities but it can be an alternative to paraffin wax and heat treatments masks are useful when used in conjunction with an exfoliation treatment.

There are many brands of hand masks on the market each having different effects. Choosing the right one will depend on the condition of your client's skin. There are deeply moisturising masks for dry or calloused skin, collagen masks to help plump up the skin and make it look more youthful, stimulating masks to help skin tone by increasing the circulation, toning masks to refine the surface of the skin and many others.

As with all products, the manufacturer's instructions must be followed. Some masks need to be kept moist and, therefore, after application the hand should be wrapped in film and a towel; others need to dry out so the hand must be left exposed.

Warm oil treatment

While a paraffin wax treatment is beneficial for the hands, a warm oil treatment concentrates just on the nails and cuticles. It is a quick, effective treatment for dry and brittle nails that have a tendency to snap off in a clean break (as opposed to split). It will also help to improve the condition of dry skin around the nail and an overgrown nail fold. In the same way as with paraffin wax, the nail plate will absorb the oil and may make painting less effective, with a tendency to peel off.

Soaking the nail in oil is more effective if the oil is warm as it encourages better penetration into the nail plate and skin. There are several ways of achieving this, both in the salon and as a mobile manicurist:

1 Place the oil in a small bowl that is big enough to accommodate all the fingers and place this in a larger bowl containing hot (not scalding) water.

2 Soak cotton wool pads in the oil, wrap these around the fingers, and then wrap in foil and a towel. The heat from the fingers will be trapped and will aid the penetration of the oil. A desk lamp that gives off heat can be placed above the hands to increase the warmth.

3 Small electric heaters are available that heat the oil to the correct temperature. The oil is placed in a small disposable bowl and then in the heater. After the treatment oil and bowl are discarded.

4 Heated mitts can be used in place of the foil and towel as above.

This treatment will soften the cuticles very effectively so should be carried out before this stage in the manicure, but after the hands and nails are cleaned and the nails have been shaped.

There are some proprietary oils available for this treatment but an inexpensive alternative is to mix wheatgerm oil with almond oil (slightly more wheatgerm oil).

Thermal mitts

Heated mitts

These are a convenient way of using heat to increase the benefits of the application of moisturising creams and oils. It is also soothing and relaxing for the client. The heat opens the pores of the skin and softens the cellular membranes allowing nourishing ingredients in the creams to penetrate to a deeper level and so benefit the lower layers of the skin. Only ingredients of a small molecular size can penetrate deeper and manufacturers create formulations that take this into account. Products like paraffin have large molecules of hydrocarbons so cannot penetrate to any depth.

Thermal mitts are readily available and although they may represent a substantial outlay initially, they will last a long time if looked after. As with all electrical equipment in the salon, they must be regularly checked by an electrician to ensure their safety.

General guidelines

- Make sure they are ready for use before the manicure.
- When heating, it is inadvisable to put one on top of the other as they may overheat. Place them side by side.
- Most mitts have three heat settings: low, medium and high. If the high setting is chosen for a speedy heating time, check that they are not too hot before placing the client's hands in them and do not leave them on this setting while in use. Medium or low is usually sufficient.

Procedure for a heat treatment

1 When hands and nails are cleaned and the nails have been shaped, lightly apply the appropriate cream to the hands and oil or cream to the cuticles. Do not massage in.
2 Wrap hands in disposable gloves or cling film and place them into the protective plastic bag that is supplied with the mitts.
3 Check that the mitts' temperature is right and place the wrapped hands into the mitts.
4 Make sure the client is comfortable and leave the mitts on for 10 minutes.
5 Remove and unwrap one hand and massage with the cream remaining on the hand. Discard disposable wrapping.
6 Repeat with the other hand.

Helping with exfoliation
Courtesy Beauty Express

Exfoliation

Exfoliation is a treatment that has long been associated with facial treatments but, as the skin on the hands is the same as the skin on the face, it is an obvious step to include this in some luxury manicure sequences.

The uppermost layer of the skin is composed of keratinised skin cells that form a protective layer. They are held together with natural fats or lipids. As more are produced by the epidermis, older cells become detached and are continually being shed (desquamation). Sometimes it is worth removing this layer of older cells (exfoliation) to speed up the cell renewal process and create clean, brighter looking skin.

This treatment also helps to unblock the pores and soften and dry areas on the skin. The skin on the hands is not prone to the problem of dead skin cells in the same way as, for example, the face or the feet because hands are always being washed and exposed to detergents and other harsh chemicals. However, the treatment will improve the texture of the skin and help to treat dry areas.

Another benefit of exfoliation is that as well as removing dead skin cells, it removes other debris from the surface, leaving the skin exceptionally clean and able to absorb moisturisers. This means that the treatment that follows will be more efficient.

Exfolients are usually creams containing a stimulating ingredient such as menthol and small particles that feel quite rough. The stimulant helps to increase blood circulation to the area, which aids cell renewal and also increases the efficiency of absorption. The particles will physically remove the dead skin cells on the surface as the cream is massaged into the hands.

General guidelines:

- When removing the cream from the container, always use a spatula that can be disposed of or sanitised. Never use your fingers as this will contaminate the product.
- Massage the cream into the hands, but do not over massage as the skin could become sore.
- Avoid using an exfolient on delicate or sensitive skin as it could cause an irritation.
- When removing the exfolient, make sure to remove all the grit. Dipping the hands into a bowl of water will do this or use a wet disposable towel to clean the hands, including in between the fingers. If this is not done effectively little particles of grit will interfere with the massage sequence.
- If your manicure product brand does not have an exfolient, then you can use a soft facial brush in small circular movements to remove the dead skin and aid desquamation.

Procedure for exfoliation treatment

- Remove a small amount of product from the tub or tube, using a spatula as necessary.
- Place the cream onto the back of one of the client's hands.

- Supporting your client's wrist with one of your hands, gently spread the cream over the hand with the pads of your fingers, using small circular movements.
- Turn the hand over and repeat on the palm, paying extra attention to any hard skin areas.
- When all areas of the hand have been exfoliated, remove excess cream with a disposable towel and either wash the client's hand in a bowl of warm water or use a wet towel to remove all the grit.
- Repeat with the other hand.

MANICURE TREATMENT ALTERNATIVES

The sequence of the manicure treatment depends on two main factors, the practice of the salon and the manicure brand being used. There are many alternatives that suit different situations, and this section includes a list of sequences that are logical progressions for various types of treatment. They are offered as guidelines, and you should be careful to follow the sequences supplied by the manufacturers of the products you use.

General (i.e. for all treatments)

- The work area must be prepared before the client arrives with all relevant tools and equipment clean and ready for use.
- A consultation with the client must be carried out, even if a specific type of treatment has been booked. An alteration to this booking is acceptable following the consultation.
- It is also acceptable that, following the consultation, additional equipment is collected and prepared for use.
- Make sure the client is comfortable and has clean hands before starting the treatment. The client can either be asked to wash their hands or to use a sanitising hand cleaner.
- The client's jewellery should be removed and placed close to her where it can be seen.
- Sleeves should be rolled up and protected if this is appropriate.
- Your hands should be clean and you should be sitting comfortably and safely.
- Any existing varnish should be removed before the consultation so the condition of the nails can be seen.

> **NOTE**
>
> Timings for specific stages, e.g. massage, soaking, heat treatments, etc. have deliberately not been given. This is because these are stages that can take more or less time as required. Some clients want minimal shaping or cuticle work; others will need more. The manicurist must learn to keep an eye on the timing and make up time if necessary.

Desk set-up for a manicure

Manicure system products
Courtesy of Grafton

EQUIPMENT LIST
hand sanitiser
varnish remover
nail wipes
orange sticks
base and top coats
coloured varnish
nail oil
file

EQUIPMENT LIST
hand sanitiser
varnish remover
nail wipes
cuticle softener
file
cuticle knife
cuticle nippers
hoof stick
hand cream
orange sticks
three-way buffer
base and top coats
coloured varnish
nail oil

Reshape and varnish

Timing: 15 minutes

1 Shape nails on all 10 fingers
2 Clean under the free edge with a disposable orange stick
3 Apply base coat, coloured varnish and top coat
4 Apply oil.

Mini manicure

Timing: 20 minutes

1 Apply a cuticle softener to all 10 fingers
2 Shape nails on all 10 fingers
3 Remove the cuticle on each finger and tidy the nail fold
4 Wipe nails to remove cuticle softener
5 Apply hand cream to both hands
6 Clean under the free edge with a disposable orange stick
7 Wipe nails with remover
8 Either apply varnish or buff nails

Varnish removers for natural and artificial nails   Courtesy of Beauty Express

Nail wipes, a fibre free alternative to cotton wool   Courtesy of Beauty Express

Manicure 1

Timing: 30 minutes

1 Shape nails of one hand

2 Place hand in a bowl of warm water to soak with or without cuticle softener and shape nails of other hand

3 Remove first hand and place into a towel

4 Place second hand into bowl and dry first hand thoroughly

5 Remove cuticles and tidy nail fold

6 Remove second hand and dry thoroughly

7 Remove cuticles of second hand

EQUIPMENT LIST
hand sanitiser
varnish remover
nail wipes
file
cuticle softener
bowl of warm water with softener
cuticle knife
cuticle nippers
hoof stick
hand cream
towels
orange sticks
three-way buffer
base and top coats
coloured varnish

8 Provide a short massage using the appropriate hand cream to both hands

9 Clean under nails with orange stick

10 Wipe nails with remover, apply varnish or buff

Manicure 2

Timing: 40 minutes

This is similar to manicure 1, but involves a full hand and arm massage and, if time, the nails can be buffed and varnished.

EQUIPMENT LIST
hand sanitiser
varnish remover
nail wipes
file
cuticle softener
hand cream
disposable wrap/gloves
heated mitts
cuticle knife
cuticle nippers
hoof stick
towels
orange sticks
three-way buffer
base and top coats
coloured varnish

Treatment manicure 1

Timing: 45 minutes

1 Shape nails of both hands
2 Apply appropriate cream and oil to both hands
3 Wrap hands and place in heated mitts
4 Remove one hand
5 Remove cuticles and tidy nail fold
6 Remove second hand and repeat
7 Provide hand and arm massage to both hands
8 Clean under nails and wipe them with remover
9 Apply varnish or buff

Treatment manicure 2

Timing: 60 minutes

1 Apply cuticle softener to cuticles
2 Shape nails of both hands
3 Apply exfoliation treatment
4 Apply appropriate mask
5 Wrap in disposable material and then a towel to keep warm
6 Remove all traces of mask with wet disposable towel
7 Provide massage to hand and arms with appropriate cream
8 Buff nails
9 Tidy nail fold and clean under edge of nail
10 Apply varnish

EQUIPMENT LIST
hand sanitiser
varnish remover
nail wipes
file
cuticle softener
exfoliating cream
mask
disposable wrap
wet towels
cuticle knife
cuticle nippers
hoof stick
towels
orange sticks
three-way buffer
base and top coats

Male manicure

Timing: 15 minutes

1 Shape nails of one hand. Follow shape of the end of the finger and leave a very short, even free edge (unless otherwise requested)
2 Put the fingers in a bowl of warm water to soak, with or without the application of cuticle softener
3 Shape nails of second hand
4 Remove first hand and place in towel
5 Put fingers of second hand to soak
6 Thoroughly dry first hand
7 Remove cuticles of first hand. Avoid nipping the skin as it will just get harder
8 Repeat sequence with second hand
9 Apply hand cream with a short hand massage to both hands
10 Buff nails but check with the client if he wants a shine. Some men like shiny nails while others prefer them just smoothed.
11 Clean under the free edge

EQUIPMENT LIST
hand sanitiser
varnish remover
nail wipes
file
cuticle softener
bowl of warm water with softener
cuticle knife
cuticle nippers
hoof stick
hand cream
towels
orange sticks
three-way buffer

Male treatment manicure

Any of the treatments are appropriate for a man's hands. Men often have very tough skin that can benefit from the softening effect of, for example, paraffin wax or heat treatment.

MANICURE TREATMENTS FOR COMMON

NAIL AND SKIN CONDITIONS

Conditions that restrict the manicure

Minor nail separation

There are several things that cause the nail to separate from the nail bed (see Chapter 4). If the separation is very slight and there is no evidence of an infection under the nail, the manicure may continue. However, if separation is present, the seal at the edge of the nail bed (hyponychium) has been broken and this can allow bacteria under the nail that could cause an infection.

To prevent passing or spreading bacteria during treatment, make sure every piece of equipment is disinfected and do not, under any circumstances, put any tool under the free edge of the affected nail. Advise the client that they must do the same and keep the nail clean. The use of tea tree oil can sometimes help this condition as it has mild antiseptic properties.

Minor eczema and psoriasis

If there is some eczema present and the skin is not broken or sore the treatment can continue. Avoid the use of perfumed products and proceed as if you were dealing with sensitive skin. Be very gentle over the affected area and avoid heat treatments. These conditions benefit more from moisturisers.

Damaged nails

As it is impossible to list all the possible forms of damage to nails, it easier to list some general guidelines:

- do not treat where there is broken skin
- do not treat where there is any evidence of infection
- do not treat if there is any pain
- be very gentle in the area in case the problem can be made worse.

Bitten nails

A manicure can often help a nail biter to give up the habit. Obviously, there is nothing that can be done to the shape of the nails, but a biter usually also has cuticles in very bad condition. Spending extra time on making the cuticles and the skin around the nail look better is sometimes all the encouragement the client needs.

If the cuticle area is particularly bad, the extra skin that is lifted could be nipped off, but the client must be made to understand the implications and what after care treatment will be required.

Even though there may be little or no nail to shape, the nail plate will benefit from buffing to stimulate growth and improve its appearance.

Sometimes, even on a tiny nail, it is worth painting. The paint must be very neat and a colour that the client particularly likes, but it is another incentive not to bite and the taste of the varnish will remind the client when biting is done without thinking. A series of manicures will result in a vast improvement in the appearance of the hands and nails and, eventually, even the worst set of bitten nails will look natural.

Broken bones

If a client has broken bones in the hand or arm, it can make a manicure very difficult, but a client wearing a cast may want the nails to look good almost as compensation for the inconvenience of the break. It is possible to very gently deal with the cuticles and nails without causing any movement. Painting the nails in a bright colour can cheer up the client.

CONDITIONS THAT CAN BENEFIT FROM

A MANICURE

Weak nails

A client may have thin and weak nails in the same way as they can have thin weak hair – either as a natural characteristic or as a result of a systemic condition. Weak nails can also be due to external effects, for example damage from artificial nails, the effect of chemicals, bitten but growing nails, etc.

Whatever the cause, the treatment is the same. The nails must be treated gently and buffing should be avoided other than with the final side of a three-sided buffer as a stimulation. Filing should also be kept to a minimum.

Weak nails benefit from wearing varnish, whether coloured or clear. This will offer some measure of protection by providing an extra thickness to the nail and also by sealing the edge to help prevent peeling. Several layers can be applied to the nail and reapplied every two days. If the nails are bending, the polish may peel away but can easily be reapplied. Applying nail oil and massaging it into the skin and nail is also essential to help nourish the nail and replace any oils lost.

If a base coat for weak nails is used, care must be taken that this is not used for too long as it can cause the nails to become brittle and snap. Alternating its use with a different base coat and using nail oil will help prevent this.

Brittle nails

Like weak nails, brittle nails may be a characteristic or caused by external influences. A manicure can proceed as usual for this condition, which would obviously benefit from the treatments that use plenty of creams and oils, for example warm oil or heat treatments.

Basic base coats can be used for this condition and, of course, those for brittle nails. The most useful treatment would be the application of a nail oil every day and hand cream several times a day. If the nails are very brittle then it is best to keep them quite short to avoid painful breaks.

Ridged nails

There are different types of ridged nails. Those that are found on thick, usually brittle, nails and those found on thin nails. It is important that you know which type you are dealing with. If the nail has thickened into ridges and minimising the appearance of them by buffing will not result in the overall thickness of the nail plate becoming too thin, they can be treated. However, if the nail plate is the same thickness throughout and the ridges are folds created by the nail bed or matrix, they should not be buffed as the ridges will become splits.

AFTER CARE ADVICE

During all manicure treatments, you should explain to the client exactly what you are doing, why, how this benefits them and how any improvements can be maintained following the treatment.

At the end of the manicure, the specific recommendations you are making that are relevant to the client's nail and skin condition should be repeated and reinforced. These should be supported by suggestions of retail products that will help and suggestions of other or further treatments. Treatment manicures should definitely be followed by further treatments as the improvement in condition is a relatively slow process. As improvements become visible, the treatment may need to be varied slightly. Remember to note your after care and retail recommendations on the client's record card.

If your client's nails are very slow to grow and she wants quicker results, you could recommend that she has a set of artificial nails for a short time while work continues to improve the condition of the skin. The natural nails will grow with the artificial set and they can then be removed.

General tips:

- apply hand cream several times a day, especially last thing at night
- massage nail oil into the nails and surrounding skin
- reapply a top coat every few days to refresh the varnish
- wear gloves when using cleaning materials
- wear a barrier hand cream if gloves are impractical
- do not use nails as tools to open things
- do not pick or bite the skin or nails
- use a hand cream that has some sun protection, even in the winter.

Possible retail recommendations

- hand cream
- nail oil
- top coat
- nail treatment base coat
- varnish remover
- gentle nail file
- varnish colour.

Manicure retailing opportunity
Courtesy of Grafton

SUMMARY

This chapter has provided the information on all manicure techniques, products used, alternative treatments and homecare advice.

Assessment of knowledge and understanding

1 What are the correct methods of filing natural nails?

2 Describe the nail plate with regard to the layers.

3 Why should the nail plate layers be kept sealed and how can this be achieved?

4 What is the cuticle and why should it be removed?

5 Name three ways of softening the cuticle.

6 What are the benefits and effects of massage?

7 What is a paraffin wax treatment and what are the benefits?

8 What would be your recommendations to a nail biter?

9 How would you treat:
   - weak nails?
   - brittle nails?
   - peeling nails?

10 Why is after care advice important to the client?

chapter 6

PROVIDING A PEDICURE TREATMENT

Learning objectives

Learning objectives

In this chapter you will learn:

- **what a pedicure is**
- **all the techniques used in a treatment and their purposes**
- **the purposes of the products being used**
- **additional treatments, their procedure and purpose**
- **various treatment alternatives and their timings**
- **after care advice**

INTRODUCTION

There are many treatments that can improve the condition of the feet and toenails. This chapter explains in detail the various techniques that may be used during these treatments, their purpose and value, and gives procedural steps for a variety of treatments.

WHY A PEDICURE?

Our feet are obviously a very important part of our body and should be kept in good condition: not only to make them look attractive (as they are not usually the prettiest part of the anatomy) but also to keep them in good condition for our comfort. Appearance is important to most people and good looking feet and nails are a part of good grooming; and paint on the toenails is very much part of today's fashion culture. It is a fact that those who are not comfortable wearing coloured varnish on their finger nails often wear colours on their toes, or perhaps a much brighter or bolder colour on their toes. This is probably more to do with the distance away from their face and painted toes do, usually, look more attractive.

A **pedicure** is still often thought of as a real luxury, but those who regularly receive one consider it to be an essential; not only for the sake of grooming but it is also a perfect form of relaxation with a result that improves comfort.

Pedicures have many similarities to a manicure: treatment of skin, nails, cuticles, massage, painting, buffing, etc. However, there are a different set of conditions.

The hands suffer greatly from external influences, for example detergents, sun damage, accidental damage to nails. The feet have different problems: in summer they need to look attractive, in winter they need to be maintained for comfort and at all times they need treatment and protection from some very common foot conditions such as fungal infections (easily picked up from others, by wearing the wrong shoes and as a result of ineffective hygiene) or hard skin (due to the nature of their job). The feet do not often suffer from dry nails and cuticles (although this is possible) and dry skin is usually found on the soles rather than on the hairy skin on top of the foot (conversely the hands are usually dry on their backs). Other conditions such as ingrown toenails and excessive sweating are also common.

Pedicure products Courtesy of Grafton

FOOT AND TOENAIL TREATMENTS

There are several levels of treatment that are relevant to the feet and toenails. The manicurist can carry some out, but others will need qualified medical advice.

- The simplest treatment (other than good homecare) is a short pedicure that temporarily improves the appearance of the foot and/or nails. This would be appropriate for a client whose feet and toenails are in excellent condition and wants this to be maintained plus perhaps having the nails painted. Alternatively, it would suit for a client who has time or financial restrictions and needs a fast or inexpensive treatment maybe in the form of an application of moisturiser or a reshape of the nails and some paint.

- The next level would be a pedicure that was part of a treatment plan that improved the condition of the skin and nails suffering from common conditions such as dry, rough skin or long nails. The condition of the feet and toenails cannot be dramatically improved immediately, so this type of treatment would form part of a plan for the client that was working towards permanently improving these skin conditions. It could also be a one-off treat for a client who wanted a bit of pampering.

- A manicurist cannot diagnose or treat more serious foot or toenail condition and the client should see a chiropodist. A pharmacist can treat some conditions, such minor fungal or bacterial infections.

- If a condition is difficult to diagnose or treat by a chiropodist then the client will be referred to a dermatologist who may recognise the condition or conduct various tests in order to accurately diagnose and treat the condition.

Pedicure or chiropodist?

As a general description, a pedicure will improve the appearance of the foot and the toenails. It will also treat very minor nail and skin conditions. A **chiropodist** is a foot specialist and is able to medically treat a number of foot and toenail problems, having studied a 3-year degree course. They do not, however, work towards improving the appearance of the feet! In fact, they often want to cut the nails down to a length that is unacceptable for fashion. A chiropodist or **podiatrist** (there is no difference) carries out a variety of treatments and it is important to understand their role so that recommendations can be made.

Chiropodists treat people of all ages and from all walks of life. For example:

- children sometimes have pains in their legs or feet as they grow or have problems walking

- diabetics may have problems with the circulation or sensation in their feet

- sports men and women often suffer from injuries to the legs and feet

- dancers who spend long hours rehearsing and performing put stress on their feet and legs that can cause injuries

- people needing minor surgery such as nail surgery or laser treatment

- some people do not need treatment but just want advice about footwear or foot health.

Chiropodists will:

- assess and treat ailments that may, range from problems such as verrucas to deformity

- analyse a person's walk or run and correct misaligned anatomical relationships between the different segments of the foot; orthotics – custom made soles – are often prescribed to achieve this

- monitor and manage foot problems and deformities caused by diseases such as rheumatoid arthritis

- advise and treat patients at high risk of foot problems and amputation such as those who suffer from diabetes

- carry out nail surgery using a local anaesthetic.

The following section looks at each stage of a pedicure treatment, explains its purpose and benefits and describes how the procedure is carried out. Although the stages are in a logical order they do not necessarily relate to a complete treatment.

NOTE

A manicurist must never diagnose a skin or nail condition that has a medical or systemic basis. Simple environmental damage, such has minor hard skin, are part of the manicurist's remit, together with individual characteristics that result in similar, common conditions such as weak, thin nails or delicate skin. The manicurist will come across many different conditions on many different clients and must be able to recognise all the more common ones and know when a pedicure can continue and improve the condition, when a pedicure can continue but with certain restrictions (e.g. when bruising or minor eczema are present) or when a pedicure treatment cannot be carried out and a client should be referred to a pharmacist or GP (e.g. for ingrown toenail, fungal or bacterial infections).

PEDICURE TECHNIQUES

Foot preparation

As with hands, feet must always be clean before you touch them. There are various methods of cleaning feet and this is something the manicurist must do (unlike with hands, where a wash with soap and water or sanitising hand gel is carried out by the client).

The method will depend on the products used in the salon. The feet could be dipped into warm water with an antiseptic additive and then dried or sprayed with a foot cleanser or wiped over with an antiseptic wet wipe. Whichever method is used, it should be done first before the feet are touched. During this cleansing process, the feet can be inspected for any conditions that may prevent treatment such as fungal infections or viral infections.

When the feet are clean, any varnish should be removed and the nails inspected for any problems.

Filing

It is easier to file a nail into a good shape when it is at its hardest (that is before it is soaked in water or soaked with oils). This is because an over-hydrated nail will have a tendency to bend and it will be difficult to achieve a smooth and even edge. Also, the moisture may disturb the natural bonds between the nail plate layers and filing could cause the layers to separate.

For all natural nails, a very fine file or emery board must be used. Causing trauma to the layers easily damages the edge of the nail and a harsh abrasive will splinter the layers and cause them to part.

Remember the comparison of nails to plywood in Chapter 5 (p.100). The toenails are constructed in the same as fingernails but they do have some minor differences. The big toenail is usually much bigger and often thicker than any other nail. It protects a very important part of the foot: the big toe is essential for balance. Remember the discussion of the arches of the foot in Chapter 2 (p.37): it is a shaped like a tripod, that is there are three main points of contact with the ground. The big toe is a crucial part of this shape and it is also important in gripping. Without a strong toenail the big toe would not be so efficient.

The nails on the next three toes are usually quite small and thinner. Their role is protection and they do not suffer the wear and tear of finger nails or the big toe nail. The little toe nail differs because it often suffers from pressure from tight shoes. It may have a misshapen, thickened nail or sometimes a nail that can barely be seen. This toe frequently suffers corns, again from rubbing against tight shoes.

If nails need to be shortened, cutting with a sharp pair of scissors or clippers followed by filing with a fine emery board is safe. When using clippers on the big toenail do not cut the whole width of the nail in one cut as this could cause the nail to split and also puts pressure on the sides of the nail.

Make small cuts all along the nail from one side to the other. For minor length reduction, a file is all that is needed.

Toenails do not suffer from the same abuse as finger nails. They are not continually plunged into water and detergents, etc., but they can suffer from being enclosed for long periods.

The shape of the filed nail should be to the preference of the client who may follow the current fashion or have a personal preference. If the client has real preference and leaves the decision to the manicurist, the nail shape can be straight or slightly curved. The important point to remember is not to file down the side of the nail. Let the sides of the nail reach the top of the toe before you shape the free edge. Taking the sides of the nail away may cause a problem when the foot is in a shoe that will squash it. The nail can then grow into the skin and result in an ingrown toenail. If the sides of the nail are already below the top of the toe, just round the corners of the nail so there is not a sharp point that can dig into the skin.

During the winter months, the toenails should be no longer than the toes. Closed-in shoes can press on the nails, particularly the big toenail or the longest toe. Continual pressure on the nail in this way can cause it to start to separate from the nail bed and infection under the nail can result.

In summer, when open-toed shoes are predominantly worn, the nails can be kept slightly longer if the client wishes. However, if the client wears closed shoes or trainers, the nails must be kept short.

Hard skin removal

This is an essential part of a pedicure treatment and is the main difference between this treatment and a manicure. Nearly all feet have some areas of hard skin to varying degrees. It is most common on the heel and the ball of the foot; on the pressure areas of the feet, in fact. It can also occur on the sides of the heel and either side of the foot near the toes.

The hairless skin on the soles of the feet and palms of the hands has the structural ability to become very hard and tough. Those who use their hands for hard manual work develop thick, hard skin that can withstand a great deal of abuse. People who walk barefoot have a very thick layer of hard skin on their feet to protect against rough ground. This is an example of the body's natural protection systems working.

However, clients requiring a pedicure are unlikely to be the 'barefoot' type of person as they want their feet to look and feel attractive. Hard skin on the feet tends to look very dry and can even start to 'crack' on the heels.

Although many people associate pedicures with summer and wearing sandals, it is important that the feet are also looked after in the winter as enclosed shoes and man-made fibres cause the feet to sweat. The dry, dead skin should be removed regularly to prevent a build up resulting in thick patches of hard skin.

A manicurist can only deal with superficial hard skin. If the areas are very thick, it is worth recommending that the client visits a chiropodist who can remove hard skin to a deeper level using scalpel blades. The alternative to

Cutting toenails

Square toenail

Rounded toenail

Soaking in foot spa

Removal of hard skin

this is for the client to have more regular pedicure treatments and maintain the hard skin prevention treatment at home.

Manicurists should only use an abrasive and exfoliator during a treatment. An open blade should *never* be used to remove hard skin. Most insurance policies and local authority licensing does not allow for instruments of this kind at this level of treatment. There are many excellent abrasives available on the market designed for this use, plus many pedicure brands that have very efficient hard skin removal products. These produce excellent results without the need for cutting skin away.

Hard skin can only be removed when the skin has been softened. The usual method is a soak in warm water containing a small amount of liquid soap, for cleansing and softening, and an antiseptic solution. (Many inexpensive foot soaking solutions are readily available.) Feet can be soaked in a clean plastic bowl but, ideally, a specific piece of equipment with a thermostat to control and maintain the temperature of the water is preferable for the comfort of the client.

After the toenails have been filed and shaped and cuticle remover (if used) has been applied to the toes, the feet are placed in the water for around 5 minutes. This is very relaxing for the client, especially if the bowl has a massaging facility. Five minutes should give sufficient time for the hard skin to soften, especially if a suitable solution has been added.

Remove one foot from the bowl and place it onto a clean towel. Feel with your fingers for the areas of hard skin and, using the rough side of the abrasive, buff off the skin until the area feels smooth and soft to your fingers. Feel all around the foot taking care not to miss any areas.

After all the areas of hard skin have been removed with the harsh abrasive it is important to smooth the skin. As with using a three-way buffer on the nails, the abrasive leaves the surface feeling rough and, when the skin dries out, this will be unpleasant. Most foot files have a hard and soft side, so buff over all areas with the softer side to smooth and 'polish' the skin.

If an exfoliator is used, manufacturer's instructions should be followed.

When all the hard skin has been removed and the skin feels smooth, return the foot to the bowl so any debris can be washed away. This will also serve to keep the foot warm while the process is repeated on the other foot.

If a heated bowl is not being used, the water will get too cold for the foot to be returned. In this case, after the hard skin removal, continue to the cuticle removal then wrap the foot in a towel to keep it warm while the second foot is treated.

It is advisable to remove the bowl of water at the end of this stage.

Cuticle removal

As for manicure, it is important to understand this area of the nail unit. The structure on the toes is the same as on the fingers.

The cuticle (as its name implies: a thin layer on the surface) is a layer of epidermal skin that grows from under the nail fold and sticks to the nail plate. It is this that can be removed, but not as far back as the seal of the eponychium.

As in a manicure, this skin should be removed and it is usually very easy to do so. On toes, the nail fold is not always so evident, but there is plenty of cuticle waiting to be removed.

When the cuticle is softened with water, oil or proprietary removers, it is very easy to remove it from the surface of the nail. Usually, the correct use of a good cuticle knife will make an efficient job of this with the very occasional use of a pair of clean, sharp cuticle nippers. Often there is so much cuticle that the use of nippers is desirable after the skin has been lifted from the nail plate.

This is an important part of the treatment. It will make the toes look better, neater and well looked after. It will also make painting easier and more effective.

Cuticle should only be removed when it has been softened. During a pedicure this is almost always after the feet have been soaked.

The methods used during any kind of pedicure will depend on salon procedure or the brand of pedicure products being used. It is always advisable to closely follow manufacturer's instructions.

Wrap foot and remove cuticles

Buffing

This is a useful procedure for several reasons:

- the stimulation to the nail plate increases blood circulation in the area
- it can remove superficial staining caused by polish
- it produces a very healthy looking shine that will last several weeks
- it will minimise ridges
- it helps to make the nail plate less porous
- polish bonds better and is therefore less prone to chipping
- when used on the free edge, it will help to seal the layers and make the edge smooth and rounded.

A three-way buffer is a tool that has progressively finer abrasives on its three surfaces. Usually it is coloured black for the first and most abrasive side, then white for a finer abrasive and finally grey for a smooth surface.

Care must be taken not to over-buff as this can thin the nail, particularly over ridges. The full three-side buffing should only be done about once a month as any more could thin the nail. The last two sides can be done more often to bring up the shine.

Sometimes the big toenail has excessive ridges. If the nail itself is quite thick these ridges can reduced before the use of a three-way buffer. This can be done with a clean white block buffer or a 240 grit file. Be careful not to buff too much and thin the nail. Never do this to a nail that is thin and delicate.

TIP

Buffing the toenails makes varnish stay on much longer.

The end of this stage is a good time to clean under the nails. Buffing dust has probably collected there and the nail bed on the toes sheds dead skin cells. Use a clean orange stick and have a tissue or cotton wool disc in your hand to wipe the orange stick after cleaning under each nail. Take care not to break the seal of the hyponychium.

Massage

Clients often say that the massage is the best part of the pedicure as it so relaxing. It is also definitely the only stage that they cannot carry out effectively at home and it can turn a pedicure into a real treat and luxury treatment.

Apart from keeping the client happy, there are many reasons why a massage of the foot or, time allowing, foot and lower leg is beneficial. The hands and feet are the extremities of the body and often the first to feel the cold or suffer from sluggish or poor circulation. The benefits of massage include the following:

- blood circulation is stimulated and, therefore, during the period of the increase, becomes more efficient at delivering nutrients and oxygen to the cells of the area and removing cellular waste

- the improved circulation will also help with muscle tone, skin tone and colour

- lymphatic drainage is improved by the manual friction, so waste from the tissues is removed and the body's mechanism for dealing with infection has a period of increased efficiency

- absorption of the nourishing cream used during the massage is improved so its nutrients reach deeper tissues

- a good massage can relieve tension in the muscles and joints

- it is relaxing and soothing for the client.

There are situations and conditions when massage must be avoided or restricted. Avoid massage:

- over open cuts or wounds, as cross infection could occur or bacteria could be introduced to the open skin

- over recent scars as they could be stretched

- in inflamed or infected areas

- over areas of bruising.

Restrict massage:

- over painful, inflamed joints, for example in clients with arthritis whose joints should be avoided during the massage

- at any joint that is painful.

Movements

See Chapter 5 (p.107) for the main movements.

A massage routine

- Make sure you have sufficient massage medium in your hands for the complete massage of one hand and arm. Knowing how much to use will only come from experience with the specific product and your client's skin.

- Depending on your working conditions, the massage may be carried out with your client's foot on your lap or resting on a foot stool. Make sure your lap or the stool are covered with a clean towel.

- Once you have started the massage, do not take both hands away from the area at the same time. This can be disconcerting for the client. One hand may be removed to move position but never both.

- When the massage is coming to an end, slow the movements down and finish by placing the client's foot down on the floor. Make the final stroke down the foot and off at the toes.

- Encourage the client to keep her feet very relaxed and remind her if the foot or leg starts to tense.

1 With the chosen massage medium on both hands, take your client's foot with one of yours to support the foot and leg and, with the other, spread the massage medium up the leg to just below the knee. Repeat with the other hand so the area to be massaged has been spread with sufficient medium for the treatment. Repeat these actions 2 or 3 times as a relaxing start to the massage.

2 Support the foot and leg on your lap or stool with one hand and, using the fingers and thumb of the other, gently squeeze and release the calf muscle near the ankle on one side and repeat this up the leg to just below the knee (petrissage). Slide your hand back down to the ankle. Repeat this once or twice more then repeat with the other side of the leg.

3 Holding the client's foot in both your hands, apply effleurage movements over the top of the foot in a rhythmic movement. Apply more pressure on the stroke towards the ankle.

4 Supporting the foot, use your thumb to apply small friction movements between each metatarsal on the top of the foot from the toes to the ankle.

5 Repeat, but use a deep sliding movement with firm pressure on the upward stroke. This is a lymph drainage movement.

6 Hold the toes between the palms of both hands (using the heel of the hand, that is the part of the palm nearer to the wrist) and 'grind' the toes. This is very relaxing.

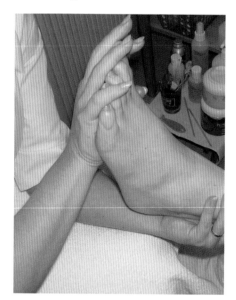

7 Supporting the heel of the foot, flex the foot up and use your thumbs to apply deep friction movements all over the sole of the foot. With the side of your forefinger and thumb, squeeze the outside edge of the foot.

8 With both your hands, place your fingers on the top of the foot and with your thumbs on the sole just below the toes, spread the foot while applying small friction movements with your thumbs.

9 Grasp the client's ankle and rotate the foot from the ankle a few times in each direction.

10 Apply a few gentle effleurage movements to the foot and leg becoming slower, and finish off with the last down stroke coming off at the toes as you place your client's foot down on the towel.

Wrap your client's foot in the towel to keep warm. Repeat for the other foot and leg.

Painting

Not every client will want painted nails, but those who do should be delighted with the result and the colour or effect achieved. A beautiful, professionally painted set of nails should be better than most clients can do for themselves. The paint should last longer and the finish should be perfect.

Clients will often choose a colour that is bolder than one they would wear on their fingers. If they are unsure, follow the general rules given for a manicure to help them decide.

Skilful painting, like all other skills, needs plenty of practice. An excellent pedicure can so often be let down by bad painting and the client takes away the proof of that lack of skill to be seen several times a day.

The results of good painting are:

- colour that stays on for more than five days; it should stay on for seven or more. (Paint on toes usually lasts longer than fingers as it is not immersed in water several times a day)

- a smooth and even surface

- a neat, even edge that neither touches surrounding tissue nor shows any unpainted nail

- a layer that is not so thick that it takes an unreasonable time to dry.

There are no magic tips about painting. There are no foolproof steps to follow to produce a perfect result. Each varnish will be different to use depending on the brand, the colour, the brush and the temperature. There are, however, some guidelines that may help, but practice is what really counts – and then more practice.

General guidelines for painting toenails:

Paint nails

- Toes need to be kept apart while painting and drying. Use a clean pair of toe separators for each foot or roll a tissue up and wind it around the toes (the tissue can be discarded once the varnish is dry).

- Make sure you and your client are in a comfortable position and that the foot is at an angle that allows you to see the toenails properly.

- Practise holding the bottle in the palm of the hand that is holding the client's toe. This is safer than using the bottle on the desk top where it can get knocked over by your brush. It is also quicker to reload the brush and it is useful to be able to do this comfortably as sometimes there are situations when you will not be working on or near a desk.

- When removing the brush from the bottle, lift it out in a spiral motion wiping the shaft of the brush on the neck of the bottle. This will prevent varnish on the shaft running down and flooding the brush or dripping off.

- Wipe the brush away from you on the neck of the bottle. This will leave the brush with sufficient varnish loaded on the side you are going to place onto the nail.

- Try to load the brush with sufficient varnish to cover the nail and so avoid the need to go back in the bottle for more. Varnish is drying while you are painting so you want a good coverage quickly. Remember to be aware of the size of the nail being painted, i.e. a small toenail will need much less varnish than the big toe.

- Avoid over-working the varnish on the nail. Use the minimum number of strokes, as over-working will start to drag the varnish off and make it bumpy.

- Whatever the colour, don't worry if the coverage is uneven after the first coat. Keep the layers thin and, if necessary, apply a third coat of the colour to get a good, even coverage.

- Always use a base coat. These products are formulated differently from coloured varnish. They are developed to create a stronger bond with the natural nail than coloured varnish and help to form a barrier between the nail and the varnish. Deep pigments can stain the natural nail but pale colours can also have this effect, especially when worn in sunlight or on a sunbed. The barrier of the base coat may not prevent this, but it will certainly minimise it.

- Special base coats are also available and can be used if appropriate. Ridge fillers can be useful, but remember that the thicker the layers, the longer the varnish will take to dry. Ridge fillers work by being slightly thicker and smoothing the ridges. This should not be a problem with a thin varnish, but it will create a very thick layer with a thick, densely pigmented varnish.

- A top coat should also be used. Like the base coats they have a different formulation as their job is to create a good shine and be hard wearing. In addition they are often quick drying. After painting the nail plate, run the side of the brush around the edge of the nail. This will seal the nail plate and also the layer of varnish to help protect the nail and avoid chipping.

- Painting is the last stage of the pedicure treatment and the client will need to wait for a while before collecting their belongings, putting their coat on etc. It is a good idea if a client brings sandals with her for a pedicure treatment. This means that she does not need to wait until the nails are dry before leaving. As varnish takes a long time to dry, putting on shoes will almost always leave dents in the varnish, even if the surface is dry.

- This is the final stage of the pedicure and it is essential that there is no trace of any oil or moisture on the surface of the nail plate, as it would cause the varnish to peel off the nail very quickly. Thoroughly wipe the nail with varnish remover from the free edge towards the cuticle (this direction will avoid any moisture from the skin being wiped onto the nail plate) to ensure it is clean and dry. Some removers have oily conditioners in them and these can leave a film on the nail plate and cause a problem with the varnish. It could peel off very quickly or sometimes bubble. This is when small imperfections in the surface of a newly painted nail can appear.

- If the varnish does not look good or if you make a mistake, it is far better to remove the varnish and reapply (even if the next client is waiting). The client must leave with proof of a first class pedicure that took a little longer rather than a second rate one that was rushed.

- It is a good practice to apply a small drop of oil after painting to the cuticle area with the nail angled down to allow it to run over the surface of the nail. This will ensure maximum hydration of the skin, and the coat of oil on the surface will stop the varnish being tacky and attracting fluff or hairs, etc.

Procedure for painting

1 Wipe over the nail to remove any trace of moisture
2 Apply a thin layer of base coat or appropriate treatment base
3 Apply two thin coats of the chosen colour
4 Assess the coverage of the varnish and apply a third coat if necessary
5 Apply a top coat and seal the edge
6 Apply a drop of oil to the cuticle and let it run down the nail
7 If appropriate, escort your client to an area where she can wait for a while until her nails are dry enough to leave.

French pedicure

See Chapter 5 (p.115) for details on French manicure, which can be applied to the feet.

Paraffin wax treatment

This is an additional treatment that is offered in many salons either as part of a luxury pedicure or as a specific treatment for conditions such as dry or rough skin. It can be very soothing for arthritis sufferers.

This treatment in a pedicure has all the same benefits as in a manicure:

- it is very relaxing and soothing
- it will soften dry, rough or calloused skin
- it temporarily gives the skin a younger-looking appearance
- it improves blood circulation during the treatment
- it softens cuticles ready for removal
- it soothes aching joints and tired muscles.

It is not always advisable to paint the nails after a paraffin wax treatment as the nail will have absorbed oils and the paint will probably peel off very quickly.

See Chapter 5 (p.117) for details on types of wax and heaters.

> **NOTE**
>
> Paraffin wax treatments should not be used if the foot has any infected areas or open wounds of any kind.

Procedure for a paraffin wax treatment

1 Make sure the heater is on for sufficient time before it is needed

2 Have a disposable wrap ready (this could be plastic bags, cling film or foil) together with clean towels. (This treatment can be used with heated bootees, in which case have them ready to use with relevant accessories)

3 The feet need to be soaked to make sure they are very clean. After this, it is usually advisable to remove hard skin with an abrasive. This will allow the wax to have a better softening effect on the skin

4 Check the temperature of the wax

5 If the heater is big enough, hold the client's ankle and dip the foot in the wax and remove, keeping the foot over the heater. Repeat this several times until a thick coat of wax is covering the foot. If the heater is too small for this, place the foot on the disposable covering that is being used (e.g. foil or cling film) and paint several layers of wax onto the foot

6 Wrap the foot in the prepared disposable wrap and then either in a towel or place it in the heated bootee

7 Repeat with the other foot

8 Leave wax in place for approximately 10 minutes

9 Remove one foot from wraps and peel away wax. Discard used wax and disposable wrap. Repeat with other foot

10 Continue with the pedicure treatment.

Masks and exfoliators

As with manicures, there are many brands that have a full range of pedicure products that loosely follow the treatments of a facial (after all, it is all skin).

It is important that manufacturer's instructions are followed for the sequence of these treatments and their recommended usage.

See Chapter 5 (p.118) for general observations about masks.

Warm oil treatment

On the feet, as on the hand, hard, brittle and dry nails and dry cuticles benefit from an oil treatment. It is not possible to dip just the toes into a heater and it is not very practical to fill a whole foot bath with oil especially as it should be discarded after use! Fortunately, there is an easy method for providing an oil treatment:

1 Soak cotton wool pads in the oil. Apply a generous amount of a moisturising foot cream to the foot. Wrap the oil-soaked cotton wool around the toes, then wrap the foot in foil and a towel. The heat from the foot will be trapped and aid the penetration of the oil. Meanwhile the benefit of the foot cream can be enjoyed.

2 Heated bootees can be used in place of the foil and towel, as above.

As with paraffin wax, oil will be absorbed by the nail plate and may make painting less effective, with a tendency to peel off.

Thermal bootees

See the details on thermal mitts in Chapter 5 (p.119).

Heated bootees

Procedure for a heat treatment

1 When the nails have been shaped, the feet have been soaked and most of the hard skin removed, lightly apply the appropriate cream to the feet and oil or cream to the cuticles. Do not massage in.

2 Wrap the feet in disposable plastic bags or cling film and place them into the protective plastic bag that is supplied with the bootees.

3 Check that the bootees' temperature is right and place the wrapped feet into the bootees.

4 Make sure the client is comfortable and leave the bootees on for 10 minutes.

5 Remove and unwrap one foot and massage with the cream remaining on the foot. Discard disposable wrapping.

6 Wrap the foot in a towel to keep it warm.

7 Repeat with the other foot.

PEDICURE TREATMENT ALTERNATIVES

The sequence of the pedicure treatment depends on two main factors, the practice of the salon and the pedicure brand being used. There are many alternatives that suit different situations, and this section includes a list of

NOTE

Timings for specific stages. e.g. massage, soaking, heat treatments, etc., have deliberately not been given. This is because these are stages that can take more or less time as required. Some clients want minimal shaping or cuticle work; others will need more. The manicurist must lean to keep an eye on the timing and make up time if necessary.

sequences that are logical progressions for various types of treatment. They are offered as guidelines, and you should be careful to follow the sequences supplied by the manufacturers of the products you use.

General (i.e. for all treatments)

- The work area must be prepared before the client arrives with all relevant tools and equipment clean and ready for use.
- A consultation with the client must be carried out, even if a specific type of treatment has been booked. An alteration to this booking is acceptable following the consultation.
- It is also acceptable that, following the consultation, additional equipment is collected and prepared for use.
- Make sure the client is comfortable before starting the treatment and has removed all footwear.
- Trouser legs should be rolled up and protected if this is appropriate.
- Your hands should be clean and you should be sitting comfortably and safely.

Set-up for a pedicure

EQUIPMENT LIST

antiseptic wipe/spray

varnish remover

nail wipes

file

hoof stick

orange sticks

base and top coats

coloured varnish

nail oil

Reshape and varnish

Timing: 20 minutes

1 Thoroughly clean feet with an antiseptic wipe or spray
2 Shape nails on all 10 toes
3 Clean under the free edge with a disposable orange stick
4 Apply base coat, coloured varnish and top coat
5 Apply oil.

Mini pedicure

Timing: 30 minutes

1 Thoroughly clean feet with an antiseptic wipe or spray
2 Apply a cuticle softener to all 10 toes
3 Shape nails on all 10 toes
4 Remove the cuticle on each toe and tidy the nail fold
5 Wipe nails to remove cuticle softener
6 Apply foot cream to both feet
7 Clean under the free edge with a disposable orange stick
8 Wipe nails with remover
9 Either apply varnish or buff nails

EQUIPMENT LIST
antiseptic wipe/spray
varnish remover
nail wipes
cuticle softener
file
cuticle knife
cuticle nippers
hoof stick
foot cream
orange sticks
three-way buffer
base and top coats
coloured varnish
nail oil

Pedicure

Timing: 45 minutes

1 Ask client to place her feet in the prepared bowl for 2–3 minutes. Remove one foot and roughly dry while inspecting the condition of the skin. Wrap in the towel leaving the toes exposed

2 Remove any varnish and inspect the condition of the nails. Clip, file and shape the nails

EQUIPMENT LIST
antiseptic wipe/spray
varnish remover
nail wipes
foot spa
towels
cuticle softener
file
cuticle knife
cuticle nippers
hoof stick
foot cream
orange sticks
three-way buffer
base and top coats
coloured varnish
nail oil

3 & 4 Apply cuticle remover. Return the foot to the bowl and repeat with the other foot

5 Remove the first foot from the bowl, pat dry and remove the hard skin

6 Remove the cuticles

7 Buff the nails. Return the foot to the bowl and repeat with the second foot

8 Remove the first foot from the bowl and dry thoroughly. Apply the appropriate massage medium and provide a foot and lower leg massage. Wrap the foot in a towel to keep warm. Remove the second foot from the bowl, move bowl away and repeat massage sequence on second foot

9 Clean under nails with orange stick. Wipe nails with remover

10 Apply varnish

Treatment pedicure (thermal bootees)

Timing: 60 minutes

1 Ask client to place her feet in the prepared bowl for 2–3 minutes. Remove one foot and roughly dry while inspecting the condition of the skin. Wrap in the towel, leaving the toes exposed

2 Remove any varnish and inspect the condition of the nails. Clip, file and shape the nails

3 Return foot to the bowl and repeat with the other foot

4 Remove the first foot from the bowl, pat dry and remove the hard skin. Wrap foot in towel to keep warm

5 Remove second foot, pat dry and remove hard skin. Apply foot cream and cuticle treatment and wrap the foot in the disposable covering

6 Apply foot cream and cuticle treatment to first foot and wrap in disposable covering

7 Place both feet in thermal bootees for 10 minutes

8 Remove first foot from bootee and briefly massage in any remaining cream

9 Remove cuticles and buff nails. Wrap foot to keep warm. Repeat with second foot

10 Massage foot and lower leg of second foot. Massage foot and lower leg of first foot

11 Clean under nails of the first foot with orange stick. Wipe nails with remover

12 Apply varnish if required. Repeat cleaning and polishing on second foot

EQUIPMENT LIST
antiseptic wipe/spray
varnish remover
nail wipes
foot spa
file
cuticle softener
hand cream
disposable wrap/gloves
heated bootees
cuticle knife
cuticle nippers
hoof stick
towels
orange sticks
three-way buffer
base and top coats
coloured varnish

Treatment pedicure using a mask

Timing 60 minutes

You should follow the manufacturer's recommended procedure for a pedicure using a mask.

PEDICURE TREATMENTS FOR COMMON

NAIL AND SKIN CONDITIONS

Chapter 5 (p.126) discussed conditions that restrict manicure treatments, and these are all – with the exception of bitten nails! – applicable to pedicure treatments. Similarly, conditions that can be improved by manicure can also be helped by pedicure.

AFTER CARE ADVICE

Following a pedicure treatment, it is pleasant for the client to apply a product suitable for the condition of the feet. This may be a refreshing foot spray in the summer or a foot powder in the winter to help keep the feet dry in shoes.

During all pedicure treatments, you should explain to the client exactly what you are doing, why, how this benefits them and how any improvements can be maintained following the treatment.

At the end of the pedicure, the specific recommendations you are making that are relevant to the client's nail and skin condition should be repeated and reinforced. These should be supported by suggestions of retail products that will help and suggestions of other or further treatments. Treatment pedicures should always be followed by further treatments as progress is relatively slow. Remember to note your after care and retail recommendations on the client's record card.

General tips:

- Apply moisturising foot cream last thing at night, paying attention to the areas of hard or dry skin, such as the heels
- Massage nail oil into the nails and surrounding skin
- Reapply a top coat every few days to refresh the varnish
- Do not pick the skin or nails
- Wear well fitting shoes
- Visit a chiropodist if there is any sign of corns or bunions, infections or ingrown toenails.

Possible retail recommendations

- moisturising foot cream
- refreshing foot spray
- nail oil
- top coat
- foot file for use in the bath at home
- varnish colour
- varnish remover.

SUMMARY

This chapter has provided the information on all pedicure techniques, products used, alternative treatments and homecare advice.

Assessment of knowledge and understanding

1 Explain a pedicure treatment and what can it achieve.

2 What treatments can a chiropodist provide?

3 What skin and nail conditions prevent treatment?

4 What skin and nail conditions restrict treatment?

5 Explain the four main massage movements.

6 Describe the benefits of heat treatments.

7 What after care advice is appropriate following a pedicure?

8 Why are feet more prone to fungal and bacterial infections?

chapter 7

ESSENTIAL CHEMISTRY OF ARTIFICIAL NAILS

Learning objectives

In this chapter you will learn about:

- the artificial nail 'systems' used in the professional nail industry
- the critical differences between the 'systems'
- ways to choose the right one for you
- the basic chemical processes in all artificial nail products
- how to find the cause of a problem and put it right

INTRODUCTION

Every person who considers themselves to be a professional should strive to be a master of their craft. A nail technician should be skilful at applying nails to all types of nails; they should also be knowledgeable about the products and tools they use. This chapter provides the nail technician with a basic understanding of the chemicals, chemical processes and generic products that underpin all aspects of artificial nails.

In the nail industry, the information available about the products in use tends to be provided by manufacturers of brands and this information is usually tied up with marketing exercises. A technician needs to have a basic knowledge of the chemistry involved and then add specific product knowledge to this, almost as 'post-graduate' learning. You may use the same products every time but the client, their nails, the circumstances and the environment will differ every time. By understanding how the chemistry of the products works and what can influence the chemical reactions and performance, the professional technician will be equipped to use all products to their best potential and solve any problems that may arise.

'SYSTEMS' IN THE NAIL INDUSTRY

Although all types of artificial nails result in either longer or stronger nails that, hopefully, look natural, there are several different ways of achieving these results using different sets of products. These different methods are called '**systems**' in the nail industry. The name 'system' has evolved as a group of specific products working together to produce artificial nails: there is a system of using them together and a chemical system that makes them work.

The three main systems in use

There are three main 'systems' that the industry is familiar with – **acrylic**, **UV gel** and **fibreglass** – but the names that are now in common usage are inaccurate and can be misleading. The inaccuracy of the names of the systems is unimportant as they are widely accepted and understood, but an understanding of the underlying chemistry will show the discrepancies. The three main systems have several derivatives that confuse the situation even more, but the different systems refer more to application methods than the system components and chemistry. We can briefly look at each of them.

- *Acrylic* – This system uses a liquid monomer and a powder polymer that, when mixed together, form a solid. This should more accurately be called liquid and powder.
- *UV gel* – This system uses a gel that is supplied as a 'pre-mixed' product and forms a solid when exposed to ultraviolet (UV) light.
- *Fibreglass* – This system utilises the additional strength of a **fibre** mesh – that can be man-made fibreglass or natural silk or cotton – together with a resin that hardens.

The way in which each of these systems works from a chemistry point of view is actually very similar. The application and type of product differs enormously.

A fibre system Courtesy of Beauty Express

When a nail technician starts their career, or is thinking of starting, one of the most confusing and difficult decisions is which system to learn. It is important, in spite of any advice to the contrary, to concentrate on one system at the beginning. The application of artificial nails is a practical skill that needs lots and lots of practice. Experience can be achieved only by working with different clients, as experience cannot be taught. A deep understanding will provide the knowledge of how to deal with every situation. While these skills and understanding are being gained it is better to avoid the complication of trying to understand system differences and characteristics. Once the skills have been achieved and the technician has plenty of experience of different situations and problems, it will be a very easy matter to 'add on' another system. In this way the intricacies of the system can be concentrated on.

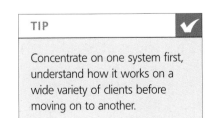

TIP ✔

Concentrate on one system first, understand how it works on a wide variety of clients before moving on to another.

Choosing a system

When choosing which system to learn, there are five main things to take into account:

- **Which one you enjoy**. This is the most important. When learning anything new, an enjoyment of the subject or skill will aid learning enormously. There will be one system that an individual will enjoy or find easier than another. The best way of making this decision from an informed point of view is to look at every system, watch their application by an experienced nail technician and, if possible, have a go yourself. A good technician will make every system look incredibly easy, but a few minutes of trying it out will show you that none of them is as easy as it looks.

- **Your existing confidence and knowledge**. It may be that you have been a client of a technician and have been impressed with the system that has been used. You will also have an amount of knowledge as you have been watching the process. Perhaps you work in a salon where a specific system is used very successfully. These are good reasons for choosing a system but remember that every system is only as good as the technician: every system will work in the correct hands.

- **The financial cost**. Starting any new career or skill can be very expensive. It may be that the cost of a student or starter kit influences this decision. This need not be a problem as the basics are the same for all, and the basic knowledge will provide a good foundation for any system. It is also worth knowing the cost in terms of products for a full set of artificial nails, as this will influence what you can charge your clients for your services.

- **Availability**. Nail products, like hair and beauty products, are available in several ways. There will be one way that suits you better or a combination of several. There are many items that are required for nails, not just the system products, such as cotton wool or nail wipes, disposable towels, terry towels, tools and much more (see Chapter 3). Products are available from direct sales companies that supply them via mail order. Some of these outlets will only sell their products to those who have taken training courses with them or can prove that they are already trained. Others will supply products to anyone. When buying via mail order, you will need to find out: what charges are made for postage and packing; whether there is a minimum order level; how long deliveries take; and how payment is made. You will also need to be available to accept delivery of packages. Direct sales companies do not always sell basic items, such as cotton wool, so you will need to go to a wholesaler for these items. If you prefer to see products before you buy, you will need to go to trade shows. However not all the direct sales companies attend these shows, so you will need to rely on their catalogues.

Another way of buying products is via a local wholesaler. There are hundreds of these all over the country and, as they are professional wholesalers, most of them require proof that you are in the trade.

Many wholesalers operate a delivery service and always sell the additional items needed for 'nails'.

What is convenient for you may affect what system you choose. Some direct sales companies only sell one system of a specific brand, others sell more than one system of specific brands. You may choose the brand rather than the purchase method, but take into account what is the most convenient for your situation and how much extra you are prepared to pay (and wait) for delivery or how much time (and petrol) you are prepared to pay for visits to wholesalers.

- **Company advice**. Most product companies are more than willing to give you lots of advice on what to buy. One word of caution here: the company may advise you that a specific system is the only one for you. This may be the case but if the system is the only one that the company sells there may be another reason why they are promoting it.

As a general piece of advice, do not rush into anything when choosing a system. Do your research, gather information, talk to others, attend trade shows, buy trade magazines. When you have lots of information you can decide for yourself from an informed position rather than being persuaded by others.

The chemistry of nail products

The chemistry of nail products for all brands is similar. In the same way as beauty therapists who learn how moisturisers work on the skin and how various electrical currents affect tissues, as hairdressers learn how perming solutions curl or straighten hair and hair colours work on the hair, nail technicians need to know how nail products work together and on the nail. Once this is understood, the specific product knowledge provided by manufacturers and distributors will enhance your skills and understanding and make you a better and more professional technician – especially if you have the essential attitude that a technician never stops learning.

When the word '**chemicals**' is mentioned, many people immediately think of danger! This is not so. Everything in the world is made of chemicals, including us! The only exceptions are heat, light and electricity, which are energies that affect chemicals.

Atoms and atomic structures

The smallest state in which a chemical can recognisably exist is an **atom**. This is a microscopic piece of matter that is organised in a way that is specific to the simplest chemicals in existence, that is **elements**. Examples of elements are oxygen, carbon, hydrogen, calcium; there are over 100 different elements, each with its own kind of atom.

TIP

Understanding how systems work will allow you to 'trouble-shoot' when things go wrong.

TIP

Never underestimate the value of product company training provided for technicians. They are not always the right people to provide training for beginners, but technicians should always attend a session for product knowledge and application techniques. Update these sessions regularly and never stop learning.

The atomic structure is specific to the different elements but each atom can have a negative or positive charge. As we all know from playing with magnets, a negative charge will attract a positive charge and vice versa. When a negative charge is joined to a positive charge a **chemical bond** is created. It is the joining together of these elements in various combinations and configurations that creates all the millions of chemicals that make our world.

Molecules

When an atom joins other atoms it forms a molecule. An example of a molecule is H_2O (1). The letter H is the symbol for the element hydrogen, the letter O is the symbol for the element oxygen; H_2O means 2 atoms of hydrogen joined to 1 atom of oxygen – which makes 1 molecule of water.

(1) Water (H_2O)

This specific molecule is the smallest form in which the chemical known as water can exist. How many molecules there are in a space or how they are joined together determines the form that the water is taking:

- lots of molecules tightly packed together will be water but in the form of ice (2)
- fewer molecules loosely packed together will be flowing water (3)
- very few molecules with only some packed together will be steam (or vapour gas) (4).

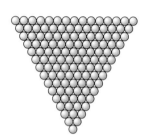

(2) Molecules of water forming a pyramid of ice (solid)

Water has the chemical symbol of H_2O but, if only one more element is added, for example carbon, and the number of hydrogen, oxygen and carbon elements varied, the chemicals that are formed are vastly different from simple water: alcohols (such as the one found in alcoholic drinks: ethanol C_2H_5OH), fatty acids (such as acetic acid in vinegar: CH_3COOH) and even solvents (such as acetone, widely used in the nail industry).

(3) Molecules of water forming a liquid

Ethanol C_2H_5OH

Acetic acid CH_3COOH

(4) Molecules of water forming steam (gas)

We are very familiar with each of these chemicals in their liquid form but should already be aware of possible dangers. Water is quite safe to drink, but too much of it in the wrong circumstances is dangerous; we can drown in it. The ethanol in our favourite alcoholic drink is good in small quantities, but a little too much has very unpleasant effects and considerably too much causes alcoholic poisoning and death. There is no one who would wish to consume too much vinegar and no one who would want acetone in their stomach, but we are quite happy to use it remove nail varnish. Chemicals used correctly and in suitable quantities are neither dangerous nor harmful.

Vapours, fumes and odours

Molecules of chemicals can escape into the air and become **vapours**. Water does not smell, but is present in the air all the time. Some chemicals can escape into the air much more easily than others. For example, water under normal conditions does not escape too readily, but if left long enough will evaporate. Other types of liquid chemicals, such as solvents, can escape very easily are known as 'volatile' and this property is useful for fast drying. Molecules of the actual chemical are in the air when this happens but they cannot necessarily be detected by smell. These molecules are called vapours and the liquid is said to be vaporising. Volatile liquids vaporise very easily so should be kept in containers that prevent this.

The smell of these liquids are often called **fumes**. This is very inaccurate. We refer to car exhaust fumes and this is accurate. Fumes are burned particles in smoke. What is often found in the context of nails is vapour – that is, the volatile chemicals escaping into the air.

Smell or **odour** is different again. We can detect some chemicals via our noses, others we cannot detect, but that does not mean they are not there. A strong smell of nail products suggests that the chemicals have escaped into the air as vapours and are now being breathed in. (The effects of this were discussed in Chapter 3.)

Bonding

A basic understanding of how molecules bond together to create something different will be useful in understanding the chemistry of nail systems. It is also important to understand that some molecules will bond together naturally owing to their positive and negative attractions; others need help. The help required could come in the form of heat, light or another chemical to speed up the process. This process is a crucial part in the understanding of nail systems, as the methods used and the speed of reaction affects the results and the application.

Acrylics, polymerisation and monomers

Almost every product used in the various nail systems belongs to a vast family of chemicals called 'acrylics'. An acrylic is a man-made type of plastic and those that are used in the nail industry use the same chemical process to form a solid from a liquid or from a semi-liquid: this process is called '**polymerisation**'.

- Polymerisation is a process that joins single but complex molecules called monomers together to form a solid even more complex structure called a polymer. The term 'monomer' is made up of 'mono': single + 'mer': unit; 'polymer', similarly, is 'poly': many + 'mer': unit. If we think back to the water molecules discussed earlier, single molecules can flow around as a liquid; when their temperature is drastically lowered, they join together to form a solid that is ice. It is the lowering of the temperature that has made this happen. (This reaction is not strictly the same as polymerisation, but thinking of it in this way makes it easier to understand.)

- Monomers are present in some form in all nail system products. As explained, the single units or molecules are monomers; there is also a slightly different arrangement where a few units are formed together. These are called '**oligomers**'. As a general rule, monomers are the products that are liquid in form and oligomers are in a semi-liquid form, such as a gel or **resin**.

Monomer (liquid)

Oligomer (semi solid)

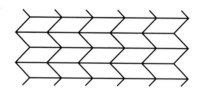

Polymer (solid)

Thinking back to how proteins are formed, you may remember that amino acids join together in long chains and these chains are linked together by amino acid bonds. These too can be described as polymers as they are single units (the amino acids) joined together to form long chains. Nails are made up of keratin so therefore nails are also polymers.

● The cells that are formed in the matrix on the nail unit have in the nucleus (or 'brain') of the cell the instructions to create the keratin. The nucleus initiates the process by collecting the relevant amino acids and causing them to link together in a specific format that will make the protein, keratin. This is a process of polymerisation, but notice that an instruction from the nucleus was needed to make it happen. To relate this to nail products is now a simple exercise. Monomers (or oligomers) are present in a nail product. When the polymerisation process is initiated, the single units join together to create long chains with bonds linking them together and a solid is formed. This solid is what becomes the artificial nail. The precise way in which this happens is different for each of the systems.

The chemistry of systems

The acrylic system

This system is the most popular in the UK and the US, holding probably about 50 per cent of the nail market. It is also popular in Europe, but other systems hold the largest market share in some countries, such as Germany, where a UV gel system is favoured. The acrylic system was the first to be used commercially, and came, as we saw in Chapter 1, directly from the dental industry. Even the colours that are used came from dentists, as they used pink for dental plates and various shades of white for dentures. (Pink and white is often used to create a natural-looking nail with a white free edge.)

The acrylic system is a two-component system using a liquid monomer and a powder. As already explained, the monomer (liquid) needs to polymerise and become a solid, and it needs an instruction to do this. If a liquid monomer is left exposed to light at room temperature, it would start to polymerise of its own accord, but this reaction would occur very slowly and the resulting polymer would be very soft and jelly-like.

The initiator and the catalyst: The instruction, or **initiator**, must come from somewhere. The solid that is to be formed must also be a strong solid rather than a soft jelly. This is where the powder comes in. The powder in an acrylic is, in fact, tiny polymer beads that have been manufactured to exact specifications. It is the powder that usually carries the initiator to start the polymerisation process.

Two conditions are needed for the process to be successful for the nail industry. An initiator is needed to start the process off and a **catalyst** is needed to determine the speed of the process. Two different chemicals, when they come together, create these two conditions. They start the process by giving the monomers a 'blast' of energy. This comes from the **chemical reaction** that occurs when the two come together – a release of energy that 'kicks' the monomers into linking together.

The two chemicals are both essential. The amount of each is also an important factor, and a balance that was created for a different application (such as making dentures) could produce problems. The blast of energy that is produced needs to be controlled, as too much would speed up the process too quickly, not enough would result in a very slow polymerisation.

The catalyst process: The most commonly used catalyst system (the two chemicals that start the process) are **benzoyl peroxide** in the powder and an '**amine**' in the liquid. When these two react together they create the 'instruction' for the monomers to join together. A similar reaction is used in permanent or semi-permanent hair dyes. Hydrogen peroxide and amines are used to create the necessary reaction to allow the pigments in the hair dye to enter the hair shaft. Every acrylic system needs an initiator and catalyst to create the acrylic polymer used for artificial nails.

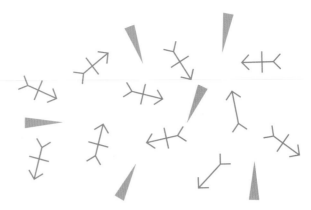

Acrylic monomer with initiator to 'kick-start' the polymerisation process

+

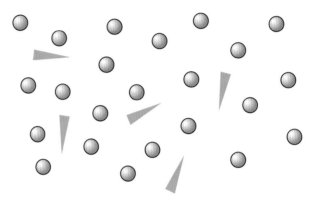

Acrylic polymer powder with catalyst to regulate the speed of the process

=

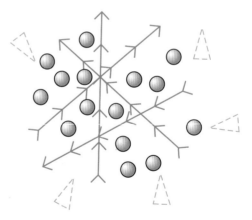

A solid acrylic with polymer chains and polymer beads. Catalyst and initiator used up

The polymer beads: The polymer beads have several roles, including the delivery of the 'instruction' to polymerise. The polymer beads remain as beads during the process and after polymerisation is complete. They stay in among the long polymer chains that are being formed and give support and strength to the final structure. The monomer alone would produce a soft and flexible structure but, with the polymer beads, the structure remains flexible but also has the strength of the supporting spheres.

The liquid and the powder: The amount of the liquid and powder that is mixed together, that is the 'ratio', is important to the finished solid. Too much powder can make a very hard solid that may be brittle. Too much liquid can result in a soft and weak solid. The correct ratio plays an important role in the performance of the system and needs practice, together with some guidance from the manufacturer.

Another role of the powder is to carry coloured pigment. Technicians and their clients like to have the choice of a natural nail or a permanent 'French manicure' (with a very white free edge that is often created by nail varnish). This can be achieved on artificial nails by using a pink powder over the nail bed and a white powder on the tip. There are also some powders that provide a peach tone for sallow and dark skins. It is possible to use powders that have strong colour pigments and are designed to take the place of coloured varnish. (If these are used, the whole overlay should be removed every few weeks to make sure that there is no problem with the natural nail, as this will not be seen through the opaque overlay.)

Methacrylates – EMA and MMA: The chemicals used in this system commonly belong to the methacrylate family. The two most common are **ethyl methacrylate** (or **EMA**) and **methyl methacrylate** (or **MMA**). Both of these were used at one time as monomers, as they were in the dental industry. However, it was discovered that MMA caused a great many allergic reactions and was too aggressive for skin. As a liquid monomer, it is now banned in the US although the very low-cost acrylic systems available there are sometimes MMA. MMA is a stronger polymer but, as a monomer, produced very hard and brittle overlays.

EMA is now the substance most commonly used for monomers. It can cause allergic reactions but by working correctly this should not cause a problem. Monomers are a highly reactive substance in that they have a great deal of energy, with the molecules rushing about all over the place. They want to polymerise and, as stated earlier, will do so given enough time. This is one of the reasons why they can cause allergic reactions if they touch the skin too often. When they are polymerised, their energy has gone and it is then less likely that clients will react to them.

Powders in acrylic nail systems: Powders in this nail system are usually made from the same chemicals, as members from the same family tree will have very similar characteristics. Powders are already polymers and they can be a 'homopolymer' – that is, it is made from one polymer, either MMA or EMA, or, more usually from two or more polymers, MMA plus EMA, which is called a '**copolymer**'.

EMA will form a softer, more flexible polymer so, when used as a monomer, it needs the strength of a good polymer powder to support it. However, a homopolymer reacts faster with a monomer that is the same. Therefore, an EMA liquid monomer will react faster with an EMA powder polymer, but will produce a relatively soft overlay. An EMA monomer reacts slower with a MMA powder polymer, but can produce a stronger overlay. A regularly used mixture is an EMA monomer with a copolymer of EMA and MMA. This will result in a reasonably fast reaction with a good combination of flexibility and strength.

When a liquid monomer and a powder polymer are mixed together, the resulting product goes through several stages, which are 'stage managed' by the catalyst system. Timings are infinitely variable:

- The first stage is when the monomer meets the powder and the additives to the powder, or beads, are released, which can be called 'swelling'. This is when the reaction really gets going and it happens quite quickly. It can be seen as the product starts to melt.

- The next stage is when the polymerisation starts and the mixture stops melting. It begins to have more of a gel consistency. At this **gel stage**, the product can be moved around the nail. The length of this stage varies for different brands.

- The next stage is when the product leaves the 'gel' stage and goes into the beginning of the final 'cure' or setting stage. The product cannot be moved around easily now without leaving dips or bumps. Once this stage has been reached, the final cure will not be far away. This whole process can take anything from 3 minutes to over 10 minutes and finishes when the product is hard enough to file (or produces a clicking noise when tapped with a brush handle). However, do not be fooled! The overlay may be hard enough to file but the polymerisation process will continue within it for many hours. Harsh abrasives or hard knocks to the overlay can interfere with this process and create weak areas in the artificial nail.

Temperature and polymerisation: There are external factors that can influence the process, the most obvious of which is temperature. Higher temperatures will speed up the process.

Fast polymerisation can create a heat sensation on the nail. The process itself produces a small amount of heat as it is an '**exothermic**' reaction (one that gives off heat), but this is too small to be felt by a healthy nail plate under normal circumstances. Fast polymerisation can also create a brittle overlay with weak areas. Normal room temperature is ideal, and this is one reason why technicians are not advised to work under desk lamps that get hot.

A low temperature will slow down polymerisation. The result of this can be seen when the liquid monomer is cold or the client's hands are cold. When the overlay is applied, crystals or frosting can be seen in the area near the cuticle. This occurs because the process is slow to start and the volatile monomer evaporates leaving some of the powder on the nail. Using the monomer at room temperature and keeping your client's hands warm can prevent this.

When the chemical engineering is unbalanced: The acrylic nail system, as can be seen, is a delicately balanced piece of chemical engineering. Several things can affect this balance. The addition of extra chemicals, for example, can have disastrous results – the most common chemical is brush cleaner, which can contaminate the mix.

The traditional acrylic system (with benzoyl peroxide as a catalyst system) is prone to discoloration, or yellowing, caused by ultraviolet light from either the sun or sunbeds. Some brands of the system have an additive (called a **UV absorber**) that prevents this type of discoloration by working in a way that is similar to sunscreens for the skin. Some have a blue or violet colour added to the liquid. This is present as an **optical brightener**, to make the white look whiter and the pink look pinker, but it will also cover any slight yellowing.

Some brands of the system require the application of a UV block, in the form of a varnish, over the finished nail. The block needs to be reapplied regularly. Acrylic systems that do not use benzoyl peroxide do not suffer from this problem of discoloration. However, all brands are prone to discoloration owing to **contamination**, which is dealt with in Chapter 9.

The chemical balance in this system is crucial to its performance. You are strongly advised not to mix brands – that is, a liquid monomer of one type with a powder from another. The catalyst system may not be compatible and other additives may not work together. Always use products that are designed to be used together.

The UV gel system

This system is sometimes called a 'pre-mixed' system, as it does not need another product or chemical for it to work. What it does need, however, is ultraviolet light to make it cure, or set. Like the acrylic system, it has, for the most part, been derived from the dental industry where light-cured materials are used to seal teeth.

The initiator and the catalyst: Like the acrylic system, the semi-liquid gel that is applied to the nails needs to polymerise or cure. The acrylic system uses a catalyst system that initiates the process with a blast of energy. The energy needed to start the polymerisation process in this system is ultraviolet light. Light, as we saw earlier, is a form of energy. You may remember learning about light from your school days. Light energy either comes from the sun, or from electrical energy converted into light. We see the visible light spectrum – that is, light from red to violet, as in a rainbow. At either end of this spectrum, but just outside of the visible range, there is ultraviolet at one end and infra red at the other. Also outside the visible spectrum are microwaves, X-rays and radio waves.

Cure for recommended time

Ultraviolet light: There has been some concern about using ultraviolet light in a nail system, as it is perceived to be harmful. Ultraviolet light can be very harmful, but in the case of nail systems this is not the case. There are three different 'strengths' or wavelengths of ultraviolet light: UVA, UVB and UVC. All of these are emitted from the sun in various amounts. When getting a tanned skin from the sun or a sunbed, the skin produces a pigment called melanin that protects the underlying tissues from the harmful effects of the dangerous wavelengths of ultraviolet light. This process needs relatively large quantities of UVA, which is safe, and smaller quantities of UVB, which can be harmful. In sunbed tubes, the percentages of these two wavelengths are such that the process of melanin production will work without being harmful (unless exposure to the light exceeds safe levels for the individual). 'Fast-tan' sunbeds sometimes have a higher percentage of UVB to speed up the process. The size of these tubes are usually 100 watts and an average sunbed has about 24 such tubes: a blast of 2400 watts of UV light!

The story is different for nail systems. The tubes in most nail lamps emit only UVA, it is not necessary to have UVB. Tubes are usually 6 or 9 watts and lamps can have from 1 to 5 tubes, depending on the design. The maximum 'blast' is therefore only 45 watts of UVA.

It is worth remembering these brief facts in case your client asks, 'Will my fingers get a tan?' or 'Is the UV light harmful?'

UV gel, oligomers and polymerisation: So now we understand a bit about UV energy, how does it affect the UV gel? All the nail systems need some form of energy to make them form a solid structure on the nail. An acrylic system needs the energy generated from a chemical reaction. UV gel needs UV energy to turn it from a semi-liquid into a solid. The process of forming a solid, as with all other systems, is called polymerisation.

- The gel used in this system varies between the brands, but all are from the acrylic family. The liquid in the acrylic system has single units of monomer, hence the liquid form. Gels have short chains of units, called oligomers, that are not long enough to be called a polymer. This gives the gel its consistency and makes the creation of polymers from light energy easier as they are partially formed already.

- When a UV gel is subjected to the energy of ultraviolet light, the polymerisation process starts and continues in much the same way as with acrylics. As with acrylics, the process is exothermic – that is, the chemical reaction gives off heat. This is relatively easy to control with acrylics as it is the carefully balanced chemistry that does most of the controlling. This is not always the case with UV gels as there are many variables that can cause a much stronger exothermic reaction.

- When a blast of energy is applied to the oligomers, they literally rush around at great speed, linking up with each other. All this rushing about creates a heat that is similar to the friction caused by rubbing two things together: the faster the rubbing, the greater the heat. This happens in the gel if the energy blast is too high, if the output of the UV lamp is too high for the specific gel – for example, a lamp with a 45 watt output would be too strong for a gel that is designed for a 9 watt lamp. It can also happen if the layer of gel is very thick. This is because there are more oligomers rushing around in a greater space and creating the friction effect. (To put this picture into perspective: if the nail was the size of the UK, the oligomer would be about the size of an ant!)

- This excess heat is a problem, for two reasons. First, the heat can be so great that it is felt by the nerve endings in the nail bed and the pain can be very severe and very frightening. This is obviously unpleasant for the client and it can damage the nail bed. Some clients are more prone to feeling this heat sensation than others and the nail bed will be particularly sensitive if it is damaged or thinned owing to excess buffing. Second, such a fast polymerisation will create a very brittle polymer that could easily crack or shatter. This can be avoided by using the correct UV lamp and avoiding thick layers of a gel. Always follow the manufacturer's instructions.

UV gel and oxygen: Polymerisation does not like oxygen! The presence of oxygen slows down, or inhibits, the process. This is the case with polymerisation in the acrylic system, too but the method is not so sensitive to it. Gel, however, is sensitive to oxygen. There are many gels available on the market that, when cured under the UV lamp, still have a sticky surface. There have been stories that this happens because the gel cures from the bottom up and liquid is pushed to the surface. The truth is due to the role that oxygen plays in its hindrance of the process. Oxygen is all around us; the surface of the gel is exposed to oxygen and therefore does not polymerise as the oxygen inhibits the process.

This sticky layer is not a problem if it is removed correctly and thoroughly. It is the oligmers that are not polymerised and, like the liquid monomer in the acrylic system, are likely to cause allergic reactions if the skin is touched. There are some gels on the market that do not have this sticky layer, this is owing to a total cure where the problem of oxygen inhibition has been solved.

Viscosities of gels: The chemical make-up of the gels is very complicated and the different types of gel that are available all have variations in both their characteristics and their make-up. One of the first things that can be seen about the gels is the thickness of each of them. This thickness is called '**viscosity**'. A thick liquid is described as viscous; water or any liquid that is free flowing has a very low viscosity.

Gels, depending on their nature and on the manufacturer, are available in various viscosities. The low-viscosity gels are used for painting thin layers onto nails and building up a sufficient coating to strengthen a natural or artificial nail. They are also used, depending on their characteristics, as a finishing layer that has a very high gloss shine.

Thicker, or more viscous, gels are applied in fewer layers and, again, depending on their characteristics, can be applied to create a specific structure to provide maximum strength to the nail. Some gels do not hold their shape for long before curing and care must be taken to avoid the gel running into the sides of the nail and onto the skin. Other types of thicker gels do hold their shape and stay where they are placed. These, however, have a consistency that is similar to that of petroleum jelly and can be difficult to apply without plenty of practice.

Shrinkage of UV gel: Polymerisation of any kind is prone to some shrinkage as the chains form. Gel is particularly prone to this and, if the shrinkage is severe, the overlay will lift from the nail plate or the client may feel a tightness that can make the finger tip throb. A good-quality gel should not shrink too much, but thicker layers will shrink more that thinner ones.

'American' and 'European' gel: There are two distinct types of UV gel on the market, often known as 'American' gel and 'European' gel. Every gel will have different characteristics and every manufacturer will have created a specific formula.

- As a general rule the 'American' type of gel, is based on an epoxy and urethane **acrylate** oligomers. Although the viscosities can vary enormously, they tend to be self-levelling so can usually be used only in thin layers as thicker layers would run into the side walls and cuticles. They are usually very resistant to solvents and so will keep their shine through many changes of nail varnish colour, although they cannot be removed easily with solvents.

- The type of gel that is sometimes known as a 'European' gel, also usually has urethane acrylates plus esters of acrylic. This style of gel often has a component system that uses more than one type of gel. The components may have a bonder gel that will make sure the gel does not lift from the nail plate, a building or sculpting gel and a sealer gel. There could also be a gel that can be used alone to build in thinner layers like the 'American' gel. The main gel will have a much higher viscosity and a creamier consistency. When applied, the gel will tend to stay in place and not run.

Applying fibre

The fibreglass system

Rather than from the dental industry, this system has been developed from the beauty industry! Before artificial nails and all the accompanying products, manicurists developed a way of repairing split nails that involved using tissue paper and clear varnish. A split in the nail was sealed by painting the nail with a clear varnish then applying a small piece of tissue paper to hold the split together and then painting several layers of clear varnish over the top to give it strength and a smooth finish. This method could work, but was not always satisfactory as it was not very strong, could peel off and came off with nail varnish remover. If the split was close to the end of the nail, however, it could be saved temporarily in this way until it could be filed away.

Stick-on nails were introduced into both the retail market and professional market where a whole plastic nail was attached with strong glue over the natural nail. These **glues** or adhesives were useful to repair natural nails and also to stick on the paper used to hold the edges together.

The three-component system: This is called a three-component system because there are three products necessary within the system – **fabric mesh**, **resin** and a **resin activator**.

● **Fabric mesh**: fabric is used to provide a cross-linked structure and to give the overlay strength (a bit like the polymer beads in the acrylic system). Any thin fabric will work, but those in common use and produced specifically for the job are a fibreglass mesh and a natural silk. These are both supplied as a fine mesh with a sticky back and are used to reinforce the overlay. The one you use is a matter of personal preference.

– *Fibreglass* is, as the name suggests, fibres with a high glass content. Of the two, this is slightly stronger as the glass remains untouched by the resin as a linked structure, but it is more difficult to 'wet' than silk.

– *China silk* is a very fine mesh of natural silk fibres. It does reinforce the structure, but the resin soaks into the fibres and the silk becomes an integral part of the resin. It is easier to 'wet' than fibreglass.

The mesh is supplied either as strips that are cut, using special scissors, to the width of the nail or in pre-cut 'fingers'.

● **Resin**: The second component of this system is a resin. This, again, belongs to the acrylic family of chemicals and is a **cyanoacrylate** of a specific chemical structure and viscosity. It is used to 'wet' the fibre, so that it cannot be seen, and then built up to an overlay. Cyanoacrylate is a monomer, but it has a different chemical structure to the ones used in other systems. It is sensitive to air and moisture and will cure (polymerise) when exposed to either.

Cyanoacrylates are used in a great many industries as an adhesive, in the motor industry, plumbing, woodworking and many others including the medical industry where it can be used as a skin or bone adhesive. Obviously, there are different kinds of this adhesive and different grades or qualities. The type most suitable for nails is an **ethyl cyanoacrylate**. The viscosity is infinitely variable, as is the speed at which it cures. A high-grade cyanoacrylate is preferable. This chemical is used as an adhesive for nail tips but a specific viscosity and chemical make-up is called a resin and is used in the fibreglass nail system.

- **Resin activator**: The resin will set, or cure, in time, on its own as it uses moisture from the air to set. As this takes at least 15 minutes and results in a very pliable coating that can peel off easily, it is not practical for the technician. To speed up the process and produce a strong overlay, an activator is used. The activator is usually an alcohol-based product, or an alkaline, of a dilution that will cause a controlled set.

Polymerisation: As with other nail systems, this system is based on acrylic polymers. When the resin is polymerised, it forms long chains but does not have any **cross-links** and needs the added strength of a fibre mesh. Owing to the lack of cross-links, it needs special care when removing nail varnish or using household cleaners.

The process of polymerisation, as we know, gives off energy in the form of heat. When the process is properly controlled at the right speed, this heat cannot be felt. If the process occurs too quickly, then excessive heat is produced, which can be very uncomfortable for the client and produce a weak overlay.

By applying the resin and spraying it with **activator**, the polymerisation process is started as the reaction is given the blast of energy required. To control the speed of the process, a very small amount of activator should be sprayed from a distance of about 30 cm. If the client feels any heat at all, the spray is too close. A fast cure is not only uncomfortable but also produces a brittle and cloudy overlay that has thousands of tiny cracks.

Fibre mesh: When introducing the fibre mesh into this system, it is important that the mesh is not visible through the overlay. To make it invisible it needs to be '**wetted**'. This is the term used to describe the application of resin to the fibre to make sure it penetrates the mesh and makes it invisible. It is essential that this is done with care as an artificial nail with the fibre showing through does not look natural. The mesh must be soaked with the resin before any further layers are applied. (This method is described in Chapter 6.)

OTHER IMPORTANT CHEMICAL REACTIONS IN NAIL SYSTEMS

Tip adhesives

The chemical reaction that takes place within tip adhesives is closely associated with the fibreglass system as it involves cyanoacrylates. Tip adhesives are almost always an ethyl cyanoacrylate that is sensitive to moisture and the cure of which is inhibited by oxygen. The viscosities can vary from a water-like liquid to a thick gel. As a general rule, the thicker the adhesive, the slower the cure and variations will apply to personal preference and to the job in hand.

- Tip adhesives, as the name implies, are used to stick a plastic tip to the natural nail. As the adhesive is sandwiched between the tip and the nail, the oxygen is expelled (therefore no inhibition to the cure) and there is sufficient moisture in the nail to encourage polymerisation. Thin adhesives cure very quickly, in a couple of seconds, the thicker ones take a little longer.

- Personal preference relates to how quickly the technician wants the tip to stick firmly. Beginners tend to prefer to have a bit longer to position the tip before it is too late, experienced technicians like to work as fast as possible. However, speed is not always the main consideration. A thin adhesive can produce only a thin layer of adhesive between the tip and the nail, which is fine if the tip fits the nail exactly and the nail plate does not have any irregularities. If this is not the case, air pockets are created that not only look bad but can also create problems later. A thicker adhesive can form a thicker layer and fill up any irregularities. The gel-like adhesives are an invaluable help when dealing with a severe nail-biter or a nail shape that tilts upwards, as the surfaces can be safely filled with adhesive (see Chapter 6).

- Cyanoacrylate adhesives can, over time, break down in water, so, in the artificial nail you should not put too much confidence in the strength of the bond between the tip and the nail. The strength needs to be between the overlay and the nail.

Primers

Function of a primer

There are some brands that do not require any help for the overlay to bond to the natural nail; they may just need a very clean, oil-free surface that has had the shine removed. Some systems have a built-in method of bonding a man-made plastic to a natural surface of keratin. The majority need some help to create this bond and the product is generally known as a '**primer**'. Primers are seen in many areas: metal, wood and ceramic tiles all need a primer before they can be painted; natural nails should have a base coat before varnishing; even teeth need a primer before a veneer can be applied. A primer is necessary in these cases as whatever is being applied to the surface must bond with it, otherwise it will peel or fall off. A primer prepares the surface to accept a substance that does not naturally bond with it. Shiny surfaces do not bond together and a roughened surface will accept another substance more readily. Nails, when shiny, almost have a seal on the surface that prevents too much penetration by substances. When the shine is removed, the surface bonds more readily with adhesive or overlays and allows a small amount to penetrate and create a stronger bond.

Methacrylic acid

Some nail systems require extra help in the form of a separate primer. The most common primer in use is a chemical called **methacrylic acid**. As can be seen from the name, this chemical belongs to the acrylic family and therefore will have an affinity to the overlay. The acid part of it, although mild, will gently etch the surface of the nail and encourage it to accept the overlay. It forms both a chemical and a mechanical bond by holding the overlay onto the nail plate.

Methacrylic acid is a strong irritant and is corrosive. Care must be taken when using it not to allow it to touch any soft tissue. Bottles must be kept with the lid on and spillages dealt with carefully.

Acid-free primers

There are other primers available, which are generally called 'acid-free'. They will work in such a way as to hold on to both the natural nail and the overlay. They 'interface', or soak into, the nail plate and, as a type of monomer, will polymerise with the overlay to create a complete structure.

The best primer to use is the one that is recommended by the manufacturer of your system, as they will have developed the primer to give the best results with its own system. As with all nail systems, information on how to use products efficiently and safely must come from the manufacturer. A technician should spend some time learning, in depth, all there is to know about the products and a reputable company will provide this information. There may also be some application techniques that are best to use with specific brands and that make an application quicker or more effective. Do not consider that such training is a waste of time or money – it is the complete opposite, every product that is on the market will work properly in the right hands; in the wrong hands, where there is insufficient knowledge, most products will not work.

ARTIFICIAL NAIL REMOVAL

A final explanation of the chemistry of artificial nails is their removal. The most commonly used method of removal is to soak the nails in acetone or some other solvent. The solvent does not dissolve the overlay but breaks down the bonds between polymer chains. The stronger the bonds, the more difficult it is to break them down.

Using a solvent

In the various systems, the cyanoacrylate resin in the fibreglass system has the weakest bonds as there are no cross-links in the structure. UV gel is usually the most difficult to remove, as the bonds are exceptionally strong. There are many gels that cannot be removed with solvents and the only way is to buff them off.

When the nails are soaked in the solvent, the bonds break down and the structure becomes soft. While in the solvent, the overlay can be scraped off quite easily. If the nails are removed from the solvent before this is done, the softened acrylic immediately becomes hard again.

In order to imagine what happens to the acrylic in the solvent, imagine putting paper in water (those with children may have had to fish out a roll of toilet paper from the lavatory in the past!). The paper becomes very soft and liable to break up, it is still, however, paper and does not dissolve in the water. When the paper is removed from the water and dries out, it may feel a little harder and the separate sheets may have moulded together, but it is still paper. This is very similar to the effect that acetone has on acrylic.

The use of acetone

There have been some worries about using acetone to remove acrylic nails. All solvents are classed as hazardous chemicals and all chemicals, even water, are hazardous if care is not taken in their use and storage. Over-use of any hazardous chemical is a danger but sensible use should not be a problem. Continually soaking skin in acetone, or any other solvent, could cause health problems, but there should be no need to continually remove artificial nails. Usually, the only reasons to remove artificial nails are if a problem with the natural nail or skin is suspected or if clients decided that they no longer want or need them. Correctly maintained artificial nails do not need to be removed. Occasional removal by soaking in acetone or similar solvent is not a problem, as long as the correct procedures are followed and the used solvents are disposed of carefully.

SUMMARY

This chapter has explored the chemical reactions that underpin the three main 'systems' – acrylic, UV gel and fibreglass – used in artificial nail technology and what the choice of system entails for both the technician and the client.

Assessment of knowledge and understanding

1 What are the three main artificial nail systems available?

2 Explain: (a) vapours, (b) fumes, (c) odours.

3 Ventilation is essential for the safe removal of (a), (b) or (c) in Question 2?

4 What is the name of the chemical process that changes an artificial nail overlay into a solid?

5 How can room temperature affect artificial nail products?

6 What is the purpose of an initiator in any artificial nail system?

7 What are the initiators in each of the three main systems?

8 Name some problems that could occur as a result of contamination of artificial nail products.

9 What is polymerisation?

10 What is the sticky layer on a cured UV gel and why should it be removed?

chapter 8

APPLYING TIPS TO THE NAILS

Learning objectives

In this chapter you will learn:

- **how to prepare the natural nail plate for artificial nail products**
- **about the different types of tip and their uses**
- **how to apply and blend a tip**
- **how to apply a tip to various nail shapes in a way that improves their appearance**
- **how to apply tips to bitten nails**
- **the use and application of tip varieties**

INTRODUCTION

There are two methods of lengthening nails: one is by applying a plastic tip to provide the length and then an overlay over the top; the other is by 'sculpting' the overlay onto the nail to provide the length (see Chapter 10). This chapter deals with the application of plastic tips and is relevant to all the different nail systems, as it forms the basis of this method of applying artificial nails.

PREPARING THE NATURAL NAIL

Before any artificial product is applied to nails, they must be carefully prepared. If steps in this stage are missed or done inefficiently a problem with the artificial nail will result, for example lifting of the overlay. This procedure must be carried out before any artificial product is applied and precedes tip application.

Sanitise hands

Wipe nail from the edge to the cuticle

Step 1: Sanitise the nail plate

The nail plate must be perfectly clean before any work is carried out. There are many specific products available for this purpose and every system brand usually has one. In effect, the nail plate is cleaned of surface debris and oils using a solvent. It is possible to use a varnish remover as long as it does not have conditioners, as these can remain on the nail plate.

A cotton wool disc or a disposable nail wipe is used and the nail should be wiped from the edge to the cuticle. In this way oils from the skin will not be drawn onto the nail plate.

Step 2: Removing the cuticle

The true cuticle is a thin, clear layer of skin that is attached to the nail plate. It grows continually and there is always some to be removed. It is possible, if a client has not had a manicure or any nail treatment for some time, that the cuticle could be covering the lower part of the nail. As it is so thin and transparent it is difficult to see. Removal of this is essential as any overlay products will not bond to this skin, they will bond only to a clean nail plate. A little area of missed cuticle will cause lifting of the overlay that, in turn, can result in other problems. The nail fold at the base of the nail must never be pushed or forced, especially when it is not softened. Applying products to soften the nail fold at this stage is not recommended, as they will be difficult to remove and may be absorbed by the nail plate. If the nail fold is unsightly, the technician should recommend that the client has a few manicures first to minimise the skin.

Remove cuticle

Before applying artificial nails, the most efficient method of removing the cuticle is with a clean cuticle knife. Some can have a very sharp blade, but every metal tool needs to be used carefully as they can cause severe damage to the nail plate.

This stage must never be missed and the whole nail must be checked for cuticle. With practice, it is often easier to feel the cuticle rather than see it. With so many different cuticle tools available, it is advisable to get advice from the distributor on their correct use.

As a general guide, hold the cuticle knife reasonably flat on the nail plate and, starting around the centre of the nail, gently scrape down towards the nail fold. Any cuticle on the nail plate will be easily removed if the knife is held at the correct angle and the nail will not be affected. If the knife is held upright it is possible to dig into the nail. Once the whole nail has been checked for cuticle, special attention needs to be paid to the sides of the nail. The skin can be pulled back by a finger and thumb and the cuticle knife can check for cuticle down the side walls.

The nail fold at the base of the nail should be gently lifted, never forced. An efficient cuticle knife in the correct hands should accomplish this without any problems. The knife should then be used to clean away any debris from around the edges and nail fold.

Some technicians like to use a cuticle softener at this stage. However, remember how porous the nail plate is and unless the product is removed thoroughly, including under the lifted skin of the nail fold, there could be a problem with lifting later.

A wooden orange stick is not suitable for removing the cuticle. It is good for gently lifting and shaping the nail fold during a manicure, but is not able to remove cuticle as efficiently as a good cuticle knife.

TIP ✔
If the client has a nail fold that has grown too far down the nail, it may be necessary to suggest a manicure first.

Step 3: Removing the shine

A nail plate is naturally smooth and fairly shiny. This helps it to resist moisture absorption. Two shiny surfaces do not bond together well with an adhesive as there is not enough 'grip'. (This could be likened to a shiny leather sole on a new shoe and a smooth pavement. There is no grip, but if the sole is scored to make it rough, it will grip much better.) The adhesive or overlay has more surface to hold onto if the shine of the nail has been removed.

The nail plate, like the skin all over the body, has bacteria living on the surface. Some of these bacteria are harmless and sometimes useful. Other bacteria may not be so friendly so, when applying artificial nails, it is safer to try to remove all the bacteria. Using a gentle abrasive to remove the shine on the nail will also help to remove some of these unwanted 'visitors'.

The natural nail should never have an abrasive used on it that has less than a grit of 240 as it would cause too much damage. The end of a file of 240 grit or less is ideal to remove the shine. The end shape can get very close to the nail fold without causing damage to the soft tissue, and the sides of the file are perfect for getting down inside the side wall and ensuring there is no

Remove shine

Shape free edge to fit stop point on tip

area of nail missed. The file should be used in the direction of nail growth, that is from the cuticle area towards the free edge. Keeping to this one direction only will minimise any trauma to the nail plate and help to avoid any more of the surface being removed than is necessary. It is literally only the shine that needs to be removed and not a layer of nail or any amount of nail that will make the nail plate thinner.

When the entire surface of the nail has been gently filed the free edge, if there is any present, can be tidied up and shaped to fit in to the tip. At this stage the nail plate should look dull all over.

Dehydrate nail plate

Step 4: Dehydrating the nail plate

It is essential that the nail plate does not have any trace of oil or moisture on the surface immediately before application of the overlay. Oil or moisture could be carrying bacteria or fungal spores that could cause problems, and any overlay or adhesive will not bond to the nail if there is any oil or moisture present.

Obviously, the nail bed is excreting natural oils and moisture that keep the nail healthy and flexible and this will continue. This moisture will not affect the overlay once it is bonded to the nail, but the bond must occur while the nail plate is moisture-free.

As the nail plate has a surface that is slightly more porous than usual, owing to the removal of the shine, any dehydrator used on it will penetrate the upper layer very slightly and remove excess moisture that is present. Dehydrators used on the nail plate not only remove excess moisture, but they also act as sanitisers. Most bacteria and fungi require moisture to live, and by removing this essential moisture any organisms that are present will not be able to survive. The mild products used for this purpose will not necessarily kill the organisms, as the products must be mild enough to be used on the skin, but they will stop or inhibit their growth.

As before, the product designed for this job (or acetone) should be applied following the manufacturer's instructions. Alternatively, the dehydrator can be wiped over the nail on a cotton wool disc or nail wipe towards the finger. This will remove the dust that has been generated by filing.

System nail preparation products
Courtesy of Beauty Express

The nail is now perfectly clean and prepared and ready for the application of artificial products. It is at this stage that the client must be prevented from using the prepared hand and the best way to avoid this happening is to ask the client to keep their hand flat on the towel. It is so easy for the client to touch their face or head then all the preparation work has been lost as oil, moisture or make-up could have been transferred to the nail plate.

If the nail system being used does not involve a UV lamp for curing, it is best for each hand to be prepared and all artificial nails applied before the next hand is started. In this way, the client has one hand free and there is no chance of contaminating the prepared nails.

If a UV system is being used, both hands must be prepared, as one hand is worked on while the other is under the lamp. The technician must ensure that the nails are kept away from any contamination.

ADHESIVES

Tips are applied to the nail with an adhesive (glue is an incorrect term as this describes a product made from natural materials). The adhesives used in the nail industry are cyanoacrylates, specifically ethylcyanoacrylates. It is widely used in artificial nails, as it is used for applying tips and is also the basis of the resin in the fibre system.

Adhesive is manufactured in several viscosities (thicknesses) and speeds of cure. It also has several grades. The highest grade is used in surgical procedures. That used for nails should be high grade, while its viscosity and speed are another area for personal preference.

As a general rule, thin adhesives cure very quickly and thicker versions more slowly. For the purposes of tip application, a thin adhesive will bond quickly but is prone to air bubbles and will not fill up any irregularities in the nail surface; a thick adhesive will take longer to bond and will cushion the nail and fill irregularities (this type is ideal for a bad nail biter).

Adhesives are broken down with solvents, the most efficient being acetone. If any skin in bonded together during its use, cotton wool on an orange stick soaked in acetone will quickly solve the problem.

APPLYING A PLASTIC TIP

Plastic tips come in many shapes and sizes, colours and lengths. Some of them are amazing to behold and all of them, to the beginner, look impossible!

Applying the tip is a skill in its own right and one that is often hurried during training in an effort to get on with overlay application. The application of the tip must be perfect and, on completing this stage, the nails must look like they actually grew on the finger and are not a piece of plastic stuck to the end. If the tips are not a perfect fit, they cannot be corrected by the overlay. The shape of the overlay has its own rules and requirements, and must not be concerned with correcting a badly applied tip.

The tip plays only a small part in the strength of the finished nail. The most important area of strength is provided by the overlay. The tip alone is only as strong as the bond between it and the natural nail and this is not a good bond. If the real strength is not provided by the overlay, the tip will snap off. A well-applied tip does provide some strength in one area and that is the side wall near to the free edge. This area of nail, either real or artificial is very vulnerable, and is the most usual place for a nail to break. A tip will add some strength here.

ABS plastic or acetate tips

A good-quality tip is made from 'virgin' ABS plastic. ABS is a plastic within the acrylic family; it is relatively strong and can be made in many different

> **ANECDOTE**
>
> I used to work with a very good technician, but one who was prone to accidents, large and small. A common occurrence for her was to get adhesive on skin, usually her own but sometimes the client. When adhesive dries on skin it can be easily peeled off without any damage although, ideally it should be soaked off with acetone. On one memorable occasion, I heard noises coming from my colleague that were obviously designed to attract my attention and sounded a bit panicky. When I looked, her finger was in her mouth. I quickly understood what had happened. She had got some adhesive on her finger and had tried to peel it off with her teeth (not recommended on any occasion). The adhesive was still wet and promptly stuck her finger to her teeth! The bond was not strong and her finger came away but not before the moment of panic!!

Various tip shapes

Nail with area of tip highlighted to demonstrate reinforcement of vulnerable area

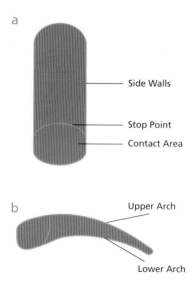

a

Side Walls

Stop Point

Contact Area

b

Upper Arch

Lower Arch

c

'C' Curve

Features of tip (a) the front (b) the side (c) the end

colours. Most tips today are made from ABS plastic, but occasionally a tip may be made from another type of plastic called acetate. These tips have a translucent quality and are usually more transparent than traditional tips. They tend to be cheaper and were originally made for the false nails that were sold for retail use to be stuck over the whole nail. These are not suitable for artificial nail systems as they are difficult to blend into the natural nail and have a higher oil content that may affect the overlay.

Making the tip

Tips are manufactured by pouring liquid ABS plastic into a mould that is shaped rather like a tree with a central 'stalk' and the tips coming out of the side like branches. The little rough bits on the end of tips show where they were removed from the main 'stalk'. The 'stalks' that are left after the tips have been removed are sometimes melted down by manufacturers and reused to make more tips (rather like remould tyres). This obviously helps manufacturers to keep costs down but, like some remoulded tyres, the tips can have weak spots. 'Virgin' plastic is a plastic that has been freshly made and not mixed with the melted 'stalks'.

Important features

Every tip, whatever its shape or size, has a number of features that are relevant to the technician:

1 **Contact area or well**. This is a thinner area and the part that is in contact with the natural nail.

2 **Stop point**. This is the demarcation point of the contact area and the actual tip. The natural nail free edge should fit snugly into this without any gaps to trap dirt and it will protect the edge of the nail and help it from absorbing too much water. When the tip is properly blended, this line will produce a natural-looking smile line.

3 **Side walls**. Tips either have parallel or tapered side walls to suit the natural shape. A well-constructed tip will have a reinforced side to the contact area in order to provide maximum strength in this vulnerable area.

4 **Upper arch**. Like natural nails, tips have differently curved upper arches from flat to very curved. Choose the one that fits the natural nail shape or, if the natural upper arch is flat, it will need some correcting and a tip with a curved upper arch will help. If the nail has a high arch, a curved tip will exaggerate this even more so a flatter tip will help compensate.

5 **Lower arch**. Like nails that have grown naturally, a tip needs to have a lower arch. This is not so obvious if the shape of the finished nail is going to be oval, but the lower arch is still there and is what makes the tip look as if it has grown from the finger and not been stuck on top.

6 **'C' curve**. As with the upper arch, this can vary between types of tip, and the shape of the natural nail should dictate which is most suitable. Unlike the upper arch, it is not advisable to choose a shape that is different from the natural 'C' curve. The tip needs to sit on the nail comfortably without distorting the shape of the tip. If the natural nail is quite flat and

a tip is applied that has a deeper curve, the tip will need to be flattened to adhere across the width of the nail. Once applied, the tip will try to return to its shape and this will put undue stress on the nail bed. When this happens, clients will feel a great deal of discomfort, as the nail bed will throb as if it is bruised. It is even possible that, if the nail plate is very thin, nail separation could occur. If the natural nail has a deep curve and a tip is applied that is flatter, the only way to stick it to the nail is to hold the sides of the tip onto the nail and make it follow the natural curve. Again, after application the tip will try to return to its original shape that may not necessarily cause discomfort but may result in lifting down the side walls.

a

b

c

'C' curve of a nail looking from the nail down the length of the finger (a) flat 'C' curve (b) natural 'C' curve (c) deep 'C' curve

Choosing the correct tip

Some guidelines

- The first thing to look for when choosing the correct tip is the 'C' curve of the natural nail. Match the shape of the natural nail.

- The next area to take into account is the natural upper arch. Again, match the natural shape, or choose a tip to correct an over- or under-exaggerated arch.

The above guidelines will help save some time in trying several tips. However, the best way to choose a tip is to try it on the nail. If it follows the curves it is the right one. It is worth a technician having at least two different types of tip available, and more if finances allow.

Size and width

a

X

Placing the tip (a) tip too small for nail

Tip too narrow for nail plate

(b) tip too wide for nail

Tip too wide for nail plate

(c) tip of correct size

Tip width perfect fit

TIP ✔

If you are not sure if the tip is the right size, hold the tip against one side wall and look across at the other side wall. This will show a tip that is too narrow. Sometimes, when looking down onto a nail, the tip will look right but is actually too narrow when this technique is tried (see picture).

TECHNICAL TIP ✔

If a client has a very flat nail and the flattest tip still has the wrong 'C' curve, choose a much wider tip, which will be flatter, and the sides can then be filed until it is the correct width.

TIP ✔

Always **pretailor** or shape a tip to fit before application as it cannot be changed when it is on the finger

Once the correct tip has been chosen, the right size or width must come next. Most tips come in ten different sizes with 1 being the biggest and 10 the smallest. Sizes 4 – 6 are the most commonly used.

When choosing the correct size, the width of the contact area must be ignored as it is the width at the stop point that is important. This must be exactly the same width as the nail at the smile line (or **onychodermal band**) without any gaps when the skin is pulled back from the sides. It is a very common mistake to fit a tip that is too narrow. It cannot always be seen on a new set but, when the nail grows, there will be a step at the side with some natural nail exposed. Some clients have puffy or thick skin at the sides of their nails and unless this is firmly pulled back, the full width of the nail will not be seen.

If one size is too wide and the next is too narrow, choose the wider one and file away a very small amount from either side until it fits perfectly. If there is any doubt as to the correct size, one side of the tip can be 'tucked down' into one side wall and the other side looked at. Very often this will show that a tip that looked right is actually too narrow.

Full contact area versus reduced contact area

Most tips have a full contact area. These can be applied directly to the nail plate with adhesive or they can be tailored beforehand. There are eight main reasons why it is worth removing most of the contact area before application:

1   When applying a tip with a full contact area it is easy to get bubbles under the tip. If this happens, the tip must be removed. The bubbles are unsightly and are areas where bacteria or fungus could grow.

2   The bond between the nail and the tip relies on the adhesive used. This will be a cyanoacrylate and this can eventually break down in water. If the bond covers most of the nail (1) there is a larger area to be broken down.

3   The strongest bond in the artificial nail structure is between the nail and the overlay. If most of the nail plate is left exposed, as in the first diagram, the bond will be more effective.

4   A full contact area needs blending until it is invisible and there is no shadow that can be seen through the overlay. This involves more work and there is a greater risk that the natural nail will be buffed. Blending a small area is very quick.

5   When any tip is applied to a nail with a flat upper arch, the contact area must be completely in contact with the nail. A full contact area will cause the tip to be tilted upwards at a very unnatural angle (2).

6   By having a minimal contact area, the angle of the tip can be placed so that the finished nail looks most natural (3).

7   By placing the tip at the correct angle with a reduced contact area, the line to be blended will be at the top of the upper arch curve and therefore easier to blend without touching the nail plate (4).

8   Sometimes the contact area is almost as long or longer than the client's nail plate and there is very little room left to blend the area without damaging the soft tissue. This is particularly the case with nail biters.

Tip and upper arch (a) tip with complete contact area producing wrong upper arch curve (b) tip with reduced contact area producing correct upper arch

(1) Tip with full contact area on nail

(2) Wrong angle of tip with full contact area

(3) Corrected angle of tip with reduced contact area

(4) Tip with reduced contact area on nail

Removing the contact area

There is no rule that states that the contact area must be removed or left in place. However, it is a very useful skill and a thorough understanding of the question allows individual technicians to make up their own mind what is right for their client. The most important result is a natural-looking, strong artificial nail that has been applied without damage to the natural nail and under safe and hygienic conditions.

There are two methods of removing the contact area:

1 *Using a file*. By holding the tip and the file at the appropriate angle (see picture), the contact area can be removed very quickly leaving a curved edge. By leaving this shape as opposed to a straight edge, the side walls of the free edge of the natural nail are provided with extra protection and support.

2 *Using scissors or clippers*. Scissors with a curved blade are ideal for snipping around the contact area, following the shape of the stop point. Nail clippers can also be used to cut out a 'V' shape.

Removal of contact area using a file   Removal of contact area using scissors

Applying the tip to the nail

Once the tip had been chosen and any necessary tailoring carried out, it must be applied to the nail with adhesive. The choice of adhesive is for the technician unless the client is a severe nail biter or has a damaged nail plate. If this is the case, a thick adhesive or gel should be used that will fill and cushion the irregularities of the nail plate or, in the case of a nail biter, fill the area where the nail has been bitten down below the hyponychium. If this area is left as an air space, there could be problems with bacteria or excess moisture.

A small amount of adhesive should be carefully placed in the contact area of the tip. Placing adhesive here is preferable to it being placed directly on the nail. When placed on the nail, it can easily run down into the side walls or over the edge of the finger. When placed on the tip, it starts affecting the plastic of the tip immediately, softening it ready for accurate placement.

The tip should be brought to the free edge of the nail at an angle of around 45°. This will allow the nail to be placed correctly in relation to the nail plate and then levered down onto the nail, expelling any air bubbles as full contact is made. As soon as the excess adhesive is seen being squeezed out onto the nail plate, the tip should be held in place for a few seconds until the bond is made. At this stage, the finger should be pushed up from underneath by the hand that is holding it rather than the tip pushed down. If the tip is pushed down it is very easy to lift it too high and therefore break the contact at the free edge and pull in air. The lack of oxygen present between the tip and the nail encourages the adhesive, to cure quickly, much quicker that when exposed to the air. However, the thicker the adhesive the longer this curing takes.

This should be repeated for each finger on one hand. When all five tips are applied, they can be cut to slightly longer than the desired finished length. The length should be decided by the client, but with advice from the technician if the requirements are unreasonable, such as too long for the nail bed or life style. At this point, it is worth asking the client what shape is required – oval, square, rounded square or tapered. If the client has no preference, the shape of the base of the nail should be followed to create a good-looking nail.

Cutting techniques

There are several tools on the market designed to make cutting tips easier. They are adaptations of a tool used for clipping animal claws but instead of a round hole that the claw fits through, they have a curved hole for the tip. These clippers are quick and efficient and allow the tip to be shortened with one movement. When using cutters, the metal plate that has the curved hole must be nearer the finger. This will protect the finger from being cut as the blade is on the other side. If the cutter is angled under the client's hand, a slightly curved shape will be cut on the tip. The more upright the cutter is held, the straighter the edge. Care should be taken not to hold the cutter away from the client as this will result in an edge that curves in the wrong direction and, if the cutter is moved during cutting, could result in pulling the tip off.

Scissors or nail clippers can be used for cutting tips. Plastic tips are easily 'stressed' or bent which results in white areas. When using clippers or scissors, the tip should never be cut across in one action as this will cause the stress lines. Each side should be cut separately (see picture). The angle of the clipper blade will produce an outline of the finished shape – that is, oval, square or tapered. The piece of tip should be discarded as it cannot be used for anything else.

Angle of application of tip on nail – 45°

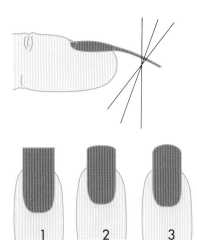

Angles of one-cut tip cutter
1 = square
2 = rounded square
3 = oval

Cutting tips with clippers

Applying the tip

(1) Choose correct size

(2) Remove contact area

(3) After replacing adhesive in contact area, apply tip to nail

(4) Cut tip to appropriate length

> **CAUTION**
>
> Only a fine grit of 240 or more should be used on the natural nail. Great care must be taken to avoid buffing the nail plate. This is the stage that causes many problems for beginners and removing the contact area of the tip may help.

> **TECHNICAL TIP** ✔
>
> During training, this stage often causes damage to the natural nail due to inexperienced blending. To help avoid this, apply a thin layer of adhesive to the nail plate and allow to cure in the air or activate to protect the nail before applying the tip.

Blending the tip

Once all the tips have been cut to the required length and the unwanted ends discarded, the tips must be blended to the natural nails. The result should be perfectly natural in appearance and look as if the nail grew there. More importantly, there must be no damage to the nail plate.

There are two methods of blending the tip: manually – that is with a file – or chemically with acetone or a branded tip blender.

Manual blending

During training, procedures are easily learned if eight easy steps are followed. These steps will help to produce a perfectly blended tip:

1 Holding the file parallel to the finger, 'tuck' it down in the side walls and, with a few strokes, blend the sides of the contact area of the tip so that it is the same width as the nail plate. By keeping the file parallel, the sides of the free edge will remain straight (1).

2 Shape the free edge to the approximate shape and length required. Look at the tip on the finger as a whole and not just the nail plate to check that it is a suitable length and shape and that it is straight to the finger (2).

(1) File sides of tip

(2) Shape free edge

(3) Blend contact area

3 Holding the file flat to the tip, gently start buffing the surface, starting at the tip and working backwards towards the contact area. The shine of the tip must be completely removed (3).

4 Using at least two-thirds of the length of the file, gently buff the contact area. Care must be taken not to buff in the same place for too long. Keep moving the file all over the area but avoiding the nail plate. It is not necessary to press hard with the file as gentle pressure is much more effective. The contact area will become much thinner until it is transparent and cannot be seen. A little nail adhesive often squeezes out onto the nail during the tip application and becomes shiny. This is can be a very useful guide to help know when the tip has been blended and the nail is being avoided. The tip must be completely invisible and there must be no evidence of a 'shadow' where the contact area is.

5 Refine the shape of the free edge until it is perfect and even, and remove any debris that may have collected underneath during filing.

6 Look at the nail from the side to check that the upper arch is correct and even, and that the lower arch is correct.

7 Gently refine the 'smile line' area to produce a neat and natural-looking effect.

8 The tip should now look like a perfect natural nail and is the ideal 'canvas' on which to apply the overlay.

Chemical blending

This method works by melting the plastic of the tip as an alternative to blending with a file. Some people, trainees in particular, like to use this method as they feel that damage to the nail plate can be avoided. To a certain extent this is true, but other problems may occur if it is not fully understood. It is not necessarily quicker than manual blending as, once mastered, manual blending is very fast.

Acetone may be used or there are a number of branded products on the market.

1 Once the tips are applied, paint a small amount of the tip blender with either a disposable cotton bud, or a brush used solely for this purpose, over the contact area. Wait a few minutes while the plastic melts. This time can be used to apply the blender to other tips to help speed up the process. Do not apply too much, as any liquid can be absorbed into the nail plate and could cause unnecessary dehydration. Too much liquid will also run into the side walls and cause dehydration.

2 While waiting for the blender to work, the free edge can be shaped to the required length.

3 When the tip starts to look very shiny, use a fine file to file away the melted plastic. The blender can be reapplied if necessary, but too much solvent on the nail plate should be avoided.

4 Follow steps 5 to 8 for manual blending now to ensure a perfect nail.

5 Make sure that there is no melted plastic covering the nail plate, as this could prevent a good bond with the overlay and could result in lifting in the centre of the nail leading to an air pocket.

6 Brush the file as the melted plastic can stick to the abrasive and make it less effective. Discard the file if the plastic cannot be removed.

Although skilful manual blending is usually faster, chemical blending is an excellent standby for the client who has very sensitive nail beds and cannot take any buffing on the surface. It is also useful for a nail biter who has such a tiny nail plate that it is difficult to use a file without damaging the soft tissue.

Removing the dust

Once all the tips are perfect, the dust that has been produced must be removed from the nails. A bristle brush may be used, but thorough hygiene procedures must be followed to keep this very clean. Remove dust inside the nail folds with care, making sure that oil from the skin is not brought onto the surface of the nail. The product being used for preparing the nail plate is often very useful for this job as the moisture will remove the dust and the product will ensure a clean, oil-free nail.

Once the tips are blended and cleaned, they should look like perfect natural nails. If this is not the case and there are shadows on the contact area or the free edge is curving up and not down, they are too wide or too narrow, they cannot be corrected by applying the overlay. No amount of clever overlay application will correct a badly applied tip. It will only make it worse.

PROBLEM NAIL SHAPES

AND HOW TO CORRECT THEM

Clients come in all different shapes and sizes, and so do their nails. It is a very lucky technician who is presented with lots of nails that have beautiful long nail beds with parallel side walls and neat free edges. Most clients present their technician with all manner of horrors and it is the job (and often challenge) of the technician to make the artificial nail look perfect. It is not enough to apply nails that follow the natural shape. Many natural shapes are not perfect and are not always very attractive. The technician must correct natural imperfections. Many natural imperfections or problem shapes can start to be corrected with the tip application. This, followed by a planned overlay shape, will result in the desired perfection.

Practice is the only real way to perfect the art and skill of correcting problem shapes, but the following suggestions are a starting point to help that practice along.

Fan-shaped nail

Looking at the nail from the top, the side walls of a good shape should be parallel to each other. A **fan-shaped nail** is very common; this is where the edge of the nail is wider than the base, that is, the side walls 'fan' out. This nail plate is usually quite short and artificial nails can look very wide and clumsy and not at all elegant if the shape is not corrected by the skilful technician.

The correct tip size should be chosen carefully and the width of the nail plate at the free edge is the area which will decide the correct tip size. A tip with a full contact area usually appears much too wide as the contact area will often be wider than the centre of the nail plate. This does not matter as the contact area can be removed. The stop point of the tip must be the exact width of the free edge (a). Once the correct size is chosen, the contact area can be removed. It is likely that most of the area will need to be removed to avoid it being wider than the nail plate. Sometimes it is also necessary to angle the remaining contact area inwards so that it fits the nail.

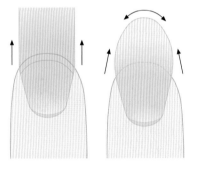

(a) Fan-shaped nail: fit tip to width at free edge (b) Fan-shaped nail with blended tip: tapered sides and oval shape

The tip being tailored should keep being fitted to the nail to make sure the shape is right. This shape of nail is also usually quite flat with little or no upper arch or 'C' curve. A tip that has a flatter shape should be chosen so as to avoid any stress being put on the nail bed by a curved nail. If the flatter tip is still too curved to comfortably fit the nail without pressing it flat, a wider tip should be chosen and the sides filed to the correct width. When this has been achieved and the tip has been applied at the correct angle for a gentle upper arch (remembering that the tip will need to be angled down slightly to help create an upper arch), it can be cut to length. It is inadvisable for the free edge to be any longer than half the length of the nail bed. Anything longer than this will not look attractive and will not be as strong as a shorter nail.

When shaping the free edge, the side walls need to be tapered in to compensate for the wide free edge. An oval is often better for this shape of nail as the base of the nail is usually oval, but a square can be achieved if required that does not look too wide. This is achieved by making the parallel side walls taper slightly towards the tip of the free edge. If done correctly, the sides will still look parallel but more elegant than if left, as this can accentuate the 'fan' shape of the natural nail. The square edge can then be achieved, and the overlay applied.

Claw nail (a) claw nail with no free edge (b) tip applied to edge of nail at correct angle (c) tip blended and overlay applied to correct poor upper arch

Ski-jump nail (a) ski-jump nail with no free edge (b) tip applied to give better upper and lower arch (c) tip blended and overlay applied to correct poor upper arch

Hooked or claw nail

A **hooked** or **claw nail** has an exaggerated upper arch and the free edge has a tendency to curve over the end of the finger. Clients with this shape of nail are often unable to grow their nails as the downward curve is unattractive.

The solution for this problem is to remove any free edge on the natural nail, choose a tip that fits (this is often one with quite a deep 'C' curve) and remove a great deal of the contact area. When the tip is applied to the nail, the side view should be checked and the upper arch corrected. Care must be taken that the underside of the tip does not have a gap between it and the nail plate, as debris could collect and cause problems.

The length should be quite short as, the longer the free edge, the more the curve will appear. Adjustments in the structure of the overlay will further compensate for this shape.

Ski-jump or spoon shaped nail

A relatively common shape, the **ski-jump** is a nail that curves up towards the tip. If a tip was put onto this shape without any correction, the nails would appear to be pointing upwards.

The corrective solution is very similar to that of the claw nail. The free edge should be as short as possible and the contact area of the tip removed. As the strength of the finished artificial nail is in the overlay and not the tip, the contact area can be tiny, if necessary, in order to achieve the correct upper arch. As before, when applying the tip, look at the side view and make sure the tip is curving down, even though the nail bed is curving the other way.

The length should be quite short and the overlay will need to be adjusted to compensate for the unusual shape produced by tip application.

Bitten nails

Bitten nails are probably the biggest challenge for the technician. If a good-looking set of artificial nails can be achieved from a set of severely bitten 'stubs' the technician can do anything! Obviously there are many degrees of nail biting, from the occasional nibbler to the person who bites their nails down past the hyponychium and on to the nail bed. The worst scenario is the experienced biter who not only bites down onto the nail bed, but also chews and picks at the soft tissue around the nail. The technician can do their best with the nails but can do little, other than offer advice, for the surrounding skin.

Obviously, recommending a course of manicures before applying artificial nails is preferable, as the cuticle and nail fold can be improved and some nail growth will help the strength of artificial nails; however, it is unlikely that the client will agree to this or succeed if they do agree. Biters do not usually bite deliberately and often try to stop the habit. They will try quite hard and achieve a little growth but then, while watching a good film, reading a good book or after a stressful day, will unconsciously nibble and spoil all the hard work. When this happens, there is often little point in leaving the other nails so they all go and the biter is back to the beginning.

Having a set of artificial nails can often be the answer for several reasons. A skilful technician can make the nails and hands look so good that the client does not want to spoil them. Having paid for the service, the client is more likely to make sure the money is not wasted. The unconscious move to the mouth is immediately noticed as the teeth come across hard plastic instead of soft skin. Nails applied well need determination to bite off, although the biter who is determined will do it whatever it takes!

Bitten nails

Preparation

Although it is a challenge that will take the technician longer than usual, even the worst biter can have a set of very good-looking nails. The challenge starts with the preparation.

A biter will often have a very obvious layer of cuticle and a pronounced nail fold. The cuticle can be removed relatively easily, but the nail fold will take more time as it must not be forced. Manicures would help a great deal, but this may not be an option. If the nail fold cannot be lifted, it must be left to be dealt with after the artificial nails have been applied, either during homecare or manicures.

The remaining nail plate will be soft owing to the length of time it spends soaked in saliva. There may also be dents and crevices where bacteria can breed. Preparation must be efficient and thorough with the nail and surrounding skin very clean and the nail plate dehydrated as much as possible.

The skin around a bitten nail is usually puffy, again owing to the amount of time it spends soaked in saliva. The end of the finger is often slightly swollen from this puffiness, the sides of the nail plate hidden from view and the overall shape flattened. All this will change dramatically after a couple of weeks with artificial nails.

Applying the tips

Milder cases of nail biting need to have the tips applied in the usual way, remembering all the rules about leaving most of the nail plate exposed for the overlay bond and creating good curves. If the nail plate is bitten down past the hyponychium, the skin that is exposed will usually be swollen and higher than the nail plate and the tip will need a great deal of pretailoring before application. A tip, even with the contact area removed, when applied to this type of nail will point upwards as the skin will not allow it to lay flat.

A flat tip needs to be chosen and, if necessary, a wider one made narrow to provide the right 'C' curve (or lack of it). To find the right size, the skin at the sides of the nail must be pulled back very firmly with the finger and thumb of the technician so the full width of the nail plate is exposed. Like the fan nail, the width at the edge of the nail and the stop point must match exactly, regardless of any other part of the tip.

When the correct size has been chosen (or made) the contact area must be removed so that only a minimal amount of tip will be on the nail plate, leaving the maximum amount of nail plate exposed for the overlay bond.

a

b

c

Bitten nail (a) Badly bitten
(b) Side walls of tip removed to
form 'bridge' over end of finger;
contact area also drastically
reduced (c) Tip cut short and
blended with overlay to
compensate for poor shape

Tip pretailored for a nail biter

Wrong placement of French
white tip and unsuitable natural
nail shape

At this stage the tip will still not sit on the nail properly, as the skin will push it up. The sides of the tip from the stop point down the sides of the free edge need to be carved out for the puffy skin to fit into (b). This will form a 'bridge' that will curve over the puffy skin and create a reasonable arch that curves down instead of up. This 'bridging' is necessary as, without it, not only will the nails look unattractive, but the skin that has been pushed down to fit the tip to the nail will push the nail upwards and make it very weak and liable to breakages.

When applying the tip with adhesive, it is advisable to use a much thicker adhesive than usual. With the skin in the way, the tip cannot be angled onto the nail and needs to be placed from the top. There is also usually an area around where the hyponychium should be that is lower than the nail and the skin. If using thin adhesive, it is difficult to avoid air bubbles when placing the tip in this way, which might allow a space where bacteria can thrive. A thicker adhesive will help to avoid the bubbles and fill up and cushion the area of the hyponychium.

The length must be very short, just to the end of the finger is ideal. The artificial nail will not be as strong as that on an unbitten nail and the client will be unused to having nails and will be clumsy for a few weeks.

Blending the tip on a small area can be tricky and if it is difficult to avoid the usually delicate soft tissue, it may be advisable to use a chemical tip blender. Although some people prefer an oval-shaped nail, a free edge that is slightly square usually better suits the wider fingertip of a nail biter.

The overlay will further improve the appearance of the nails and the homecare advice must be specific, as must the need for maintenance visits.

ALTERNATIVE TIPS

French white tips

A **French white tip** is an opaque white, it is designed to create a quick and easy permanent 'French manicure' look. Although this tip can be used with any system, there are restrictions as to who can wear this tip. The tip must be applied to the end of the nail and not blended. The shape forms a perfect 'smile line' and the overlay will create the necessary strength. This tip is not suitable for:

1 A client who has a different 'C' curve from the tip (there are now several shapes of white tips available, so having a selection is worthwhile)

2 A short nail bed, as the extra white tip, when correctly placed, will make the nail look unattractive with too much white and not enough pink

3 A client without any free edge; the tip's 'smile line' will need to be placed onto the nail bed instead of where it would naturally be and would result in an unattractive nail

4 A natural nail that does not have an upper or lower arch that matches the tip.

There is a correct placement for this type of tip that can create a perfect French manicure appearance. There is also a wrong placement that can make the finished nail look very unattractive.

A client wearing this type of tip must have the growth of natural nail covered during maintenance treatments.

Correct placement of French white tip on suitable natural nail shape

French white tip prepared for overlay

Clear tips

These are tips that are totally transparent and are usually used for various types of nail art. They are dealt with in exactly the same way as traditional tips. When they are blended in they will look dull and scratched, but as soon as an overlay is applied the dullness and scratches will disappear.

These tips should only be applied to nails that are very neat and without any free edge at all, as every irregularity will be seen through them.

Various clear tip shapes

Clear tips applied to nails

Clear tips blended and prepared for overlay

Designed tips

There are many pre-designed tips coming onto the market for quick and easy nail art. Some of them are in the form of tips with a small contact area and some have a larger contact area. Obviously these cannot be blended, as this would ruin the design.

The nail should be prepared in the usual way and the tips applied to the nail. There is usually no need to do anything else to the tip at this stage and the overlay can be applied directly over the tip.

SUMMARY

This chapter has explored the stages in the process of lengthening a client's nails by plastic tip or overlay techniques – choice, application and safe removal – and how to cope with the many types of 'problem' nails that a client may present to the technician.

Assessment of knowledge and understanding

1 What are the features of a plastic tip?

2 How is a tip type chosen to fit a client's nail?

3 Why is the correct width of tip so important?

4 How can any damage to the natural nail during blending be avoided?

5 How can tips be customised to fit various nail shapes?

6 Ideally, what is the maximum length of an artificial nail while still keeping the nail balanced?

7 What would you do if there is a bubble under the tip?

8 How would you apply a tip to:

(a) a nail biter

(b) ski jump nail

(c) hooked nail

9 When would you avoid using French white tips?

10 Why is it so important that the tip fits perfectly?

chapter 9

APPLYING OVERLAYS

Learning objectives

In this chapter you will learn:

- **about the critical differences between the 'systems'**
- **how to structure the overlay for strength and appearance**
- **how to apply a liquid and powder overlay**
- **how to apply a UV gel overlay**
- **how to apply a fibre overlay**
- **how to correct problem shaped nails with overlays**

INTRODUCTION

This chapter explains the differences in all the **overlay** systems available on the market today. It provides an unbiased information base and explains application techniques with ways to practise and perfect technique.

The perfect foundation has been created with the application of tips. Now is the time to create the perfect artificial nail that looks good and is very durable and strong. The tip has provided the required length, now the overlay on that tip will provide the required strength.

WRAP TECHNIQUES

By overlaying a tip, a longer artificial nail is going to be created. The overlay can be applied to a natural nail that has some length but needs to be protected because it is weak. Some clients like to wear a natural nail overlay just to keep their nail varnish in perfect condition as it does not chip. This treatment is often known as a **nail wrap**. This term probably came from a technique that was used many years ago by manicurists before the products and techniques we know now were available. If a client had split a nail or

Weak damaged nails ready for overlay   Marco Benito

Nails protected by overlay
Marco Benito

had weak nails, a piece of tissue was placed on the nail with a clear varnish. Several more coats of varnish were applied to smooth the surface. The tissue was sometimes wrapped slightly under the free edge, especially if there was a split. This is where the term 'wrap' came from and this procedure is probably the forerunner of the fibre system. Fibre users will now sometimes wrap the fibre mesh under the free edge to seal and strengthen it.

Overlay systems

This aspect of artificial nail work can sometimes be the most confusing for the beginner. There are several different 'systems' and many different companies, all insisting that their system and brand is the best. Some companies sell all systems, others sell only one of them. For help with choosing the best system see Chapter 7.

Many clients and technicians believe that the end results of the systems look very different. This is often the case, but it does not need to be. A beautifully applied set of nails should be a perfect shape and look natural whatever the system. One system need not look thicker or more natural than another. Colours and finishes can make a difference, but the skilful technician can even overcome this with some little tricks of the trade!

The systems in use

Almost all products in artificial nails belong to the acrylic family of chemicals. Acrylics are a vast family of various types of plastic. The word 'system', when it is related to artificial nails, describes the specific method and type of acrylic that produces the overlay.

Each system has a specific collection of various components and it is this collection and the application method that differentiates the systems. The tip application remains the same for each, although various brands may recommend specific preparation products. It is worthwhile taking these recommendations as, although cheaper options are often available, specific branded products have been developed to work with the system products to help achieve a better result. Introducing different or additional products or chemicals into the system can lead to problems.

Liquid and powder

This system is probably more commonly known as 'acrylic', although the term is strictly inaccurate as all the systems are based on acrylics. The system was arguably the first to be used for artificial nails using materials from the dental industry and the term 'acrylic' has stayed since then (see Chapter 1). It uses a liquid monomer and powder polymer (see Chapter 7) that cure to form a solid polymer. Its versatility in the hands of a skilled technician is immense and it is generally considered to be the trickiest to learn. It is sensitive to many external conditions, application techniques, and the time available to get it right before it hardens is limited. It is, however, a very popular system and is the favourite in the UK and US.

Liquid and powder products with coloured powders   Odyssey

It has many advantages in that any shape can be sculpted onto a tip or a free form (see Chapter 10); it can easily be used to correct difficult nail shapes; powders are available in different colours to allow the technician to create permanent French manicures or enhance natural skin tones. The overlay can be built to create the strongest structure and the strength within the overlay is excellent.

Its main drawback is the fact that the monomer is quite volatile and has a strong odour. Many technicians do not like the smell, or strong odours may be inappropriate in a beauty salon. Working cleanly, correctly and hygienically can minimise this problem. There are some products on the market that are classed as '**low odour**'. This usually means that the evaporation rate is lowered. The newer versions of this type of product can work very well and, if odours are a problem and a technician prefers a liquid and powder system, they are certainly worth considering.

A version of this system that has some additional benefits is the UV **light-cured** liquid and powder system. These are applied in a very similar way to the traditional acrylics; the main difference is that they do not polymerise until UV light is applied as the catalyst. This can be very beneficial for beginners as they have plenty of time to apply the overlay in the correct shape. For experienced technicians, both hands can be worked on, which avoids any additional time for curing. These monomers are in the low-odour category and therefore can be more user-friendly if odours are a problem. The overlay that is produced is as versatile and strong as traditional acrylic but, with some brands, has a characteristic that must be dealt with carefully: many UV-cured materials do not achieve a total cure and a sticky residue is left on the surface where oxygen has inhibited the cure. This residue is unpolymerised monomer, which is a skin irritant. It must be carefully removed with an appropriate solvent before buffing, as continual contact with the skin for either the client or the technician can result in an allergic reaction.

Most brands of this system have powders in several colours. This gives the technician the ability to create very natural looking artificial nails that suit the client's preferences. The most usual combination of colours available are:

- *Clear*. Used for either the entire nail or over the nail bed. Suitable for a nail bed that has a good colour.

- *Pink*. A powder that has a slight pink pigment added to it to enhance the colour of the nail bed. Used in the same way as clear. There are some brands that produce different shades of pink, so the shade best suited to the client can be chosen. Some pinks can be a little 'violent' and, if there is only one choice in the brand, take this into consideration when choosing which brand to use.

- *Bright white*. This is a heavily pigmented powder for use on the free edge only. It will create the very specific appearance of a French manicure. The application of this needs lots of practice as it is essential to achieve a perfect smile line for it to look good. This is also used during maintenance to put the smile line back to the right place.

- *Natural white*. This has less pigment than a bright white and will create a more natural looking nail. The application of it in on the free edge still needs care but the smile line is not so sharp. Even if this is not used during the first application of artificial nails, it is very useful to cover up the natural nail growth at the free edge. This growth of nail visible through the overlay often prevents wearers from having their nails varnish free as it does not look attractive. When choosing brands, check that the natural white is dense enough to do this job.

- *Natural*. This is not so common in modern brands now, but is a milky version of clear. It was very common in early liquid and powder systems as a good clarity in the overlay was difficult to achieve and the milkiness hid imperfections. Some clients still like the look of a milky nail, but it should never be used to hide poor workmanship such as visible lines from previous maintenance treatments.

- *Coloured powders*. There are many brands that have introduced multi-coloured powders. These are for use either as a 'permanent' colour instead of varnish or they are used to create nail art designs. The preparation and application is the same, but various colours may be applied in different sequences rather that following the order indicated. See Chapter 12.

The liquid and powder systems are applied with a brush made of natural hair, usually sable or the better quality Kolinsky sable, by dipping the tip of the brush first into the liquid monomer and then into the powder polymer where it picks up a bead of the material. This bead is then applied to the nail and pressed into place. Polymerisation either occurs within a few minutes or when placed under a UV light if it contains a **photoinitiator**.

UV gel system products   Courtesy of Grafton

UV gel

The UV gel system could be considered to be a 'pre-mixed' system, as there is only one material that is applied. The only other necessity is a UV light source. The gels are available in many different versions, all with different features and benefits. The main differences that will be immediately noticed by a technician is the viscosity (thickness) and how it flows. Some gels are very runny, others are very thick. Some thick gels will eventually flow, others will stay where they are put. Gels are available coloured, or clear.

All gels are applied to the nail and moved around with a brush before being polymerised under a UV light source. As with all systems, there are many application techniques developed by various companies to suit their gels, but there are two basic application methods: one of them is probably the easiest method of applying overlays of all the systems; the other requires a little more skill, but allows a nail to be sculpted onto a tip for maximum strength.

Another benefit of this system is that it is virtually odour-free and therefore may be more suitable for use in areas where stronger odours are a problem. In addition, the gels can be very flexible and therefore move more with the natural nail.

The disadvantages of the UV gel system are that some gels and their application methods cannot produce an overlay that is as strong as the liquid and powder systems and are therefore suitable only for those clients who are not too hard on their nails. Many of the gels on the market can be removed only by buffing and not by soaking off with a remover. Some consider this to be a benefit, others consider it to be a disadvantage (see Chapter 11).

Following cure, most gels have a sticky layer on the surface. This is uncured oligomers and needs to be removed with care and not allowed to touch the skin. Most brands have a specific product to do this job but a solvent such as ethyl acetate or varnish remover can be used.

Gels are available in a range of colours in the same way as liquid and powder systems and their use on the nails is the same. Multi-coloured gels for nail art designs (see Chapter 12) are becoming popular, but the same warning for opaque overlays in the liquid and powder system applies to gels.

Fibre

The third main system involves the application of a fibre mesh (usually silk or fibreglass) with a cyanoacrylate resin. This is polymerised or activated with a spray or paint-on chemical. This system is quite gentle on the natural nail, as the overlay produced cannot be very thick and remains quite flexible. It needs very little equipment and the starting costs for trainees are usually relatively low. Odours are kept to a minimum and are negligible if a paint-on activator is used in preference to a spray.

This system is very popular as a natural nail wrap, as it is quick and fairly easy to apply and never produces thick, clumsy-looking nails. For manicurists, it is ideal as a natural nail repair. The overlay is easy to remove.

The disadvantages include the fact that the overlay cannot be built up to create a maximum-strength structure and imperfect natural nail shapes can be corrected only by tip application, not a combination of tip application and overlay. As the overlay is quite thin, the artificial nails are not as strong as the structured nails of other systems. Some technicians find the application techniques a bit too 'fiddly', but others love it.

A fibre system   Courtesy of Beauty Express

Choosing a system

All the systems have their advantages and disadvantages: it is the technician who makes the difference. Some will hate a specific system and think it does not work at all; another technician will love that system and produce wonderful results. When, as a beginner, the choice of system is a problem and all the marketing and advertising make the choice even more confusing, the best way to choose the right system to learn with is to try them all. (See also Chapter 7 for help in choosing a system.)

Learning a new skill is easier when the task is enjoyable. It can be more frustrating if the tasks are unpleasant. Unfortunately, trainees tend to be under the impression that applying artificial nails is really easy, which is how it looks when an experienced technician does it. But trainees often discover it is not quite like that. It is not enough to watch the various systems being applied; the best approach is to try the different systems yourself to get the feel of how easy (or not) each system may be for you.

A liquid and powder system is not ideal for the person who immediately cannot stand the smell; a UV gel is to be avoided if the 'stickiness' is annoying; fibre should be left alone if handling the fibre suddenly produces clumsy fingers. No one system will be immediately easy but, hopefully, one will stand out as being the one that may become easier more quickly.

Beginners are advised to choose a system to learn with, and stay with that system until all the various skills are mastered. At this time, when the technician is very confident in their work, another system can be added. Whatever the system, it should be easier to learn, as the outcome now will always be a beautiful set of artificial nails.

THE STRUCTURE OF THE OVERLAY

The three zones

When applying an overlay, it will help to think of the nail with its tip in terms of three different **zones**:

1 **Zone 1** is the free edge where the overlay needs to be thin on the edge so that the finished nail does not look artificial.

2 **Zone 2** is the area over the smile line and slightly onto the nail bed where maximum strength is needed. This is the area of the nail that receives the most stress. It is often called the 'stress area' and should have a highest point that is called the 'apex'. The strongest natural structure is a curve (pressure is dispersed along the curve and is not concentrated over one point). The apex should be where two curves, the upper arch and the 'C' curve, come together at their highest and thickest part. This will create maximum strength for the whole nail without putting any stress on the natural nail, the nail bed, or the matrix.

3 **Zone 3** is the area near the base of the nail. Like Zone 1, this should be thin so that any ridges on the nail bed are avoided and, by being thin, it will be more flexible and able to move with the softer natural nail in this part of the nail plate.

If these zones are always kept in mind when applying an overlay, the correct shape and strength will be easier to achieve.

The application procedure

The steps in the application procedures listed below are general and, although they will be appropriate for many brands of products, it is advisable to check with the manufacturer or distributor their recommendations for application techniques. Always follow the manufacturer's instructions when using nail products and always avoid mixing system products from different brands. Polymerisation chemistry is carefully balanced and mixing potentially hazardous chemicals could be dangerous and could cause problems.

Zones of the nail

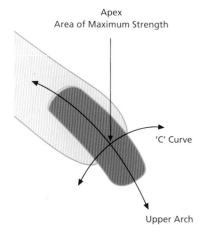

Apex
Area of Maximum Strength

'C' Curve

Upper Arch

Curves of the nail

Liquid and powder

Practising product control: Picking up the product with a brush in such a way that it can be applied to a nail is one of those things that looks very easy. It does, however, take a little bit of practice! For a beginner, picking up the perfect 'bead' can sometimes seem impossible.

- Some liquid and powder brands need a specific ratio (this is the amount of liquid to powder), others are less sensitive. There are some brands whose manufacturers recommend that a dry ratio is used in Zone 1 (more powder means harder), a medium ratio in Zone 2 (combination of hardness and flexibility) and a wet ratio in Zone 3 (maximum flexibility over the softer part of the nail).

- Usually the bead that needs to form on the tip of the brush needs to look smooth and glassy.

Practising product control for a little while is time well spent for a beginner. Understanding how the product behaves and practising picking up various beads will save a great deal of time, especially if these first attempts are placed on a nail and either have to be removed or buffed into shape.

Dipping a brush in powder

- To do this, get a piece of unwanted plastic or glass, dappen dishes with monomer and powder (use coloured powder as well as clear or pink as they behave differently owing to the density of pigment), a brush and some disposable towels.

- Dip the tip of the brush into the liquid and wipe it on the sides of the dish, dip the tip of the brush into the surface of the powder (not deep), hold it there for about two seconds and lift it out. It should have a bead of wet product on the tip.

Bead too wet

- If the bead is so wet it falls off, there was probably too much liquid still in the brush, so it would need to be wiped on the side of the dish a bit more. It may be that the brush needed to be in the powder a bit longer to pick up a bigger bead.

- If the bead that is picked up is rough, with obvious powder on the surface, the ratio is much too dry. Maybe there was not enough liquid in the brush or the brush was left in the powder too long and picked up too much powder.

Bead too dry

Practise this a few more times until a bead can be picked up that is smooth and glassy in appearance and does not fall off the brush. Different methods of dipping the brush into the liquid can be tried, such as sliding the brush down the side of the dish, noticing how far the brush goes into the liquid, squeezing both sides of the brush on the sides. As a brush is made of natural hair and many brushes are handmade, each one is going to have its own characteristics. One brush may hold much more liquid than another.

Picking up powder: There are different methods of picking up powder: little circles can be drawn in the surface of the powder or the brush can be drawn through in a line. The brush should never be dipped in further than the tip and there should be sufficient powder in the dish to avoid the brush touching the bottom. If this happens, the bead sticks to the dish and is difficult to get out. It is also worth tapping the dish on the desk to smooth out the surface of the powder. A smooth surface makes picking up a bead much easier.

Perfect bead

Bead control: When a bead can be picked up confidently, it is worth moving on to 'bead control'. This will demonstrate what the ratio of the bead is and the trainee technician can determine if this is correct.

- This is done by picking up a bead and gently placing it on the plastic or glass. If the bead is on the very tip of the brush it should come off the brush onto the surface with ease. Once the bead is on the surface, it should start to melt. How it does this demonstrates if the ratio is correct. By melting, the bead loses its shape and eventually becomes flat.

- All brands are slightly different but, as a general guideline, if the bead melts in less than 3 seconds it has a wet ratio, if it takes over 5 seconds, it is dry. A medium ratio, which is usually the one to aim for, should hold its shape momentarily and then start a slow melt.

- Doing this a few times, using the various ways to pick up a bead, will show the trainee how to pick up a bead of the right ratio.

This can now be taken a step further. Nails are different sizes and so are the zones on each nail. Now the right ratio can be achieved, it is time to practise picking up a bead that is not only the right ratio but also the right size! A step further again: the right ratio of the right size in a different colour, for example white tip powder. Coloured powder usually needs more liquid owing to the colour pigments present, so this should be tried out first to get the right ratio.

Too little on tip

After that, different-sized beads can be picked up to see how much liquid is needed in the brush, how long the brush should be kept in the powder, and so on. After this has been practised, it is worth deciding beforehand what the bead is going to be for. For example, a Zone 1 white tip for a little finger with a short free edge (very small) and then a Zone 1 white tip for a middle finger with a medium-length free edge (considerably bigger), and so on.

Too much on tip

Determining how big the bead needs to be before it is picked up will save time later and is part of the way towards creating a good structure with a brush and not correcting a bad structure with a buffer.

Condition of the liquid: During this little exercise, the condition of the liquid should be noted. If it is looking cloudy or if there is powder at the bottom of the dish, it is badly contaminated. If this liquid was used on a nail with a clear or pink overlay, it would look cloudy and mottled. This contamination must be avoided during working and is easily achieved. When working, the brush should be occasionally dipped into the liquid and taken straight out without wiping it on the sides of the dish, but then wiping it on a disposable towel or tissue. This, if done a couple of times, will remove the build-up of powder that accumulates in the hairs and then goes into the liquid. When using white-tip powder, the brush should be cleaned in this way after each nail. This is because the powder will remain in the brush and the next time the brush is dipped in and pressed on the side of the dish, the powder will be left in the liquid and the nails will become more and more cloudy. Some technicians even have a separate dish of liquid just for white-tip powder to prevent this happening.

Application on the nails: Once a certain amount of product control is achieved, the application onto the nails can start. This procedure is the same as that for a natural nail overlay.

Creating the perfect shape: One of the most important aims of applying overlays is to create as close to the perfect shape as possible with the brush and not rely on correcting mistakes with a buffer afterwards. This obviously takes practice. Liquid and powder overlays continue to polymerise for quite some time after they become hard enough to buff. Too much buffing can interrupt the polymer chains being formed and create weak spots. Also, buffing away what has just been applied can waste a great deal of time. It is much easier to try to apply it correctly in the first place and the buffing as a refinement stage.

Application using white-tip powder

> **NOTE**
>
> Zoning (that is applying the overlay in each zone) is the ideal application technique for this system. If white-tip powder is being used, the zoning principle is essential. By differentiating between Zones 2 and 3, the perfect structure can be created. However, applying the overlay in Zones 2 and 3 together is not wrong and, as long as the technician achieves the correct structure, the degree of zoning is a matter of choice.

1 The nails should have the tips perfectly blended, the dust removed and be clean and oil-free. One hand is worked on at a time from start to finish.

2 Apply primer (if instructed by manufacturers) very sparingly around the base of the nail. Make sure the primer is dry before applying overlay.

3 Clean the brush first by dipping it into the liquid, taking it straight out and wiping it on or between sheets of disposable towel.

4 Start with the little finger, pick up a bead of white-tip powder that is approximately the right size and place it in the centre of Zone 1 closer to the smile line than the edge (1).

5 Wipe the brush on the towel.

6 Holding the brush at the same angle as the upper arch of the nail and with the tip of the brush, press the bead. Take part of the bead to one side wall and create the point of the smile line (2); take part of the bead to the other side wall and create the point of the smile line; create the smile line as neatly as possible with the tip of the brush and smooth the surface of the whole zone. If the brush is angled down slightly and the overlay is gently pushed up towards the smile line, a sharper line can be created and a thinner edge of the nail (see diagram). If the smile line is uneven and needs straightening, the extreme tip of the brush (cleaned and dry) can be used to do this, making sure that the nail plate does not get monomer on it from the brush. Check the shape by looking down the barrel of the nail to make sure the overlay is even. The centre of this smile line will form the apex of the nail. (Some technicians like to apply white tip to each nail before Zone 2. This is usually to avoid contaminating the liquid. However, as the overlay starts polymerising immediately, the bond between the overlay at Zone 1 and 2 may have a weak point in it as Zone 1 has polymerised too much to blend with Zone 2. A stronger overlay is achieved if the whole nail is completed and contamination is easily avoided.)

EQUIPMENT LIST

clean terry towel on desk

three layers of disposable towels

tissues or disposable towels

hand sanitiser

nail sanitiser

nail dehydrator

cuticle knife

cuticle nippers

tips

adhesive

tip cutters

liquid monomer in clean, covered dappen dish

powder polymers in clean, covered dappen dishes

primer (if required)

clean sable brush

files of 240 and 180 grit

oil

buffers, such as a white block

three-way buffer or block

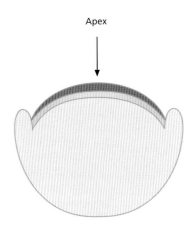

View of even overlay by looking down barrel of nail

7   Clean the brush.

8   Pick up a bead of pink or clear of the right size and place it in the centre of Zone 2 next to the white tip (3).

9   Wipe the brush.

10   The bead will have started to melt while wiping the brush and will be ready to press into shape. Making slow and deliberate movements and keeping the brush parallel with the nail, press the bead and, like Zone 1, take part of the bead out towards the side wall, leaving most in the centre and blend over the white tip; take part out to the other side wall and blend over the white tip (4). Blend the whole zone over the tip. Check down the barrel for evenness and thin sides.

11   Pick up a bead for Zone 3 and place it in the centre of the zone (5).

12   Wipe the brush.

13   Press the bead and blend up over the whole nail.

14   With the brush flattened, press the overlay towards the nail fold, taking great care not to touch the skin with the brush and leaving a tiny margin of bare nail bed. With the flattened brush between the overlay and the nail fold, gently press the overlay to thin the zone and create a good bond with the nail plate (6).

15   Check shape from both sides to make sure the upper arch is in place and the overlay is smooth. Check overlay from down the barrel (see diagram on p.199).

16   Repeat process for each finger. Polymerisation has occurred when the overlay can be tapped with the handle of the brush and a 'clicking' sound can be heard. If the click sounds dull, it is not sufficiently cured. Discard the towel that has been used to wipe the brush.

17   When all the nails on one hand are finished, go back to the little finger with a 240 grit file. Gently buff over the whole surface to smooth out any bumps and ridges. Carefully blend the edges of the overlay making sure the tiny margin of exposed nail plate is not buffed. Check overlay from all angles to ensure a perfect structure. Refine the free edge to make it as thin and even as possible (7).

18   Repeat for all nails.

19   Return to little finger and buff whole surface with a white block as this will start to refine the surface ready for the final stage.

20   Repeat for all fingers.

21   Using a three-way buffer in the correct sequence (usually black, white, grey) buff all nails to a high-gloss shine without any dull spots (dips in the overlay) (8).

22   Remove all the dust, including that which has collected under the nail and discard layer of disposable towel with all the dust.

23   Apply oil to each nail and massage into nail and cuticle (9).

24   Repeat the whole process on the other hand.

25   When both hands are completed, tidy desk by cleaning brush thoroughly and storing flat and away from dust, discard any unused monomer onto the disposable towel remaining on the desk. Make sure powder dishes are covered. Wipe the surface of the desk with a cloth dampened with a mild disinfectant and prepare for next client with clean towels, etc.

(1) Place bead on Zone 1

(2) Shape Zone 1 checking 'c' curve

(3) Place bead on Zone 2

(4) Shape Zone 2 to blend with Zone 1

(5) Place bead on Zone 3

(6) Shape Zone 3 checking strcuture from all angles

(7) Shape and refine overlay

(8) Buff nail

(9) Apply oil

If the overlay is being applied without white tip, it should still be applied in zones, but it would not be necessary to create a smile line. Otherwise the process is the same.

Troubleshooting: If the overlay looks powdery in Zone 3, it is usually because the client's hands are very cold or the liquid monomer is cold. This hinders the rate of polymerisation leaving unpolymerised powder on the surface. This can be corrected by warming the client's hands before application or making sure that the monomer is at room temperature before using. If it is an emergency, for example, the first client of the day in a salon that has not yet warmed up, the covered dappen dish with the monomer can be placed in a bowl of tepid water (not hot) to bring it to room temperature.

If the brush was not cleaned properly after the last use and has a lump of product in it, soften the product in some monomer (nothing else) and use a paper towel to try to remove the debris. Do not use your fingers as a sensitivity to the product may result. An orange stick can be used to dislodge the debris, but this will usually result in damaged hairs and a brush that does not work very well. Discard the monomer that was used.

A UV gel system   Courtesy of Beauty Express

UV gel

This system is often considered to be one of the easiest for a beginner to learn. This is possibly true as, once the tips have been applied, there is a very straightforward method of applying UV gel as an overlay. The artificial nails produced by this method are not always very strong, as it does not create a structure with the curves that produce a strong nail. This method would be suitable for those who will wear their nails quite short or who are used to having long nails and are therefore unlikely to break them.

There are many different types of gels on the market now and the technology of this area has advanced a great deal in the last few years. The range of gels now available will allow a skilled technician to do everything with gel that can be done with a liquid and powder system.

The gel 'system': Gels now come in all colours and the gel 'system' can comprise a single component – that is, one type of gel – or it can comprise several gel components, all of which are recommended as being needed to create an artificial nail. Like all other systems, the choice is down to personal preference and cost.

Gels are 'pre-mixed' system, needing UV light to polymerise rather than another chemical. There are two distinct types of gel in use: self-levelling and non self-levelling.

The bonds in gels are very strong and this usually makes them resistant to solvents. If this is the case, the overlay cannot be 'soaked' off and requires buffing to remove it. This can be seen as a benefit or a hazard – a solvent-resistant overlay is also resistant to damage and discoloration from nail varnish and remover.

Soaking nails in a solvent to remove them is very drying to the nail plate and the surrounding skin, and the nail plate especially takes time to recover from this major dehydration. If artificial nails are not being replaced, oils and moisturisers can be used after removal to help this recovery. Occasional rumours arise in the industry suggesting that this method can be damaging to health. All chemicals are damaging to health if an individual is overexposed, and the overexposure level to the solvents used in this industry, such as acetone, is very high (see Chapter 4).

Removing artificial nails by buffing needs skill and this can be achieved only by practising on real fingers. At first, it can be time-consuming and, when done improperly or excessively, can cause severe damage to the nail plate. Ideally, the removal of nails should be a rare occurrence and take place only when the client does not want artificial nails any more. There are some gels on the market now that can be removed with solvents so widening the choice for technicians and clients.

A word of warning about coloured gels (and acrylics): an opaque overlay could be hiding a problem! If lifting has occurred or if the nail plate or nail bed has become infected, this will not be visible. The only way to ensure this is not happening is to remove the overlay at regular intervals that, in itself, could cause a problem. Belief that the overlay will not lift is not sufficient, as a client may be resistant to any overlay, or may become resistant at any time owing to a change in the nail plate.

With a one-component gel system, the gel is applied to the nail in one or more layers to build up strength. In a system with two or more components, there is usually a gel that acts as a bonding layer; it is compatible with the nail plate and also with the next layer of gel; next there is a thick gel that can build an overlay with the required structure, that is curves, and then a sealer gel that provides a high-gloss shine and protection. The manufacturer's instructions should always be followed.

Application to the nails

Both hands are worked on at the same time with this system.

1 Both hands, with tips applied, must be clean and totally dust-free (gels are very susceptible to dust as it causes a lumpy overlay).

2 Apply primer to Zone 3, if required, and allow to dry.

3 Open gel and, with a clean brush, apply a thin layer of gel to each nail, taking care not to touch soft tissue (remove with an orange stick if this happens) (1). The gel is applied in this method in the same way as nail varnish, but bring the brush to the edge of the nail and wipe downwards off the edge. This will help to seal the edge and prevent any shrinkage of the overlay. If a 'whole-hand' lamp is being used, include the thumb, otherwise just apply gel to the four fingers.

4 Turn on lamp and ask client to place fingers under the lamp, making sure that the fingers are correctly placed and all are exposed to the UV light. This usually takes 2 minutes, but refer to lamp's instructions.

5 While the first hand is under the lamp, repeat the process on the other hand.

6 Remove the first hand and replace with the second.

<table>
<tr><td colspan="1">EQUIPMENT LIST</td></tr>
<tr><td>clean terry towel on desk</td></tr>
<tr><td>three layers of disposable towels</td></tr>
<tr><td>tissues or disposable towels nail wipes</td></tr>
<tr><td>hand sanitiser</td></tr>
<tr><td>nail sanitiser/dehydrator</td></tr>
<tr><td>cuticle knife</td></tr>
<tr><td>cuticle nippers</td></tr>
<tr><td>tips</td></tr>
<tr><td>adhesive</td></tr>
<tr><td>tip cutter</td></tr>
<tr><td>gels</td></tr>
<tr><td>UV lamp</td></tr>
<tr><td>primer (if required)</td></tr>
<tr><td>clean brush, either nylon or natural hair</td></tr>
<tr><td>finishing wipe (if required)</td></tr>
<tr><td>file of 240 grit</td></tr>
<tr><td>oil</td></tr>
<tr><td>buffers, such as a white block</td></tr>
<tr><td>three-way buffer (if required)</td></tr>
</table>

(1) After applying primer, apply a layer of gel

(2) Cure for recommended time

(3) Apply second layer and cure under lamp for recommended time

(4) Remove sticky surface layer

(5) Refine surface

(6) Remove all dust

(7) Apply layer of sealant/gloss and cure under lamp

(8) Finished nail

7 If a small lamp is being used, the thumb will need to have the overlay applied now and then it can replace the second hand after the cure time (2).

8 Repeat for thumb of second hand.

9 Apply second layer of gel to nails of first hand while second thumb is under lamp and cure (3).

10 Repeat until all fingers of both hands have had second layer.

11 If the nails are long or are likely to be subject to heavy use, it may be necessary to add a third layer in the same way.

12 When all nails have had sufficient layers applied and they have been cured, replace lid of gel and clean brush with nail varnish remover, or equivalent, on a tissue.

13 Many gels have a sticky surface layer of uncured monomer. This must be removed and most brands have a product that will do this job efficiently without damaging the gel. The monomer must be kept off the skin at this stage, so a new nail wipe or equivalent must be used for each nail and the nail must be wiped from the nail fold towards the tip (4). By doing this there is little chance of the monomer touching the skin. If the same wipe is used, monomer from the previous nail will come into contact with the skin and the client will develop a sensitivity and become unable to wear the artificial nails. The monomer must be thoroughly removed, as any remaining will be in the dust created at the next stage and will touch the skin of both the client and the technician.

14 It is possible to leave the nails exactly as they are now if they look a perfect shape; however, there are often small imperfections in the surface and sometimes the gel will have shrunk slightly so that the extreme tip looks more rounded than it should.

15 If the nails need refining, a very soft file should be used or a white block, as the surface of a gel is usually quite soft. The shape should be checked from all sides (5).

16 At this stage there are two options: the nails can be buffed with a three-way buffer which will produce a natural shine (not a high shine as the surface is usually too soft) or, after the sticky layer is removed, a thin layer of the gel can be applied (7), and cured to produce a high gloss. If the second option is chosen, all the dust created by the buffing must be carefully removed (6) with the finishing wipe on a tissue and the paper towel where all the dust that has collected removed.

17 Apply oil and massage.

18 Clean desk and prepare for next client.

Structuring method with a thicker gel

1 Both hands, with tips applied, must be clean and totally dust-free (gels are very susceptible to dust as it causes a lumpy overlay).

2 Apply primer to Zone 3, if required, and allow to dry or apply bonding gel if appropriate and cure for recommended time.

3 Open gel and, with a clean brush, apply a bead of gel to the centre of the nail where the apex should be (1). Take part of the bead to the side wall at the stress area and take part of the bead to the other side wall at the stress area. Ease part of the bead down towards the nail fold, taking care not to touch the skin. Bring part of the bead with the brush to the edge of the nail and wipe downwards off the edge. This will help to seal the edge and prevent any shrinkage of the overlay. The gel should now have a thin layer at the free edge in Zone 1, a thicker layer at the stress area in Zone 2 and a thin layer in Zone 3. The surface now needs gently smoothing over with featherlight movements of the brush until the shape is right from all angles (2). If a 'whole-hand' lamp and a gel that does not run is being used, include the thumb, otherwise, just apply gel to the four fingers.

4 Turn on lamp and ask client to place fingers under the lamp (3), making sure that the fingers are correctly placed and all are exposed to the UV light. This usually takes 2 minutes, but refer to lamp's instructions. It is possible that a heat reaction may be felt by the client. Polymerisation is an 'exothermic' chemical reaction (gives off heat) and the reaction in a gel is usually very fast. If the gel layer is thick or if the client has thin or sensitive nail beds the heat may be felt. The client should be warned that this may happen and to help avoid it, the fingers

should be placed under the light for 5 seconds, then removed for 5 seconds. This should be repeated at least once more and the heat sensation, if it is going to happen, may be avoided. If the heat is felt, and it is usually quite sudden, tell the client to remove her fingers and press them on the desk very firmly. This will stop the reaction and then the fingers can be replaced.

5   While the first hand is under the lamp, repeat the process to the other hand.

6   Remove the first hand and replace with the second.

7   If a small lamp is being used or a gel that can run, the thumb will need to have the overlay applied now and then it can replace the second hand after the cure time.

8   Repeat for thumb of second hand.

9   When all nails have had sufficient layers applied and they have been cured, replace lid of gel and clean brush with the finishing wipe, or equivalent, on a tissue.

10   Many gels have a sticky surface layer of uncured monomer. This must be removed and most brands have a product that will do this job efficiently without damaging the gel. The monomer must be kept off the skin at this stage, so a new nail wipe or equivalent must be used for each nail and the nail must be wiped from the nail fold towards the tip (4). By doing this there is little chance of the monomer touching the skin. If the same wipe is used, monomer from the previous nail will come into contact with the skin and the client will develop a sensitivity eventually and become unable to wear the artificial nails. The monomer must be thoroughly removed as any remaining will be in the dust created at the next stage and will touch the skin of both the client and the technician.

11   The nails now need refining as there are often small imperfections in the surface and sometimes the gel will have shrunk slightly and the extreme tip look more rounded than it should. The structure should also be checked to make sure it is correct and the same on each nail.

12   A very soft file should be used as the surface of a gel is usually quite soft. The shape should be checked from all sides (5).

13   At this stage there are two options: the nails can be buffed with a three-way buffer which will produce a natural shine (not a high shine as the surface is usually too soft) or a thin layer of the gel can be applied and cured to produce a high gloss after the sticky layer is removed. If the second option is chosen, all the dust created by the buffing must be carefully removed with a finishing wipe on a tissue and the paper towel where the dust that has collected removed (6).

14   Apply oil and massage.

15   Clean desk and prepare for next client.

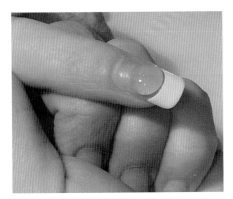

(1) Apply bead to Zone 2

(2) Work bead to create structure

(3) Cure for recommended time

(4) Remove sticky surface

(5) Refine shape

(6) Remove all dust

(7) Apply thin sealant/gloss layer

(8) Cure for recommended time

Finished nail

EQUIPMENT LIST

several layers of disposable towels

nail wipes or cotton wool

hand sanitiser

nail sanitiser/dehydrator

cuticle knife

cuticle nippers

tips

adhesive

tip cutters

fibre scissors with a very fine and very sharp blade

fibre mesh, silk or fibreglass, kept in a plastic cover or box

resin with long nozzle

activator, spray or brush-on

240 grit file

white block

three-way buffer

oil

The fibre system

This is a relatively easy system, but it relies heavily on the skilful application of the tips. Owing to the nature of the products, it is not possible to create any additional curves in the overlay, as can be done with a liquid and powder or a thick gel. Therefore the shape of the finished nail relies on the shape of the tip. It is possible to build in a little extra strength with the fibre, but this is minimal.

There are fewer actual brands of this system on the market – that is, a collection of products that make a full system under one name – than for the other systems, but the individual components are readily available.

Mesh and resin: Silk or fibreglass can be used as the mesh. The resin used in this system is sometimes called a **no-light gel**. This should not be confused with a UV gel. A no-light gel in this system is a cyanoacrylate resin that is slightly thicker and therefore more like a gel in consistency. (It is, however, possible to use fibre with a UV gel to give added strength or for free-form sculpting.) There are also two different ways of activating the resin: a spray or as a brush-on. Both are effective and usually contain similar chemicals. It is a matter of choice, but a brush-on activator will obviously put fewer chemicals into the air, which will help to avoid any sensitivity developing in individuals.

Application

1   One hand is worked on at a time from start to finish.

2   The nails with tips must be clean and dehydrated. (This system does not require any primer and the rough surface of the nail plate is enough to hold the overlay.)

3   Using the scissors and avoiding handling the fibre too much, cut a piece of fibre that is the approximate width of the nail to be overlayed.

4   Remove the fibre from its paper backing and use the backing to hold the fibre while it is put in place.

5   Place the fibre onto the nail close to, but not touching, the nail fold. Use the backing paper to press the fibre onto the length of the nail (1). Avoid touching it with your fingers as they will leave behind a small amount of moisture and this will prevent the resin from soaking into the mesh. Trim the sides if necessary by sliding the blade of the scissors down the side wall and cutting away the excess. Trim the excess length of fibre by angling the scissors backwards on the nail tip so the fibre is cut slightly shorter than the tip (2). This allows the end to be sealed with the resin. (If the artificial nail needs extra strength, a strip of fibre can be placed across the stress area. This can either be a strip placed on the nail before this stage, or it can be a double layer of the fibre.)

6   Repeat this for all the fingers, excluding the thumb.

7   Apply a very small amount of resin down the centre of the nail (3) and, with the side of the nozzle, use little circular movements to spread the resin over the nail and work it into the mesh (4). More resin can be applied if necessary but, at this stage, the pattern of the mesh should still be visible, but very wet.

(1) Apply fibre to nail

(2) Cut excess fibre with scissors and wet fibre with resin

(3) Smooth resin with nozzle

(4) Activate resin holding spray away from nail

(5) Apply second layer of resin and smooth

(6) Activate resin holding spray away from nail

(7) OR apply brush-on resin/gel

(8) Use brush to smooth resin/gel which will also activate it

(9) Wipe activator brush before replacing in bottle

(10) Refine surface

(11) Buff nail

Finished nail

8 Repeat for all fingers.

9 Go back to the little finger and apply a very small amount of resin down the centre of the nail and spread it over the whole nail with side of nozzle. (It will not need spreading if a brush-on activator is being used.) Take great care not to touch the skin and to leave a tiny margin of bare nail around the edges. Seal the tip of the nail with the side of the nozzle. (If too much resin is applied, it will run into the side walls.)

10 Repeat for all fingers.

11 If a spray activator is being used, hold it at least 30cm away from the nails and spray once (ensuring the aim is right!) (5). The resin needs only minute amounts of spray activator. If too much is sprayed or it is too close, a sudden heat reaction will occur that is very painful for the client and can ruin the overlay.

12 If a brush-on activator is being used, have the brush cleaner at the ready. (Brushes used with this product can get stuck with polymerised resin and must be put in a solvent between uses to keep them clean. It is usual to have another bottle of a similar size containing the solvent and a spare brush so they can be alternated during applications.) Spread the resin with the activator brush to cover the nail while keeping the product off the skin and leaving a tiny margin around the edge (6). This will mix the activator into the resin and speed up the polymerisation process. (This activator is usually much weaker than the spray-on version, so the process is slower.)

13 Repeat for all fingers, putting more activator on the brush for each finger. Replace brush in activator bottle.

14 Apply another layer of resin to all fingers and either spread with nozzle or leave for brush (7).

15 Activate in the same way as before.

16 Repeat the whole procedure from Step 3 on the thumb.

17 Another layer of resin may be applied if more strength is required.

18 If a brush-on activator is being used, remove the spare brush from the solvent and wipe it on a paper towel to remove most of the solvent. Wipe the brush that has just been used on the paper towel and place it in the solvent. Put the spare brush into the activator bottle ready for the next use (8).

19 The overlay should be relatively smooth and should need minimal buffing to refine and smooth the surface. If the activator has been sprayed too close, there may be pits in the surface that will need buffing out. (If this happens and by removing them the overlay is made too thin, the nail should be cleaned of dust and a layer replaced.)

20 Refine the surface further with a white block (9).

21 Bring the nails to a high shine with a three-way buffer (10).

22 Remove all dust and apply oil.

This nail system is not solvent resistant at all. If nail varnish is to be worn then a very gentle remover should be used otherwise the surface will be destroyed. If varnish is repeatedly removed, the whole nail may be undermined.

Creating the natural-looking nail

A nail correctly applied in one system should not look widely different from one applied in another. The white tip that can be used in an acrylic system may look different from others, but there are white gels available and the fibre system can use French white tips.

The finish can sometimes look different and a gel with a high gloss looks different from the high shine achieved by buffing an acrylic. However, if a client who wears acrylic nails prefers the high gloss, the gloss gel can be applied to an acrylic to give it that effect.

When applying nails, the most important aim is to create a natural-looking nail that suits the hand and is the strongest structure it can be. A technician is only as good as their last set of nails. No one can create perfection every time and a beginner needs to be able to look at their results and recognise what can be improved. An eye for balance and symmetry is not always a natural skill and needs to be learned. A trainee technician who has natural skill is very lucky; most do not have it and need to develop it. Many are not even aware that they lack this skill and send clients out with very strange shapes on their fingers.

PROBLEM SHAPES

Following on from the problem shapes encountered in Chapter 8 on tip application, there are some shapes that can be improved using overlays.

Ski-jump nails

If the tip is put on at the correct angle for a ski-jump nail, the lower arch will be good but the upper arch will be very strange. This can be very easily corrected by careful structuring of the overlay to create a good upper arch and a strong nail (see diagram).

Tip blended and overlay applied to correct poor upper arch

Bitten nails

Still the most difficult problem to overcome, like the ski-jump, the bitten nail can be further improved by the overlay. The overlay only has a tiny nail plate to hold on to and the length must be just to the end of the finger, but, the overlay can be applied so that the upper arch can look quite natural. The nail really needs to be covered with coloured varnish to hide the lack of a smile line but, if this is done, the finished nail will look very good.

Tip cut short and blended with overlay for bitten nails

Twisted nails

If natural nails were allowed to continue growing, they would curve down and twist in a clockwise or anticlockwise direction. These twists may not start until the nail has reached a decent length, but they may start on the nail bed. This can be seen if the shape of the barrel is viewed from either the tip looking towards the hand or from the hand looking towards the tip. It is difficult to see if the nail plate is very short, but the longer the nail is the more obvious the twisting becomes. Once a tip is applied and blended, a twist may become obvious. The lower arches will be uneven with one side dipping down more than the other. This can be easily rectified during the blending of the tip by matching both sides of the lower arch. The twist of the barrel can be rectified by placing slightly more product on one side than the other and making the 'C' curve of the nail even. The additional amount of product is minimal and it is very easy to overcompensate. The easiest way to see this is by turning the client's hand around and looking down the nail from the hand down to the tip.

PRACTICE MAKES PERFECT

Applying artificial nails is not just about making nails longer. It is also a skill that can solve many problems and make imperfect nails look perfect. By understanding the systems and becoming skilful at creating shapes, a technician can do many things with artificial nails. It is possible to replace nail plates that have been lost through accident or illness. It is possible to rebuild nails that are deformed through damage or an hereditary factor. It is even possible to build a nail where one does not exist, such as where the tip of the finger is missing. (If any work like this is attempted with a client who has a medical condition, it is important to get approval from their doctor first.)

The secret of the true professional and successful technician is practice. No technician can practise too much, both in perfecting shape and product control and applying perfect nails to every client regardless of nail shape, condition and lifestyle. Nothing can replace the value of applying nails to a very wide range of people. Every nail is different and every lifestyle is different. Seeing nails that have been applied two weeks earlier will teach the new technician much more than just practising shape. Also, this is work that deals with people, so practising with people is essential. When practising, technicians should aim to apply a full set of artificial nail extensions in under two hours. This is acceptable for a client receiving a treatment from a technician, as opposed to a trainee. Every technician should aim to provide a full set of artificial nails in 1½ hours or less.

Some nail salons operate very well with every treatment being carried out in one hour or less. This is the choice of the salon and their clients and can be successful as long as all hygiene rules, working practices and client care are maintained. Other salons, on the other hand, prefer to give their clients more time and a more relaxing treatment. The most important aspect of every treatment is safety and quality.

AFTER CARE ADVICE

The following after care advice should be given to clients after every artificial nail treatment:

- Return for recommended maintenance treatments
- If there appears to be discoloration under the artificial nail, return immediately
- Do not pick off the overlay
- Do not use nails as tools
- Massage nail oil into the cuticle area every day
- Do not file the surface of the nail
- It is not advisable to shorten the nail as the thin layer at the free edge will be filed away to a thicker area
- Use acetone-free varnish remover if necessary.

Potential retail recommendations

- nail oil
- varnish remover
- varnish
- hand cream
- top coat.

SUMMARY

This chapter first examined the function and structure of overlays and then demonstrated step-by-step techniques for their application to create a natural looking nail, whichever system – liquid and powder, UV gel or fibre – the technician has used.

Assessment of knowledge and understanding

1 Explain briefly the application of: (a) powder/liquid, (b) UV gel, (c) fibre systems.

2 What structure creates the maximum strength for a finished nail?

3 What is meant by perfect shape and balance?

4 What is the purpose of zoning?

5 Suggest two methods of application that could correct or improve various nail shapes.

6 What conditions could adversely affect the application of overlays?

7 In a UV-cured material what inhibits polymerisation?

8 Why is it important to provide treatments within commercially acceptable timings?

9 Why is it important to work with system products in the same brand and follow manufacturer's instructions?

10 What after care advice should be given?

chapter 10

THE ART AND SKILL OF APPLYING SCULPTURED NAILS

INTRODUCTION

This chapter looks in step-by-step detail at applying sculptured nails.

SCULPTURED NAILS OR PLASTIC TIPS?

Many years ago, when only a few individuals were experimenting with dental products the plastic tips we are familiar with today were not available in their present form. The dental acrylics were strong enough to support themselves and the nail plate could be extended using just these products. If a 'platform' was placed under the edge of the nail, the product could be continued from the nail plate onto the platform to create a longer free edge. When the product had cured (hardened) the platform could be removed and there was a longer nail.

This method is generally called 'free-form sculpture' or **sculptured nails** and there are many different versions of specially designed 'platforms' that are called 'forms', the choice is a matter of personal preference. Many technicians learned how to do 'nails' in this way only and many still prefer

Various forms

this method to the method of applying plastic tips first. Applying artificial nails in this way requires skill, but then so does applying tips correctly. The method omits the tip application stage, but needs some time spent on placing the chosen form in exactly the right place. On balance, a technician skilled in sculpting nails can complete a set in a shorter length of time than a set using tips.

The results of the two methods rely entirely on the skill of the technician. For many, artificial nails with a tip will result in a stronger nail, but only if the tip is applied perfectly and there are no weak areas around the smile line, the blending or the side walls. A sculpting technician can also produce a perfect nail that does not have any of these weak spots. This can be difficult, as there will often be a step created where the form meets the nail plate and some product can seep under the free edge. If there is no natural free edge, there may be a step up where the form does not meet the free edge. A sculptured nail must also have sufficient strength at the side walls without looking too thick, otherwise the free edge will snap off very easily. All of these features can be achieved by skilful application.

SYSTEMS AND FORMS

Systems

The liquid and powder system is the one most commonly used to create sculptured nails, as its application and **curing** methods suit the way the nail is achieved. UV gel is also used as the thicker gels will stay in place on a form for UV curing to take place, and, with the coloured gels, a white tip can be achieved. The fibre system is rarely used in this way. It is possible to hold the fibre before the excess length has been removed and coat it with resin. This will result in extra length without a tip, but it will be very delicate and would not last very long. It would also be clear and would need coloured varnish to disguise it.

Forms

There are many different types of forms available. Some are *disposable* and are used from a roll. They have a sticky back that allows them to be held in place on the finger. Technicians have devised all sorts of inventive ways of shaping these to help produce the perfect nail. They are used for one nail and then discarded. They usually have a metallic finish of some description to reflect back the small amount of heat polymerisation produces and ensures that the under-surface of the free edge is fully cured. With UV cured materials, it is usually worth removing the form after curing and putting the fingers back under the light with the palm of the hand upwards to make sure the underside is cured.

There are also an array of *reusable* forms of different shapes and sizes. Like many things in the art of applying artificial nails, the decision about which one to use is a matter of personal choice. The forms, both disposable and reusable, are not expensive, so it is worth trying out as many as possible to see which is preferred. It is also worth having several types, as some will fit a specific nail shape better than others and this will make the fitting of the form much quicker.

Fitting a form

The choice of which form to use is for the technician to make. Technicians soon find a form that they are most comfortable with.

1 Many paper forms that are supplied on a roll. A new form should be removed from the roll and the part to be fitted under the free edge as a platform for the artificial nail should be gently rolled between the thumbs to soften it and allow a curve to be easily created (1).

2 The form should be held in both hands and fitted under the free edge. When it is under the free edge, look down the barrel of the nail to make sure the form fits securely without any gaps (2).

3 Gently attach it to the sides of the finger and check the form from all angles to make sure it fits the nail correctly. Then attach securely to the finger (3).

4 Look down the barrel of the nail to make sure that a 'C' curve has been created that is the same as the natural nail and that the curve of the form is straight (4). If there is any twisting of this curve on the form, a twisted nail will be created. The shape of the form usually allows this shape to be secured under the finger. If the natural nail is wide or particularly flat, this may not be possible, but it is important that the shape is not disturbed. If this happens, then use the part of the form that has been discarded (the hole where the finger goes) to hold this shape in place.

The nail is now ready to have a sculptured overlay applied.

(1) Shape form between thumbs

(2) Put form under free edge without any gaps

(3) Secure form

(4) Check 'C' curve by looking down barrel

The application of a sculptured overlay is almost identical to that of an application over a tip. The main differences to remember are:

- With a liquid and powder system, the bead cannot be too wet as it will run down the form and be difficult to contain in the free edge shape until it starts to cure.

- While applying Zone 1, check the lower arch that is being created on the form and try to keep it as close to the finished shape as possible in order to avoid lots of reshaping when the form is removed.

- Make sure the side walls, particularly in the stress area, are sufficiently strong but without being thick.

- Check the 'C' curve and upper arch all the time.

- If the 'C' curve is too flat, it is possible to gently squeeze the form at the free edge before curing to increase the curve slightly.

- When using a UV gel system, the underside of the nail should be cured when the form has been removed. White tip gel is quite dense and the underside may not be completely cured unless replaced under the lamp.

A badly shaped sculpted nail can often be put right with a file when the form has been removed but, with plenty of practice, a perfect shape must be strived for as the reshaping process is very time consuming.

Many technicians believe this method is the quickest of all and those practised and experienced in the technique may be right.

When the form has been removed, the artificial nail is finished in the usual way.

The maintenance of sculptured nails is the same as for those with tips.

Sculpting with liquid and powder

Apply a bead of white tip powder to Zone 1

Shape Zone 1

Apply bead to Zone 2

Shape Zones 2 and 3 checking structure

Check 'C' curve

Remove form

Refine surface and buff nail

Finished nail

Sculpting with UV gel

Apply white tip to gel to Zone 1 on form and shape

Cure for recommended time

Apply pink or clear gel to Zones 2 and 3

Cure for recommended time

Remove sticky surface

Refine shape

Remove dust

Apply thin layer of sealant/gloss and cure

Finished nail

Part of nail missing

REMEDIAL SCULPTING

By using a form, a broken nail can be repaired, whether it be a natural nail or an artificial nail. Forms can also be used to lengthen a natural nail that has a good free edge but is a bit shorter than the other nails.

All the rules for application must be followed as usual.

The after care advice and retail recommendations for sculptured nails are the same as those for Chapter 9.

Apply form

Apply bead to form to repair missing area and blend into existing nail

Remove form

Refine shape

Buff nail and apply oil

Finished nail

SUMMARY

This chapter has demonstrated how to provide a sculpted nail, from fitting the form to the various techniques for applying each system. It has also showed a system for remedial sculpting.

Assessment of knowledge and understanding

1   What is the difference between a 'free form' sculptured nail and a tip with overlay?

2   Why do many forms have a metallic finish?

3   Why is zoning especially important in a sculptured nail?

4   When applying a form, what are the two curves that must be followed?

5   Does the application of artificial nail products differ in any way from their application with a plastic tip?

6   Why should the 'C' curve be continually checked?

7   What extra step should be taken when sculpting UV gel and why?

8   When is remedial sculpting appropriate?

chapter 11

MAINTAINING ARTIFICIAL NAILS

INTRODUCTION

Every client is a 'full-set' client once; after that, they become a maintenance client or a natural nail client. Skilful maintenance is as important as skilful application and will keep clients returning on a regular basis. This chapter explores in depth the value and techniques of a regular maintenance programme and examines the most common diseases and disorders the technician may have to deal with.

VALUE OF MAINTENANCE

During training, maintenance is one of the most useful learning aids and it must never be dismissed or skipped over. Many hours can be spent on learning application skills, but every client is different and every set of circumstances is different. A trainee technician will learn nothing if they do not see the results of their application a few weeks later. The preparation of the nail may have been incomplete; the client may have a nail plate that is more oily than expected; the ratio of the product may have been wrong; the shape that looked good two weeks ago may now look horrible.

It is a fact that we often learn more from a mistake or something that goes wrong than anything else. It is not enough for a trainer to explain what 'may' happen. It is essential that the beginner can see what has happened and try to work out why. If this is done with the help of a trainer then, when the technician is on their own with a client who has a problem, they will be able to work out why and will know how to put it right.

Like hair, nails are continually growing and what was put onto a nail near to the nail fold will be in a different place in two weeks' time. This is obvious if coloured nail varnish is worn for some time. There will be a gap at the base of the nail and that small area of exposed nail plate will probably have cuticle attached to it. Just as in hairdressing, when hair has been coloured or permed, the 'regrowth' is very obvious.

NEED FOR REGULAR MAINTENANCE

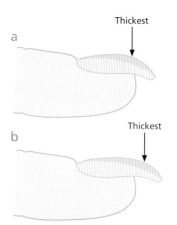

Nail growth
(a) Position of overlay at application stage
(b) Position of overlay at 2 weeks' growth

The appearance of an outgrown artificial nail is one consideration, but there are two more important reasons for regular maintenance treatments:

1 The technician will have explained to the client that they must watch out for any changes to the nail, and return immediately if anything is noticed. However, it is possible that there may be very slight changes that the client has not noticed, especially if coloured varnish has been worn. There may be some lifting of the overlay that is not very obvious. There may be a slight reaction to the products. There may be some minor nail separation owing to thin or dehydrated nail plates that was not evident before. It is important that the technician keeps a close watch on the health of the nails and skin as they should be aware of things to look for that may not be so obvious to the untrained eye.

2 After a period of natural nail growth, the structure that was created during application with the two curves (upper arch and 'C' curve) meeting at the apex or stress point of the nail to create the strongest nail possible will have moved.

The apex will have moved further away from the nail bed and could be on the free edge. This will unbalance the nail and make it susceptible to breakages. The smile line that was created either by the tip application or by a white tip overlay will also have moved and there will be a band of natural nail growth that will be a different colour to the tip.

MAINTENANCE TREATMENTS

It is not recommended, under any circumstances, to maintain a set of nails that has not been applied either by yourself or the salon where you work. No technician can be sure of the procedures followed by another technician and the preparation may not have been as thorough as it should have been. There may be a problem that the nail is hiding. The products used previously may not be compatible with the ones you use.

If a there is an infection of some kind already under the overlay that is not yet obvious, when it does become apparent you may be blamed. Either suggest the client returns to their original technician for maintenance or, preferably, explain why you cannot provide a maintenance treatment and suggest that the nails are removed and a new set applied by you. Then you can be sure of the health of the natural nail and have confidence in the products used.

Infill or rebalance?

There are two types of maintenance treatments. One, called an '**infill**', is a short treatment that allows the technician to check for any problems and fill in the small area of growth to make the artificial nail look smooth without a ridge at the base (1). The other is called a '**rebalance**', as it removes the apex that has moved to the wrong place and replaces it in the right place, it fills the regrowth area at the base (2) and, if required, will put the smile line back to where it should be and cover the band of natural nail growth (3).

The decision as to which treatment is needed should depend on the rate of nail growth. If growth is slow to average, it is likely that an 'infill' will be required two weeks after the first application and a 'rebalance' two weeks after that. These treatments can then be alternated. If nail growth is average to fast, then a full rebalance may be needed every two–three weeks. Every client is different, but the general rule is two weeks between treatments. This must be shorter for a nail biter, who must be seen at one-week intervals for several weeks. Some clients may settle down to a treatment every three–four weeks if they have slow nail growth and are used to having long nails.

Assessment of client's nails

Before the maintenance treatment can start, the technician must look very carefully at the client's nails, especially on the first maintenance visit after application of a first full set. This is especially true for trainees and beginners and much will be learned from spending some time at this stage.

The aim for every technician is to see a set of nails return looking perfect except for the small growth area at the base and at the smile line. Experienced technicians will achieve this with the vast majority of new clients and all existing clients. Beginners will experience all kinds of problems that will need solving during their first year, but must never accept that this is part of wearing artificial nails. The saying of 'no pain, no gain' is

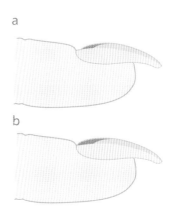

(1) Infill procedure
(a) Buff overlay near cuticle
(b) Replace overlay in shaded area

(2) Rebalance procedure
(a) Remove most of overlay
(b) Replace with complete overlay

New Nail Growth

Growth at Free Edge

(3) Smile line at 2 weeks' growth

most definitely not true in this case and, with skill and understanding, nearly every client should be able to wear beautiful and natural-looking nails without ever encountering a problem.

The incidence of an allergic reaction is probably the most worrying, but the chance of this happening to even the most sensitive client can be minimised, if not totally avoided, by good working practices.

Procedure to follow

As trainees can learn a great deal at maintenance treatments, it is a good idea to follow a set procedure. The differences between the systems at this stage are minimal.

What did the client want to achieve?

When providing a maintenance treatment, always remember what the client wanted to achieve at the beginning. Did they want to grow their own nails as soon as possible or were they happy to have artificial nails for the long term? Did they want to grow the tips off and have natural nails with an overlay? European women, generally speaking, tend to prefer natural nails or, at least, artificial nails that look natural. They also tend to like to keep the option of reverting to natural nails open. In America, and occasionally in Europe, it is more acceptable to have artificial nails that look artificial. This is a very wide generalisation, but many more women in America have their nails done. Products have improved from the harsh dental acrylics that were originally used and technical skills are improving as awareness of the industry grows. Now there is no excuse not to keep the natural nail perfectly healthy and in at least the same condition as when artificial nails were first applied.

Is the client happy?

There should be discussion with the client as to how they are getting on and if they are happy with their nails. It may be that the original plan needs changing to achieve another goal. It is not unknown for a client to admit that they cannot cope with artificial nails or cannot afford long-term maintenance. If this is the case, the nails should be removed and a course of manicures suggested. The client should always feel that the choice is theirs and the technician's main aim is to provide them with what they want to take care of their natural nails, whatever the treatment may be. Many clients like the idea that their natural nails are growing healthily and protected under the artificial covering and, when the natural nail has grown to a good length, the artificial nail can be removed. This should be true for many clients if their natural nails are capable of growing in a reasonable shape. If this is the aim, the length of the nail should always stay the same as the first application, with infills and rebalances carried out. When the natural nail reaches the desired length, it is just a natural nail with an overlay (the tip has grown out). The overlay can be infilled, but thinned on successive visits until the overlay is as thin as possible or not needed at all.

Step-by-step approach

At the start of each maintenance treatment, four steps should be followed, then nothing of importance will be missed out.

1 *Observation*: Look carefully at all the nails. A perfect, trouble-free set should look tidy. The only difference from when they were first applied should be the natural nail growth at the cuticle, leaving a gap, and at the free edge an obvious growth of natural nail. If there is anything more than this, there is a problem that needs solving and correcting and what is noticed should be noted on the client's record card. The shape of the artificial nail may not look as attractive as it did originally. It may look slightly bulbous at the sides or on the end. This will be due to the fact that the overlay was not applied in the best shape and was, perhaps over thick at the side walls.

2 *Questioning*: The client must be asked how they have managed with the nails. If there are any broken, ask how it happened. If it happened easily then the structure may not have been strong enough. If it happened during a minor incident and was painful, the structure was strong enough, but maybe the nail was too long. If it happened during a minor accident, then any nails would probably have broken.

3 *Diagnosing*: If the nails are less than perfect, the technician needs to decide what the possible causes of the problem may be and discuss this with the client. The probable causes of the problem should be explained.

4 *Treatment*: Having followed the above steps, the most appropriate treatment can be decided upon and suggested to the client. If the nails are perfect, maintenance will be minimal. If, however, some are lost, broken or lifting, they will need to be replaced in such a way that the problem will not reoccur.

Putting right the problem

It is essential that the reason why the problem occurred is understood, and how to put it right. As a guide, some common problems have been listed, with their possible causes and treatment. It is impossible to list every problem as every client is different but understanding of the system, its basic chemistry and the anatomy and physiology of the nail should provide the technician with the tools to reach a logical conclusion. The solution to these problems is often termed '**contra-actions**' as they are actions taken in response to a condition or situation.

Broken nails (if some product is left on the remaining nail plate)	
Reason	*Solution*
1 Too long	Shorten all nails
2 Weak	Rebuild stress area

Missing nails (nothing is left on nail plate)

Reason	Solution
1 Oil or moisture on nail plate	Careful preparation
2 Client picking nails	Discussion

Lifting in Zone 3

Reason	Solution
1 Cuticle on nail	Careful preparation
2 Oil on nail	Careful preparation or 2nd coat of primer
3 Overlay too thin	Add slightly more
4 Overlay too thick	Refine overlay in Zone 3
5 Overlay touching skin	Take more care in application

Chipping at cuticle

Reason	Solution
1 Overlay too thick	Apply smaller beads
2 Overlay too brittle	Use wetter ratio in liquid and powder system
	Use less activator for fibre
3 Client picking	Discussion

Chipping at free edge

Reason	Solution
1 Overlay too brittle	Use wetter ratio or less activator
2 Overlay too thin	Apply more, but taper

Discoloration of overlay

Reason	Solution
1 Contamination	Use fresh product and clean tools
2 Affected by UV light	Cover with UV-resistant sealer
3 Coloured varnish	Use base coat under varnish

Discoloration under overlay on nail plate: yellow–green

Reason	*Solution*
1 Fungal/bacterial infection	If very superficial (that is very pale colour and small area), remove overlay, dehydrate, prime and reapply; see client 1 week later. If more serious, remove overlay and refer to GP/pharmacist

Discoloration under nail plate: yellow, green, white

Reason	*Solution*
1 Possible infection	Remove artificial nail and refer to GP

Sometimes, when a client returns, it is obvious that the after care advice she was given has not been followed, even if she says it has. It is usually obvious when a client has been picking off the overlay as some of the nail plate will have gone with it. If the overlay has gone and the nail plate is perfectly clean then there has been a problem with the preparation.

The following senario is an example of many of these signs:

1 The recommended time for a maintenance treatment has been ignored. The new nail growth can be seen to halfway up the nail.

2 The remaining overlay has been picked off and the damage to the nail plate can be seen.

3 The length has been lost. This may be due to the artificial nail being out of balance and it broke off or it may be due to more picking!

Some more examples of problems experienced at maintenance treatments and their probable cause:

Missing nail – client damage

Chipping at the free edge and overdue for infill

Nail needing a rebalance (notice growth in Zone 3 and nail growth at free edge, minimal lifting)

Slight lifting in Zone 3 (solution=prep)

Localised lifting caused by thinned nail plate (probably from drilling), and tip too narrow *Courtesy Marco Benito*

Overlay touched skin on fore and ring finger, lifting on middle finger (prep), cracking on forefinger (no structure to overlay), all nails too long *Courtesy Marco Benito*

This nail plate has had an artificial overlay that has been picked off. Damage to the top layer can be seen and this is typical of this type of client damage *Courtesy Marco Benito*

Discoloration under nail plate at free edge: white

- This indicates nail separation and may be due to a number of different reasons. The correct treatment would be to remove all products and, if the condition were very minor wait and see if it improves. However, with experience, it may be possible to decide whether it has occurred owing to a very thin nail plate that may have been caused by overbuffing previously (either by a bad technician or the client). A thinned nail can break the seal at the hyponychium and this can allow bacteria to enter under the nail plate. If the nail is kept clean and without product, the nail plate should reattach itself in time and then artificial nails may be reapplied. A pharmacist should be able to suggest what will keep the area under the nail clean.

- A white area under the nail plate could also indicate nail separation that has allowed in bacteria or fungus. This must always be referred to a GP and the products removed.

- A further possibility could be a reaction to the products, either as an allergy or too much dehydration or as a result of a badly fitting tip putting too much stress on the nail plate.

In all cases the products must be removed.

Skin reaction

If there is any irritation of the skin, such as itching, swelling, redness or a rash anywhere on the body – but especially on the hands, fingers or face – the products must be removed immediately.

If this is done as soon as any slight reaction is noticed, the condition will stop. (It is very rare, but possible, that a severe reaction occurs suddenly without a warning.) The reaction will stop as soon as the irritant is removed. If acted upon quickly, the irritation will be mild and clear up quickly. If it does not stop within 24 hours or gets worse or if the reaction is more severe, then the client should visit a GP as soon as possible. This is an allergic reaction to one or more of the products or their ingredients. (If the reaction does not stop after all products have been removed, it is possible that it occurred as a result of another allergen that has nothing to do with the nails.) If the client wants to wear artificial nails after this (and many do) it is possible to slowly reintroduce some products by way of a patch test or a test nail to see which product or products must be avoided.

If a technician does not act responsibly and follow these guidelines, the condition may become serious and could result in permanent damage to the client's skin or nails. This could result in litigation, where the technician is held responsible if the correct advice was not given and the correct procedure was not followed. Public and product liability insurance will not cover a technician who has not acted in a professional manner and followed accepted industry guidelines.

The maintenance treatment

Once any problems have been addressed and notes made on the record card, the maintenance treatment can begin. The equipment required is exactly the same as for the first application. Any artificial nails that are missing will need to have a tip replaced in the same way as previously described.

Procedure for infills

Deal with one hand at a time for liquid and powder or a fibre system and two hands for a UV-cured system.

1   Have the desk prepared and all tools, equipment and products ready plus the record card completed with notes from the consultation at the start of the appointment (1).

2   Sanitise hands.

3   Sanitise and dehydrate nails with appropriate product on a nail wipe or cotton wool by wiping the whole nail from the tip towards the nail fold.

4   With cuticle tool, remove any cuticle that is on the newly grown nail.

5   Using a 240 grit file, gently blend the edge of the overlay in Zone 3 (2). This will also remove the shine. If there is any lifting of the overlay in this area it will need to be buffed away, carefully and without overbuffing the nail plate. This can sometimes be time-consuming as more overlay can lift as it is being thinned out. There is no real safe short cut to this process. Many technicians use some short cuts such as nipping with cuticle nippers (this can lift away overlay that is bonded to the nail and take some nail plate with it) or getting adhesive to run under lifting area (this could trap any bacteria that may be present) or using a solvent in the expectation that it will deal with any bacteria or fungus (the solvent can get trapped and the area will still be unattached).

6   The shine should be removed from the whole nail surface (3).

7 Remove the dust with the dehydrator, taking care to clean around the side walls and nail fold, and apply primer if required (4).

8 Apply a thin layer of the product (liquid and powder, UV gel or resin) in Zone 3 as in the original application and blend it to the rest of the nail (5).

9 With a 240 grit file, shape the overlay as in the first application, checking from all angles that the structure of curves is right.

10 Refine surface with white block (6).

11 Finish with a three-way buffer or high-gloss sealant (after removing all traces of dust) (7).

12 Apply oil.

Powder and liquid infill

(1) Assess the nails

(2) File the overlay to refine the old overlay and remove any lifting

(3) Prepared nail after filing

(4) Apply primer to exposed nail plate

(5) Apply bead to Zone 3 and shape, blending into nail

(6) Refine shape

(7) Buff nail and apply oil   Finished nail

Procedure for a rebalance:

1 Follow steps 1–4 as above (1).

5 Shorten the length of the nail to the length and shape that was originally agreed.

6 Thin out the whole overlay, removing the apex so that the remaining overlay is a thin and even coating (2). Ensure that the tip of the free edge is very thin as, by shortening the length, the free edge will be thicker than the original tip and this will need thinning. (As the overlay is old, a harsher abrasive may be used to speed up the process, but care must be taken that the exposed natural nail is not buffed and the overlay is not buffed down to the nail plate by mistake.)

7 Clean nails with the dehydrator to remove all the dust and prepare the exposed nail. Prime if required (3).

8 Apply a new overlay in exactly the same way as the original overlay was applied (4) and (5). (If it is a fibre system and the original fibre has not been disturbed, it is not necessary to apply the fibre to the whole nail as it will get too thick as time goes on. A small piece of fibre placed in Zone 3 will be sufficient.)

9 Shape, refine and bring to a high shine as usual (6)–(8).

Powder and liquid rebalance

(1) Assess the nails

(2) Prepared nail with overlay removed to thin layer

(3) Apply primer to exposed nail plate

(4) Apply bead to Zone 1 and shape checking 'C' curve

(5) Apply bead to Zone 2 and shape Zones 2 and 3 checking structure

(6) Shape and refine the shape and surface

(7) Buff nail and apply oil

(8) Finished nail

UV gel infill

Assess the nails

Prepare nails and prime if required

Apply layer of gel

Cure

Refine surface

Remove all dust

Apply thin layer of sealant/gloss and cure

Finished nail

Fibre infill

Assess the nails

File overlay

Prepared nail

Apply and smooth resin in Zone 3

Activate

Refine surface

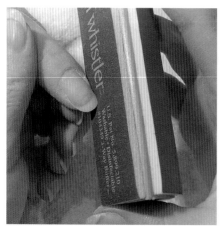

Buff nail and apply oil

Finished nail

SELF-ASSESSMENT SKILLS

Opportunities to learn

It is at the maintenance stage that the trainee technician can learn a great deal. Obviously teaching and coaching by a good trainer are essential, but the beginner can continue to improve every time a client is seen without the trainer present. This can be done by self-assessment. A dedicated technician will carefully assess their work as there is always room for improvement, but this will probably be done in an informal and basically unstructured way.

Many professional and dedicated technicians enter competitions to help them improve their standards. A good person to assess 'nails' is an experienced technician who will study them from an objective viewpoint. At the end of any competition the judges are available for a 'critique' and the best technicians will take this opportunity happily. They do not go to 'argue about the score' but they go to find an objective opinion about their nails. They may agree or they may disagree, but there is a good chance that an experienced and objective judge may see something that the technician has missed, usually because the technician is looking too hard!

Good technicians will also go to the many workshops and seminars held by various companies and trainers. They may learn something new that will improve their skills, or an assessment on their performance may be available that will prove to be useful.

Beginners need to develop many skills and they also need to cultivate an 'eye' for balance and symmetry.

A beginner should never miss an opportunity to improve their skills and should see every client as an ideal opportunity.

A self-assessment programme

The following is a suggestion of how a trainee or beginner (or even an experienced technician dedicated to improvement) can carry out an effective self-assessment. The self-assessment should be used in conjunction with a record card, and it assumes that the first application is as good as the technician is able to achieve at the time.

First maintenance

- Describe each section of each nail (*Observation*):
  - (a) shape on looking down onto nail
  - (b) shape from sides
  - (c) shape of barrel
  - (d) smile line
  - (e) clarity of overlay
  - (f) Zone 3
  - (g) general

- Client's responses (*Questioning*):
  - (a) How did the nails break? (If appropriate!)
  - (b) How have you managed with them?
  - (c) Have you followed all homecare advice?
  - (d) If not, what has been missed?
  - (e) Do you like the length and shape?
  - (f) Have they caused any problem?

- Correction of any present problems (*Diagnosis and treatment*):
  - (a) shape
  - (b) breakages
  - (c) clarity of product
  - (d) lifting
  - (e) chipping
  - (f) allergic reaction or infections

- Finished nails (this section does not need recording, just careful observation):
  - (a) free edge shape – each nail and in comparison with each other
  - (b) upper arch – each nail and in comparison with each other
  - (c) lower arch – each nail and in comparison with each other
  - (d) 'C' curve – each nail and in comparison with each other
  - (e) smile line – each nail and in comparison with each other
  - (f) clarity – each nail and in comparison with each other
  - (g) free margin – each nail.

Second maintenance

As with the record of first maintenance, look at and ask all the same points. Compare results and determine if problems have been solved and results improved. If this is not the case, make a note of what is not right as before and complete a full self-assessment.

NAIL DISEASES AND DISORDERS

There can be a great deal of confusion among technicians about the various nail diseases and disorders that may be seen on clients' fingers. Educators and information from various companies has been at best confusing, and at worst, contradictory. Even one of the most popular textbooks on the subject of nail technology contradicts itself in different chapters! How can technicians who want to do the right thing know what is the right thing to do?

There is one common and one not so common condition that technicians are likely to see during their career and available information can be confusing.

Green nails

This condition is likely to be seen by most technicians at some point but, hopefully, not too often. It is usually seen during maintenance visits or may come with a new client who has been going to another technician.

What type of 'green nails'?

At this stage it is important to describe exactly what type of 'green nails' we are dealing with. Is there a yellow/green stain on top of the nail plate but under an artificial overlay of any description? This stain is always associated with an area where the overlay has lifted from the nail plate, usually in the cuticle or side wall area and sometimes on the free edge of the natural nail plate. This type of green nail is not connected with any discoloration under the natural nail plate on the nail bed, nor is it connected with a green nail plate that has never had an artificial nail applied to it.

The differentiation between these various conditions is essential and is often where the confusion lies. An important aspect of the nail technician's knowledge and practice is to recognise skin and nail conditions, but never to diagnose them. Technicians are not medically trained and dermatologists would have difficulty diagnosing genuine medical conditions without carrying out tests.

Confusion with these conditions always seems to involve the words 'bacterial', 'fungal', **mould** and **yeast**. The next confusion is whether a technician should treat the condition, send the client to a doctor, apply nails, not apply nails, take nails off, leave everything alone to let it go away of its own accord.

This condition, as described, will always be associated with a lifting artificial nail overlay. (If the discoloration is trapped under the overlay, it will usually mean that the client, or technician, has reattached the overlay by letting nail adhesive seep under.) A lifted overlay provides an ideal environment for a certain type of bacteria to find a home, settle down and multiply! The environment is warm and moist with the water that has seeped in. It also has very little oxygen and does not get disturbed. As the first little bacterium starts to multiply it has a yellow 'metabolic by-product', but as more and more bacteria are created, the yellow colour darkens to green and, if left alone, it will eventually appear black. The nail plate can start to become soft and the nail bed can become tender as the bacteria colony breaks the nail plate down and eventually destroys it.

A good technician will make sure that clients are seen at regular and appropriate intervals. New clients should be seen no more than two weeks apart until the technician and client know exactly what to expect from artificial nails. The best technicians will sometimes experience a little lifting on clients' nails, especially new clients. If rebooking and client education is carried out properly then any sign of trouble will be detected before it becomes a major problem.

Treating a bacterial infection

If a client returns for a maintenance visit and there is a patch of yellow under a corner of the overlay, that is the beginning of a bacterial infection. It should never be any more than a pale yellowy-green if the client has returned for the correct appointment or understands that any change in the appearance of the nails needs an immediate return visit. The experienced technician can treat this condition, as it is mild and not necessarily infectious.

The artificial nail must be removed. If the natural nail is hard, very gently buff with a few strokes of a fine grit file. This may remove the colour but do not buff any more if the colour remains (it is safest to discard or disinfect the file).

If the nail feels soft where the stain is, do not replace the artificial nail for a few weeks. After gentle buffing, dehydrate the nail plate with an alcohol-based dehydrator. This will remove the bacteria and take away the environment it needs to survive. A new artificial nail can now be applied. The yellow colour will probably remain slightly and grow up with the nail plate as it is a stain. If the stain changes in shape or colour, the bacteria is still active and the process was not carried out effectively and must be repeated more thoroughly.

Some technicians recommend that the stain is removed using a mild bleaching agent. As these are water-based it is better to leave the stain to grow out, as soaking the nail plate in water and another chemical may cause a further problem with lifting and soft nail plates as the water is trapped under the overlay.

This treatment should not be carried out if the technician is not totally confident that the cause of the problem is as described. Nor should it be carried out if the infection has progressed further than a pale green colour or the nail plate is very soft. If this happens, the artificial nail should be removed in a tip remover and not replaced. If the condition continues to spread or does not start to improve in a few days, the client should go to their doctor.

Other types of bacterial, fungal or yeast infections are very rare on the fingernails. They are more common on the toenails, as the toes spend a lot of their life in the warm, moist condition of a shoe. It is possible to have these conditions on a finger nail and, depending on the type, they can affect the nail plate, the nail bed and the soft tissue surrounding the nail. A technician must never diagnose any of these conditions and the golden rule is: 'When in any doubt, don't.' Only a dermatologist who has carried out tests can accurately diagnose a genuine infection and such infections are very rare. They also take a long time to clear once diagnosis has been made.

White spots on the nails

The second condition that a technician may see and is likely to be confused about is a fungal infection that creates white spots on the nails. It is more common on the toenails, but it can affect the finger nails.

I am sure every technician has had a client with a couple of white spots on their nails who says, 'I know this is a lack of calcium'. I hope every technician has also answered that it is very unlikely that it is a lack of calcium. It is most likely that they are little patches caused by trauma to the nail plate. The whiteness is caused by the nail plate layers parting slightly. If a client suffers from a lack of an essential mineral like calcium or zinc there are likely to be other symptoms and the last of their worries would be spotty nails!

It is possible, however, to confuse this very common condition with a more serious (but rare) fungal infection. If the nail has white spots or areas that appear soft and chalky on the surface of the nail, it is possible that the client has a fungal infection called leukonychia mycotica, and this can be easily spread by buffing. This condition does not always appear on every nail and can run along a ridge rather than be a spot.

As for all conditions, the technician must not diagnose but should recommend, without scaring the client, that they should see a doctor. In the greater scheme of things, this infection is not serious, but it is contagious and can spread to other nails, the technician and other clients. It is also not very pleasant for the client who has gone to a technician to improve the appearance of their nails. They want nice nails, not white crumbly ones (or green ones), and it should be within the expertise of the technician to point them in the right direction to achieve their aim.

THE REMOVAL OF ARTIFICIAL NAILS

There are many occasions when it is appropriate to remove artificial nails, for example:

- the client wanted long nails for a short time only
- the natural nail has grown to a length the client is happy with
- the regular maintenance required is not possible for the client
- the client has had a set of nails applied by someone else
- there is a problem with the nails e.g. allergic reaction, infection, etc.

Liquid and powder and fabric nails are removed in the same way:

- Remove any coloured varnish
- Pour enough acetone into a small metal bowl (or one suitable for solvents) to just cover the nails
- Place bowl in a larger bowl of warm (not hot) water
- Make sure the client is seated comfortably, preferably at a desk (holding bowls of acetone on laps can result in accidents!)
- Ask the client to place their fingers in the acetone and cover the bowl and the client's hands with a towel to prevent vapours escaping

- Liquid and powder nails will take approximately 30 mins to come off (see Chapter 7 for an explanation of the process). This time may be longer due to the thickness of the overlay and temperature. Artificial nails that have MMA as the monomer will take a lot longer.

- The resin used in the fabric system will take only 10–15 minutes

- Do not remove the nails before the process is complete, as the product will harden immediately and then take longer

- When all the product has gone from the nail, remove the fingers and dry them

- Apply nail oil to the nails and fingers as they will look very white and dry

- Buff the nails to give them a shine

- If artificial nails have been worn for a long time, the natural nail may feel a little weak. Two or three layers of a strengthening top coat (not hardener) will help protect them until they become stronger, which will take a couple of days.

UV gel nails are removed as follows:

- Most UV gels, but not all, are not affected by acetone, so the only way to remove them is by buffing the nails off

- Great care must be taken when doing this, as it is very easy to buff the nail plate without realising

- Remove any colour first

- Using a course grit file, but taking great care when near the skin or new nail growth, remove some of the overlay

- Before the overlay gets thin, use a fine grit file

- When the overlay is thin, keep wiping the nail with varnish remover. This will show up overlay as shinier than natural nail and thus prevent buffing the nail

- When the overlay and tip have gone, buff the nail for a shine and apply oil

- The natural nail may need some protection from a strengthener

If the gel used is a type that can be removed with acetone, the procedure for liquid and powder can be followed after breaking up the surface of the gel with a coarse grit file.

There are a number of electronic devices available to aid removal. Some use a very gentle heat to keep the temperature of the acetone warm to speed up the process; others use ultrasonics to keep the acetone agitated. Only use equipment that is designed for this purpose. Do not use heaters that are meant for any other purpose as they may get too warm and cause the acetone to evaporate into the atmosphere quickly. Do not use ultrasonic equipment for cleaning jewellery, as the frequency may be dangerous for living tissue.

HEALTH AND SAFETY ✚

Always dispose of the used acetone safely and always have the room well ventilated.

TIP ✔

Applying oil or a barrier cream to the skin around the nails will help prevent the extreme drying effect of the acetone. This effect is very temporary and moisture will be replaced immediately but the skin does look unpleasant following the removal.

HEALTH AND SAFETY ✚

Always follow the manufacturer's instructions.

SUMMARY

This chapter has demonstrated the value of a regular maintenance programme for the health of a client's hands, and outlined how the technician should approach some of the more common diseases and disorders that may be encountered with a client. 'Maintenance' of the technician's expanding skill base is no less important, as the self-assessment exercises make very clear.

Assessment of knowledge and understanding

1 How is the structure of the artificial nail affected after 2–3 weeks' growth?

2 What is the difference between an infill and a rebalance treatment?

3 Why is it important that clients return for regular maintenance treatments?

4 Name four reasons for the overlay to lift in Zone 3.

5 Why is effective communication important during maintenance treatments?

6 Why is homecare advice essential and what are the main points to be covered?

7 What would you do if discoloration was noticed under the overlay?

8 Under what circumstances would you remove artificial nails?

9 Why are maintenance treatments an excellent time for learning?

10 How would you remove:
    (a) liquid and powder nails?
    (b) fibre nails?
    (c) UV gel nails?

chapter 12

NAIL ART, BASIC AND ADVANCED

Learning objectives

In this chapter you will learn:

- who nail art clients are
- how to price nail art
- how to create your own display
- basic nail art techniques
- about the variety of products and tools
- how airbrushing equipment works
- various airbrushing techniques
- embedding techniques
- about the application of coloured overlays

An airbrushed design   Marco Benito

INTRODUCTION

Nail art is a very important part of the technician's skill. Just painting colour on nails is nail art! Many technicians do not master this art and assume that they can do it naturally. Not true! It takes practice and a very good eye for detail, as this chapter will show, demonstrating both basic and advanced airbrushing techniques.

The nail art skill starts when a 'French manicure' is applied, as this is actually two colours painted very accurately. The skill becomes even more advanced when other colours and actual designs become involved. A technician does not need to be a great artist in order to create quite stunning and very commercially acceptable designs. A natural artist will obviously find this aspect of the work easy, but a 'struggling' artist can generate just as much income with some easy short cuts.

There are many products available on the market today that, with a few guidelines and hints, can create stunning 'masterpieces' at minimal cost and effort. The real effort is practising! This cannot be skipped. Nail art is visual and there are a relatively small number of basic techniques that, using readily available products, can be demonstrated in a few step-by-step pictures. Every newcomer to nail art has found that, with the right direction and range of products, a few ideas will lead on to many, many more. Technicians should aim to create their own masterpieces; it is very difficult to copy another person's work but it is easy to be inspired by ideas.

Although some more unusual designs are included, the aim of this chapter is to provide the knowledge, understanding and practical skills of the various techniques of nail art and, hopefully, spark plenty of creative ideas. The level of nail art here is that which is practical in a commercial salon or mobile situation. The skills and ideas for designs that are seen on trade magazine covers and nail art competitions are best learnt in other publications such as *Nail Artistry* by Jefford, Marsh and Swain (Thomson Learning).

Most of the techniques included here could easily be incorporated into a commercial salon if its clientele were interested. 3D and cut-out designs are the least likely to be commercially viable because, for a client, they are impractical. Most employers of technicians would welcome the additional skills involved in simple and effective nail art. However, skills in the more advanced forms of nail art will not necessarily make a technician more or less employable. Understanding the basic skills, health and safety and the materials being used is by far the most important.

> **TIP** ✔
>
> If practising nail art or creating different designs is tedious, then maybe nail art is not for you. Not everyone enjoys it and a lack of interest will show in your work. This is fine and will leave you more time to work on other nail skills. If it is for you, once you start you won't be able to stop!

NAIL ART FOR YOUR CLIENTS

First, remember that all the health and safety rules apply, as do full client consultations and an understanding of nails and all their problems. This is still a professional service and you are charging for it!

Not every client is a nail art devotee. Most will not be in the slightest bit interested, some will wear a form of nail art for special occasions and some will want the biggest, the best, the most unusual, the most bizarre all the time.

Your skills as a nail artist are obviously important in this subject, but so are your skills at understanding what people want. A suggestion of a subtle or sophisticated piece of nail art may spark the interest of an uninterested client, but pushing a full set of extravagant nail art could scare them away for ever.

If a client shows an interest in nail art the next step is careful questioning and showing them examples of designs. Make sure you understand what your client is saying and that you are clear about the degree of 'statement' she is interested in making. For example, a client usually known for her conservative taste in clothes and natural nails with sheer or delicate colours, who is interested in nail art for a special occasion, is only likely to be interested in a very subtle design. Alternatively, a client who likes to try out new ideas, such as the latest fashion trends, may be open to a more

An airbrushed design   Marco Benito

An airbrushed design   Marco Benito

TIP ✔

When allowing for time in costing a design, use an average time that the design would take. The client should not be penalised for a slower or less experienced technician taking 30 minutes where a faster technician would take 10 minutes.

TIP ✔

Create your own display board as you may not be able to copy another technician's design and make it look the same.

TIP ✔

Practise all designs on a tip and then a real finger. The appearance and application is different.

interesting suggestion such as rhinestones or some airbrushing. The client who is an individual and likes to make a strong statement of image will like lots of original (but practical) ideas. They may have a good idea of what they want and bring in a picture of a design, or they may like to let you decide for them.

Bold characters are quite rare in a traditional salon and not many technicians will be required to create 'masterpieces' very often. Masterpieces are not very practical in day-to-day salon work because (a) the time taken and material used would make the cost to the client prohibitive for such a temporary decoration, and (b) elaborate designs would be very difficult to live with on a practical basis.

However, the various advanced techniques included in this chapter are very useful for sparking ideas and creativity and many of them are effective and can be produced quite quickly and therefore be relatively cost effective for clients. The truly elaborate designs seen on trade magazine covers and in competitions are created by very artistic technicians who love to express this type of art form. It shows how the various techniques used by technicians can be extended and manipulated to demonstrate how versatile the material is and how a simple nail can become a work of art. In the real world of the salon, with its paying clients, the images created are there to amaze and enjoy and to bring attention to the skilful and visual art of the nail technician.

Some technicians will be better at nail art than others. For those who are not so artistic there is no need to think that they will not be able to provide a nail art service for their clients. There are many, many easy techniques and products that allow the most 'artistically challenged' technicians to produce some stunning designs. For those able to create the more imaginative designs, always keep in mind the practicality of providing the design in a salon or mobile setting – that is the time and cost factor.

On a practical level of offering the service to clients, the very best approach (after lots of practice on tips and real fingers) is to make a display of your own designs. Organise these in sections depending on the cost. To calculate the cost, the exercise in Chapter 3 is very valuable. On top of this, don't forget to add the cost of the time it will take.

Some designs are very quick and use little product, for example a flick of paint with a nail art brush or a simple marbelling. Other designs are very quick but use more costly products, for example polish secures that are fast to apply, but cost much more than a flick of nail art paint or a couple of 'blobs' of varnish.

Nail art is very tricky to price. If it costs too much clients are unlikely to want it as it will only last a short time. However, you must be realistic in your pricing and the most favoured designs are bound to be those that are quick to apply but look stunning. The simplest designs are often the most effective and may appeal to a wider client base.

On your display board have designs in two or three colour ways to demonstrate that a design can be customised to suit the client and how different colour combinations can change the design dramatically. Start the display with the simpler and less expensive designs and progress to the more elaborate and more involved designs.

Although designs look effective displayed on quite large plastic tips, remember that the design will look very different on a much smaller nail on a finger and some designs are much easier to apply on a tip than a real nail as the surrounding skin can get in the way!

One of the best forms of promoting the nail art service is by wearing it.

THE BASIC TECHNIQUES

All the basic techniques are easy! All they need is some ideas, a bit of imagination and the right equipment and products.

Nail painting

A collection of nail art products
Nail creations

Marco Benito

The paints used are different from nail varnishes. They are usually water-based acrylic artists' paint, as this gives a very dense colour, can be mixed and is easier to use for fine detail. There are lots of effects that can be achieved with paints, a selection of nail art brushes and a 'marbling tool'.

Nails need to be painted with a base colour that will be part of or enhance the finished design. This is usually a nail varnish that should be touch dry before painting any designs.

- Very simple but effective designs can be achieved by placing dots of colour. Use either a very small round brush or a 'marbling tool' to apply the dots (1). Care needs to be taken on the size and regularity of the dots as this can spoil a good design.

- A very long, thin brush dipped in paint can achieve fine stripes and create quite sophisticated designs (2).

(1) Steps: Base colour, flower centres, flower petals, finished design with stems added   Tracey Stephenson

(2) Steps: Base colour and stripes
Tracey Stephenson

- Abstract patterns or marbling can look stunning with a good choice of colour combinations. Flicking the colour from side to side with a fine brush or placing spots of colour on the nail and mixing them together with the 'marbling tool' achieves this effect.

Steps: Base colour, add two or more different coloured dots, swirl together
Tracey Stephenson

Designs using marbelling
Tracey Stephenson

- Those who are not so good at hand painting designs can use stencils. The types that are readily available have a sticky back to keep them in place. These are applied to a dry nail and painted over. When the nail paint is completely dry they are removed, leaving the chosen design behind.

Design with brushes
Tracey Stephenson

The steps for hand painted designs   Tracey Stephenson

Designs with brushes   Tracey Stephenson

- Pictures of all sorts can be painted on a nail with a steady hand, a good imagination or an easy picture to copy. (Most nail artists keep large numbers of pictures to copy on to a nail or just to give them inspiration to create an original design.)

- Buy or find a palette. This can be any plastic surface that can be easily cleaned with water. This can be used to place nail art paints on for use or mixing. Have a small water spray to hand then, if your paints start drying out, give a small spray of distilled water to keep them workable.

Nail art paint is water-based and any mistakes can be easily removed with a wet nail wipe, or a cotton bud will remove a small part.

In all nail art, sealing the design is very important and, when the paint is dry, a sealer or topcoat must be applied to fix the paint and also bring out the colour. The manufacturer's recommended sealer should be used, as some topcoats may react to the paints. Clients should be advised to re-seal the nails every couple of days to keep them fresh looking and avoid any chips.

Designs using brush techniques
Tracey Stephenson

Nail art brushes

There are many brushes specifically sold for nail art purposes but also remember that art shops sell many shapes and sizes too. A small collection of brushes is necessary to the technician in order to create a wide range of styles and these can be purchased relatively cheaply from suppliers and, with care, will last a long time.

Hand painted designs
Tracey Stephenson

Hand painted designs
Tracey Stephenson

Hand painted designs   Tracey Stephenson

Hand painting with a theme
Tracey Stephenson

Designs using dots and hand painting
Tracey Stephenson

Designs with French and dots
Tracey Stephenson

Brushes

- *Detail brush*. This is the smallest brush and is used for hand painting details or placing dots.

- *Striping brushes*. These are available in different sizes. Their length and the number of hairs are relevant. A shorter brush with several hairs will produce lines that are thick. The longer and thinner the brush, the finer and longer the line they produce. It is worth having at least two of these: a medium one for lines and flicks and a very long one for fine stripes.

Designs using striping brushes
Tracey Stephenson

Designs using striping brushes
Tracey Stephenson

- *Flat brush*. This is a brush with a small flat head can create several effects and is used to fill in colours. It can shade and smudge and create swirls.

- *Fan brush*. This brush can create texture and blend colours together. It is probably not as versatile as the others but worth having.

Foiling

Foiling is another very easy technique that uses various designs of a foil supplied on a roll. This is almost instant nail art, as some foils have designs on them and just need applying to a painted nail.

- Nails should be painted before using foils. They can be painted with a base coat, but it is worth spending the extra time to paint a colour, as this will enhance the effect.

- Foils are supplied with a special adhesive that should be painted onto the nail in a very thin coat. The adhesive is usually white and needs to turn clear before the foil is applied; this takes a very short time. The foil is then applied to the tacky adhesive, pattern side uppermost, gently pressed onto the nail with either a finger or a cotton bud and the backing pulled off leaving the foil behind. It is not necessary to cut any foil from the roll, as it will only stick to where the adhesive is.

- This is an amazingly quick process that can have spectacular results. As the foil only sticks to where the adhesive has been applied, patterns or pictures can be drawn with the adhesive. The foil needs a special sealer, as most topcoats will destroy the delicate layer. Several layers of sealer are also needed, as with all nail art, to keep it intact.

Polish secures

As the name suggests, this technique requires polish to secure the design. Many different products are available for this easy technique. **Polish secure** is the term for small stones or shapes with a flat back that are placed into the wet nail varnish and held secure when it dries. The products that fall into this category sometimes have different brand names. Most of them are available in different sizes and, although it depends on the design, the smaller versions are usually the most effective.

- *Rhinestones* (or *diamantes*). These are clear or coloured stones that look like precious or semi-precious stones. They are usually made of glass or crystal and cut with facets to reflect light. They can be used to encrust a design or a judiciously placed single stone can bring a simple design to life. In relative terms they are not cheap and the designs utilising them should reflect this cost. Good quality rhinestones will not dull or lose their sparkle if sealed with a top coat and this will ensure they stay on the nail for the maximum time, especially if the client reapplies a top coat. Although stunning, even the smallest rhinestone stands quite proud from the nail.

Foiled nail   Tracey Stephenson

Same foil but silver polish under one   Tracey Stephenson

Designs using foil
Tracey Stephenson

Polish secures – square rhinestones   Nail creations

Polish secures – pearls
Nail creations

Polish secures – flower beads
Nail creations

Designs using studs   Nail creations

Base colour, apply secures
Tracey Stephenson

Designs using mixed techniques
Tracey Stephenson

- *Flat backed beads*. These, like rhinestones are usually coloured glass but they are rounded rather than cut with facets. Applied in the same way to wet polish, they look like beads on the nails.

- *Flatstones*. These are a less expensive version of rhinestones. As the name suggests, they are quite flat and usually very small, but they sparkle well. They can, however, lose their sparkle under a top coat. If this is the case, then apply a thicker layer of top coat than usual and push the stones into the wet polish. This should hold them in place without the need to seal them.

- *Pearls*. These are flat backed plastic shapes coloured to look like pearls. Although white is the obvious colour, they can be obtained in pastel colours, such as pink or lilac. They can look very pretty, especially in a design for a bride. Again, take account of their size.

- *Stone shapes*. There are some interesting shapes available now, such as flower made of coloured glass.

- *Foil shapes*. These are tiny pieces of shiny or holographic plastic cut into different shapes that can look very effective incorporated into a design. The shapes may be circular, stars, moons, hexagons, even tiny hands and dolphins! These are applied in the same way, but care must be taken with the top coat. They need to be sealed as edges that are not covered by top coat can catch and be pulled off, although some top coats have a solvent that is too strong. This will cause the colour to be affected and it will often streak.

- *Metal studs*. A very effective and less 'glitzy' polish secure are metal studs. These are available in gold or silver colours and different sizes.

- After the base colour has been applied (or other design) a topcoat or sealer must be painted. While this is still wet, the 'secures' can be placed on it. The easiest way to pick up 'secures' is with a wet orange stick or with a small piece of Blu-Tack on the end of an orange stick. The Blu-Tack can be shaped into a point to make picking up the tiny shapes easier.

- When all the shapes have been placed, the whole nail needs to be sealed with a thick coat of sealer or top coat. Make sure your top coat does not affect the colour of foil shapes.

- Recommend to your client that they reapply a top coat every two–three days to keep the design fresh and avoid damage to or loss of stones.

TIP ✓

Never put an orange stick in your mouth to wet it! If Blu-Tack is not available, dip the stick into varnish remover or a small dish of water to wet it.

Designs using glitter dusts
Tracey Stephenson

Designs using transfers   Tracey Stephenson

Designs using glitter polish
Tracey Stephenson

French with a transfer   Tracey Stephenson

Designs using striping tape
Tracey Stephenson

French with a transfer
Tracey Stephenson

Glitter dusts

Glitter polishes and glitter dusts are a very versatile range of products to create or enhance nail art. Obviously, glitter can be applied to the whole nail, but it can also be used to make patterns or designs; a well-placed highlight on a painted or airbrushed design can make a simple piece of nail art spectacular.

- Glitter polishes can be painted straight from the bottle with either the brush supplied or a fine nail art brush. Glitter dusts can be used to create more specific designs by picking up the dust with a brush dipped in sealer, as this will give an effect that is denser than glitter polish. The dust will also stick to wet sealer, so the tip of a nail dipped into the pot will collect the dust on the tip only or where the sealer is wet.

- Like all nail art, glitter dusts need sealing. The sealer must to be painted on thickly and gently to avoid moving the dust.

Transfers and tapes

There are many transfers are available to apply to nails. These are ready-made nail art and can be very effective. Some need to be soaked off their backing with water (place a few drops onto the backing paper to soak through and then the transfer slides off) or they peel off their backing and stick straight on to the nail.

Designs using striping tape
Tracey Stephenson

Tapes are also available in many plain colours and patterns. They have a sticky back and must be placed on the nail and then trimmed with a small pair of very sharp scissors.

Nail jewellery

Nail piercing tool

Many different types of nail jewellery are now available.

● Some of the designs are applied to the nail as a 'polish secure', that is stuck to wet varnish. These can only be very light and small. Larger designs can be applied to the nail with nail glue. Both of these are reusable, as they can be removed with nail varnish remover.

● Other types of nail jewellery involve making a small hole in the free edge of the nail. This can be done with ease using a specially made tool that has a very sharp but tiny drill. There is no problem at all piercing an artificial nail, but care must be taken when piercing a natural nail:

  – A natural nail should be strengthened with a coating of resin as used in a fibre system.

  – The free edge must be long enough to provide a space for the hole without being too close to the hyponychium. If the hole is made on a nail that is too short the seal at the hyponychium could be damaged.

● There are two types of jewellery that require a pierced nail. One has a post that is put through the hole and secured with a tiny nut on the underside. The piercing tool has both the drill and the socket to tighten the nut. The other type has a clasp or ring that is attached to the nail through the hole. The first type usually sits on top of the nail plate and the second hangs from the edge.

To pierce the nail:

1 Make sure there is sufficient free edge to safely pierce.

2 Turn the finger over so that the underside of the nail is visible and the nail and finger are resting on a soft surface, for example, a piece of cork or several layers of tissues.

3 Place the tip of the drill on the nail, not too near the edge but also in the right place for the jewellery to fit on the nail (not too far away from the free edge for a pendant or ring).

4 Gently turn the drill until a neat hole is made; withdraw the drill by turning in the opposite direction.

5 Turn the finger over and smooth the surface of the nail with a white block.

6 Apply the nail jewellery.

7 If a pendant has been applied, advise the client to remove it while dressing, doing housework, washing hair, etc., as it is possible to catch it and split the nail.

These are some basic instructions for starting off in the realms of nail art. All the various techniques can be mixed and matched. Foil can be mixed with polish secures, paint mixed with glitter. The possibilities are endless and the only limit is imagination.

MORE ADVANCED TECHNIQUES

Airbrushing

A process that is becoming very popular among technicians and their clients is airbrushing. Unlike basic nail art, this requires relatively costly equipment and, more importantly, plenty of investment in time for practice. Like artificial nail skills, it tends to look very easy in the hands of an expert, but in reality takes a fair bit of skill.

Airbrushing nails in the salon
Marco Benito

In the US, airbrushing is rapidly overtaking traditional nail polishing and, believe it or not, some salons no longer offer nail polish as a free service! And of course, the more services your salon offers, the more valuable you are to your clientele! Airbrushing is now one of the fastest-growing nail services. It cannot only create the most amazing designs, but can take the place of traditional nail painting as colour is applied to the nails in such a short space of time.

Airbrushed artwork is a professional skill, which requires specialised techniques and methods of application. There are many products available on the market, and time should be taken to find the right package of equipment. Training courses are essential for this skill as nothing can take the place of practical instruction.

Airbrushed art has been expanding recently into other areas that have become very popular.

An airbrushed design   Marco Benito

- *Body airbrushing*. Designs are painted onto the body using stencils as a decoration, rather like a temporary tattoo.

- *Make up*. Many professional make-up artists are utilising the convenience of airbrushing. Although, at the time of writing, make-up for the face is not yet widely used, it is used by some artists and retail systems are becoming available. Used more widely is airbrushing colour onto larger areas of the body. For example, tanning the skin for photographic work and even shading in more impressive abs!

- *Tanning*. With so much publicity on the dangers of the sun, artificial tanning is very big business. Self-tanning from any number of products has grown enormously. So has salon tanning and this has now expanded into using airbrushing techniques to apply a thin and even layer of tanning liquid.

- *Hair*. It is possible to airbrush a design onto hair using a stencil and specialist paint.

Equipment

This section is designed to give technicians some idea of what the skill entails and some ideas on airbrushing designs, as well as offering an introduction to how the essential equipment works.

The electrical compressor: Airbrushing requires an electrical compressor to provide the air. These are available in many different shapes, sizes and

An airbrushed design   Marco Benito

prices. In essence, there are two main types: the compressor that produces air on demand and that which stores compressed air in a tank that is refilled as the air is used. The air is dispensed under pressure and is therefore potentially dangerous. Care must be taken at all times but note particularly the following two points:

1 Follow all manufacturers' instructions with regard to maintenance. If none are provided, the manufacturer must be asked what the procedures are. The equipment should also be serviced once a year: a faulty compressor can be dangerous.

2 The pressure of the air being dispensed should be around 30 psi (pounds per square inch) and never more than 35 psi. Every compressor should have a psi gauge and regulator to set this level. A pressure of more than 40 psi can push paint (or any other liquid in the airbrush) into the pores of the skin and possibly into the blood stream.

Compressors producing air on demand tend to be cheaper, smaller and lighter and are therefore ideal for mobile technicians or salons where

An airbrushed design   Marco Benito

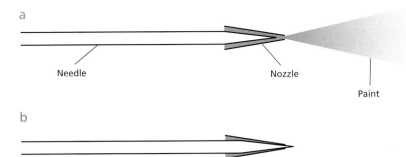

a

Needle   Nozzle

Paint

b

Flow of paint in airbrush
(a) Needle back in nozzle leaving nozzle open to allow paint through
(b) Needle in nozzle sealing nozzle

airbrushing demands are minimal. The difficulty with this type is that the compressor can only be used for fairly short periods of time before it gets too hot and the amount of air produced is limited. The storage type of compressor is more suited for use in the salon as it can be used continuously and can often provide air for more than one technician at a time. However, this type is heavier and difficult to move around and is more costly.

There is a certain amount of maintenance required for most compressors, such as draining the tanks and moisture traps and making sure oil levels are right. The least amount of maintenance is obviously better for the user, but always check with your supplier what the maintenance requirements are.

The airbrush: The crucial element is the airbrush itself. This is where the air created by the compressor is mixed with the paint and a fine mist of colour is dispensed on o the nail. There are several different types of airbrush, but the practicalities of dispensing the colour are the same for all.

On the front of the airbrush is a very fine nozzle in a cone shape. A pointed needle fits into this and when the needle is furthest forward the nozzle is blocked but, as the needle is pulled back, more and more air and paint can escape. It is the movement of this needle that regulates the flow of paint from a shut position to a small mist of paint and then to the maximum flow. The trigger that also regulates the flow of air moves the needle.

The air, supplied by a compressor, is fed into the airbrush by a hose that is usually attached under the airbrush. The trigger is sprung and, when depressed, opens a valve to allow the air in and out through the nozzle.

Gravity-fed and bottle-fed paint: The paint is dispensed into the airbrush by one of two methods, depending on the type of equipment:

1 *Gravity-fed*. These airbrushes have a hole in the top or a funnel on the side where small quantities of paint are placed as required. Flushing the old colour through and adding another to the funnel changes the colours.

2 *Bottle-fed*. On some airbrushes there is an attachment on the side where a specific bottle sits, filled with paint colour. Colour changing, after flushing, is done by changing the bottle.

The type used is dependent on the preference of the artist and other factors such as cost, availability, and so on.

Single-action or dual-action operation: The other decision a new artist must make is the type of operation preferred:

An airbrushed design   Marco Benito

A dual action airbrush
Nail creations

1 *Single action.* The trigger on this type of airbrush can only be pushed down to release the air. The regulation of the amount of paint being dispensed (that is, how far the needle is pulled back from the nozzle to open it up) is set. The needle is set at the beginning of the spraying session to the level that is appropriate for the application. It can be opened up to allow efficient cleaning, but otherwise it remains the same. This type of airbrush is good for beginners as the spraying techniques and designs can be concentrated on. However, most airbrushes of this type need two hands; one to press the trigger, the other to change the regulator and some artists are not keen on this.

2 *Dual action.* The trigger on these airbrushes can be depressed for air and pulled back to move the needle and therefore regulate the paint. The combination of air to paint regulation is infinitely variable and many artists prefer to have this option. Co-ordination is essential for this operation, and it takes a bit more practice.

3 *Combination.* Some equipment can be used in either of the above ways. The difference in these is that not only do they have a dual-action trigger, but they also have a regulator that can set the position of the needle. This is a good option, especially for beginners. The needle can be set in a position that does not allow too much paint out so no thought has to be given to regulation by the trigger. When the artist is more skilful and confident, the regulator can be left alone and the air to paint ratio can be controlled by the dual-action trigger (and a very delicate finger movement).

Paint: The paint used in airbrushes for the purpose of nail art is usually water-based acrylic artists' paint that is the consistency of milk. Any thicker and it will keep blocking the equipment; any thinner and coverage will be a problem. Most of the paints available on the market are easily washed off skin with water. Therefore paint that is sprayed over the nail is sealed with a clear topcoat, like nail varnish, and the paint on the skin can be washed off when the sealer is dry. Some paints need to be removed from the skin with a nail varnish remover.

Cleaning the airbrush: Cleaning the airbrush is essential for efficient and correct working. It is something that many artists try to short cut and then they wonder why the airbrush will not work. The paint is air-dried and little flakes of it remain in the airbrush if cleaning is not done thoroughly. These flakes are then dislodged during use and block the nozzle. Flushing through between colours takes a very short time but, more importantly, thorough cleaning after use must be carried out. Manufacturers should supply cleaning instructions and these should be followed to the letter. Most 'broken' airbrushes are caused by:

1 short-cut cleaning so they are blocked

2 short-cut cleaning so needles are removed and poked into nozzles to remove blockages. This results in bent and damaged needles and split nozzles!

For airbrushing beginners, practice and discovery are the keys to good work and enthusiasm. Every beginner should discover their own effects and colour mixes. It is very satisfying!

Techniques of layering colour

Before we look at layering colour, there are a small number of concepts regarding colour that need to be understood. Airbrushing is all about layering colour. Layering one colour on top of another will produce a different colour. This is an effect that will often be required. However, there will also be as many (if not more) occasions when the uppermost colour needs to be a true colour (as with stencil work). In order to achieve this, the lower colour must be covered up to produce a colour-free area. This is achieved by spraying white in the area to mask the lower colour. The top colour can then be added over the white.

Techniques of airbrushing

We shall now look at the basic techniques of airbrushing. This is just the beginning: experimentation and practice (and time) are what produces a skilled artist.

The working area: The first step is to collect all the necessary equipment together and prepare a working area.

Loading and cleaning: Next, basecoat plenty of tips ready to practise airbrushing (the paint will not adhere to a plain tip). Practising loading the airbrush with colour and cleaning it out is very important and manufacturers' instructions should be followed. As a basic guideline the following steps can be taken:

1 Add your chosen colour of paint to a clean airbrush.

2 The paint needs to be 'blasted' through to get it to the nozzle quickly. The method of doing this will depend on the type of airbrush being used. The nozzle needs to be opened to its maximum to let as much paint through as possible and the air also needs to be at maximum strength. This should get the paint to the nozzle quickly. Spray the airbrush onto a disposable towel until the colour appears and then adjust the level of paint spray until there is a fine mist. (Paint should not be seen coming out of the airbrush. If the spray can be seen the level of paint is too high – that is, the nozzle is open too far.)

3 With the colour loaded, practise spraying a fine straight line of dense colour onto the towel by holding the airbrush close to the surface (1). Then practise spraying a thicker, less dense line by holding the airbrush a bit further away. Adjust the amount of paint mixing with the air. Try this several times until you are aware of how the control of air and the control of paint, together with the distance the airbrush is from the surface, affects the results. Far better results are achieved if the colour is built up with several layers rather than trying to create an intense colour immediately.

4 Now practise cleaning in between colours. This should be a very quick process (major cleaning must take place at the end of the session). Spray all the remaining paint into your cup. Add clean water to the airbrush and spray it into your cup. Repeat this a few times until all paint is flushed through. It may be necessary to flush through some of the recommended

An airbrushed design   Marco Benito

Airbrush

Nozzle

Paint Spray

(1) Distance management of airbrush

Diagonal

Horizontal

Vertical

Mixed

Gradient blends

cleaning fluid. Dip your cleaning brush in water and clean the end of the nozzle to remove any flakes of dried paint that have collected there.

5 Once all the paint has been cleaned away, a new colour can be added.

6 At the end of the session, a thorough clean must be carried out. The manufacturer's instructions for this should be followed, as each airbrush has different removable parts. Never leave your airbrush without this thorough cleaning as it can make the equipment unusable.

Gradient blends:

- Choose three complementary colours, and have the bottles ready.
- Place at least four base-coated tips on a towel, using Blu-Tack to secure them.
- Get the flow of paint correct by spraying on the towel and then carry the spray across a corner of one of the tips to create a diagonal stripe. Do not spray too close to the tip. Keep spraying across the corner until the colour intensity is dense in the corner but decreasing in density as it goes closer to the centre of the tip. Repeat this on the next tip as a horizontal line, then on the next as a vertical. Finally, try to create small patches of colour on the fourth tip.
- Repeat this on other tips until you achieve lines of colour that are denser on the outer edge than in the centre.
- Clean out the paint and load the next colour.
- Spray a line of the new colour close to the first one, but making the dense colour in the centre of the line. Where the thinner colour overlays the first colour there should be another colour created as the two colours mix.
- Repeat for all other tips.
- Repeat the process with the third colour until you have tips with three colours blended on them in various ways.

 Overlap
 Overlap
 Soft Blow
 Hard Blow

Double Blow
Double Blow
Triple Blow
Triple Blow

 Graduation
 Graduation
 Overspray
 Basing the Background

More gradient blends

Note: The stripes should not have any sharp edges. The area between each colour should be soft and another colour from the two on either side.

This technique is often used as a base for many designs in airbrushing, hand painting and other nail art techniques. It is the basis of airbrushing and it is worth spending time mastering it.

Stencils: Stencils are pre-cut shapes in a thin plastic sheet. They can be abstract shapes or specific shapes. The stencil can have shapes cut into the plastic forming holes that the paint is sprayed through, or shapes cut out of the side of the plastic.

There are many ways a stencil can be used. It is not just a case of spraying a blast of paint through a hole. First the stencil must be held properly. A nail curves in two directions and the stencil must be held in such a way that allows for these curves. It must also be held so that you can see what you are doing.

The stencil must be held from the top, away from you so you are not covering your work. Choose the shape of image you want to use; if you are right-handed, you will need to use your left hand (as your right is holding the airbrush); hold your forefinger and middle finger together, then bring your ring finger and thumb together; it is with these fingers that you will need to hold the stencil. Put your ring and middle fingers on one side of the chosen image and your ring finger and thumb on the other side and bring the two sides together. This will make the stencil bend slightly, creating a curve that will sit closely on the nail. Try this a few times until you feel reasonably comfortable holding a stencil.

Have plenty of base-coated tips ready. It is easier if you now use a finger rest and secure the tip onto it. Try holding a stencil on a nail and spraying a colour. See how you get on and keep trying until you can control both the stencil and the airbrush and get reasonable results. Now you are ready to try some stencil techniques:

● *Overlap*. Choose a shape from the centre of the stencil (not the edge) and hold it closely on the nail. Spray. With a different colour, place the same shape on the stencil against the first colour but slightly overlapping and spray. Or choose a shape from the edge of the stencil and repeat the same process.

Selection of stencils   Nail creations

Selection of stencils   Nail creations

- *Soft blow*. Hold an image very slightly above the nail and gently spray. The shape produced should have soft edges.

- *Hard blow*. Hold the same image closely on the nail and spray with several layers to build up the intensity of colour. This should produce a strong colour with sharp edges.

- *Double blow*. This is where two colours are used in the one image or shape. The stencil needs to be replaced in exactly the same place to apply the second colour.

- *Triple blow*. The same principle as above, but with three colours.

- *Graduation*. This is similar to the principle of blended colours, but includes the use of a stencil. The image or shape is moved slightly and another colour added.

- *Overspray*. If an image is chosen from the centre of the stencil and the paint is concentrated around the edges, it will produce an image that is pale in the centre and more intense at the edges.

Base the prepared nail with a thin layer of white paint
Marco Benito

Hold a piece of jagged edge paper at an angle on one side and spray dense white paint   Marco Benito

Spray orange in the same way on the other edge   Marco Benito

Choose part of a stencil and spray with orange on the white area and white on the orange area   Marco Benito

Mist the whole nails with a shimmer white   Marco Benito

Seal design for the finished nail
Marco Benito

- *Basing the background*. This is one of the most important techniques and basic concepts in airbrushing. It is needed if a colour is going to be sprayed over another colour. If this is done without basing the first colour, the two will mix to create a third-colour variation. If the second colour needs to be true this technique must be used. Choose the image for the second colour and place closely on the nail. Spray white until the base colour is covered. Change to the second colour and place the stencil in exactly the same place as before and spray.

Other accessories: Other accessories can be used to create wonderful effects.

As an alternative to ready-made stencils, there is a product called Frisket Film, a sticky-backed plastic that can be used as a mask. This can be cut into any shape with a sharp scalpel and placed onto a nail that has a base colour. Colours can be sprayed over the whole nail and then the film removed. Where the film covered the nail, the base colour will show through. (Striping tape can be used for this. Several strips laid close together and then colours blended over the top look very effective when the tape is removed.)

Another useful accessory is lace. Apply a base colour to the nail. Hold a piece of lace on the nail and base it with white; than spray a second colour and remove the lace. The result is always a surprise.

Thick, fibrous paper can also be very useful (newspaper can do). If a small piece of it is roughly torn across, a jagged edge will be formed. This edge is ideal for creating effects like clouds (overspray white, move the paper to a different angle and repeat), mountain scenery or sea.

Collection of airbrushed designs using a variety of stencils
Nail creations

French manicure

Airbrushing is a very quick method of applying colour to nails. Some salons have dispensed with traditional nail varnish applications and use their airbrushes entirely.

One excellent application is to provide a 'French manicure' for clients by airbrushing the white tip. Stencils are available that concentrate on these shapes. Various-sized curves, for different finger sizes, and other shapes can create the perfect 'French' smile line without the often bulky white varnish that has a tendency to chip.

Like all nail art, the limit of airbrushing is the imagination and airbrush artists who practise are capable of creating stunning and original designs that, of course, can help to earn them a good income.

An example of a short nail with airbrushed French   Marco Benito

An example of a long nail with airbrushed French   Marco Benito

Embedding

Embedding is an interesting technique that does have a place in a commercial salon as it is effective and relatively fast to do. It also has a great advantage for the client: unlike other types of nail art which are as temporary as nail varnish, embedding is much more permanent and, depending on the design, can last many weeks. This will make the additional cost more attractive to the client, particularly if they wear artificial nails anyway.

As the term suggests, things are embedded in the overlay of the nail where they are held and protected by the product. The nature of nails means that any item for embedding must be very small and flat, otherwise the result would be a very ungainly nail. Both liquid and powder and UV gel systems are suitable for this technique (a fibre system would work only if a very thick resin were to be used). UV gel would not be suitable for very delicate items as they are very sticky and it would be difficult not to move a delicate item (such as a feather) once it had been placed.

Ideas for embedding are limited only by imagination (and of course your client's preferences!) together with their size. Craft shops can be a good source of inspiration as can looking around you every day. There are many shapes and sizes everywhere that are small and flat enough to be used. For example, look in a sewing box: threads placed in various shapes, eyelets, pieces of fabric, etc. Look in the kitchen: cooking foil can be cut into shapes. Look on your dressing table: links of broken chains, bits of earrings.

TIP ✔

Make sure any item to be used is perfectly clean before using. Spray with an antiseptic and allow to dry before use.

SOME IDEAS	
polish secures	metal thread
gold or silver leaf	metal chains
feathers	leaves
fabrics	lace

Leaf applied to a clear tip
Marco Benito

Prepared tips applied to nails
Marco Benito

Tips cut, shaped and overlay applied   Marco Benito

Overlay refined and buffed
Marco Benito

The finished nail   Marco Benito

Procedure: Have everything ready to hand before starting.

1 The item to be embedded needs a base before it can be embedded. This can be a plastic tip blended on to a nail, a clear tip so the item can be more visible or a thin base built onto a form of white, clear or coloured product. Prepare the nail in the same way as you would for an artificial nail application and apply the tip or sculpt a thin base.

2 Apply a very small amount of adhesive to the nail (if UV gel is being used, the sticky layer will do the same job) to hold the item in place.

3 Pick up the item using tweezers and place on the nail, using the tweezers to move it into the correct place and flatten it if necessary. Do not use your fingers.

4 Very gently apply a clear overlay, pressing it into the item to make sure all gaps are filled and no air bubbles remain. Ensure that the overlay has the correct curves and is of a sufficient thickness to embed the item after it has been refined and buffed.

5 Finish the nail as usual

Clear tips applied   Marco Benito

Clear tips blended ready for overlay
Marco Benito

Foil applied after an irregular pattern of adhesive applied to tips
Marco Benito

Foil removed to leave pattern on tip
Marco Benito

Overlay applied over silver   Marco
Benito

The finished nail   Marco Benito

Alternatives:

If an item or product to be used is for the free edge only (for example fabric, foil or polish secures) it is possible to apply it to the tip after the contact area has been removed but before applying to the nail.

All the usual after care advice and maintenance rules apply to this service. Obviously, the embedded items will grow with the nail and get to a stage where there is no alternative but to remove the artificial nail or buff the overlay off and remove the item.

However much your client wants to keep her design, do not allow the artificial nail to become unbalanced and therefore likely to cause damage to the natural nail for the sake of a piece of nail art.

Liquid and powder products with coloured powders
Odyssey Nail Systems

Coloured overlays

Many of the liquid and powder and UV gel product companies are bringing out their products in many different colours. Like the embedding technique, this has a good advantage for the client in that the designs last much longer.

Warning: A word of warning when using opaque coloured powders or gels on the nail plate: lifting of the overlay or the beginning of any other problem cannot be seen due to the opacity of the overlay. Ideally, the opaque coloured overlay should not be left on for longer than two–three weeks in case it is hiding a problem that needs immediate attention. This obviously does not apply to transparent coloured overlays.

Every rule that applies to the relevant application of artificial nails also applies to this technique and it is important for every technician to remember that. Just because it is nail art does not mean that any short cuts can be taken.

The only difference between this technique and that of an overlay or sculpted nail is the sequence of application. Instead of each zone being applied in sequence, in the case of liquid and powder, and the sculpted overlay, in the case of UV gel, the overlay is applied in colours.

There must be a very clear idea of the design, if not a coloured drawing prepared, before starting. The sequence of the coloured application is important. In the case of liquid and powder, the time taken is important as the acrylic will start to cure immediately and UV gels need curing in between applications if sharp definition is needed.

Some wonderful effects can be created by even the least artistic technician using this technique. Blends of colours with or without the use of glitter powders over clear tips can look stunning and are as easy to do as a usual overlay. Or pick up more than one colour acrylic powder on the brush, apply to the nail and see what happens.

TIP ✔
It is possible, with clever designing, to keep the design through several maintenance visits if the design can be added to the regrowth area without spoiling the effect.

NOTE
Very important: the theory of zones and the stress area must apply to this application too. The finished nail must be balanced and have the correct curves.

Odyssey Nail Systems

Semi-permanent polish

Coloured gels are successfully being used as a semi-permanent polish. All the rules and cautions apply, but the application will last much longer than usual polish and can be infilled if the client still wants to keep the same colour.

Nails prepared for coloured overlay

Paint a thin layer of coloured gel, taking care to create neat edges

Cure for the recommended time

Apply sealer and cure for the recommended time

Remove sticky layer and apply cuticle oil

Finished nails

Designs using coloured acrylic powders

Odyssey Nail Systems

Odyssey Nail Systems

Odyssey Nail Systems

Odyssey Nail Systems

Odyssey Nail Systems

Odyssey Nail Systems

Cut-outs

This is a technique that really is based on ideas rather than professional technique. A creative technician who understands the medium in which they work can create amazing shapes. The base of the nail can be shaped before any overlay is applied to give it a different facet of design.

The simplest way of achieving this is to take a plastic tip, remove the contact area and cut shapes into it with scissors or drill holes and other shapes through it. When you are happy with the shape achieved, buff off the rough edges with a block buffer or file. It is then ready to apply to a natural nail and be overlayed.

Cut-outs on tips are not necessarily practical for clients in a commercial salon but may, rarely, be requested for a special occasion. If this is the case and the client want to keep them on for a period of time, apply the shaped tip to the nail and apply a strong overlay, taking care to follow the cut-out shape. Where holes have been made, the same drill bit can be used to clean them up.

TIP ✔

The correct use of electric drills is not covered by this book for use in any nail treatments. A suitable practical training course should be undertaken before a drill is used for artificial nail services. For this application using a drill it is not used anywhere near a natural or finger, just a plastic tip. Care must be taken by the technician to ensure their own safety when using the drill. For example, do not hold the tip near where the drill is to be used. If this is difficult, hold the tip with a pair of pliers to ensure that the drill cannot touch your skin. Place the tip, curved side down, onto a cork board and drill, using a slow speed, through the tip.

TIP ✔

If using an electrical drill, all the usual regulations for electrical equipment apply. Keep your fingers away from the drill and make sure your hair is tied back if long.

The shaped tip can be applied to the nail and blended in for a more temporary arrangement, for example, media work or a competition. It can then have a thin overlay applied in any system just to keep it in place. This can be done for speed and ease of removal.

When the shaped tip is in place, any amount of additions can be made: coloured acrylics or gels, polish secures of all kinds, paint, fabrics, etc. This is another design idea limited only by imagination.

Design of coloured acrylics with cut-outs   Odyssey Nail Systems

3D nail art

This is a technique that utilises the properties of liquid and powder and UV gel systems and even additional accessories like lace, feathers, etc. As its title suggests, it is creating designs that are in three dimensions and stand proud of the nail. This is a technique that is not so practical in commercial salons, but may be useful for a special occasion and for technicians who want to receive recognition from their peers in nail art competitions.

For a technician who understands the medium in which they work and knows all the necessary health and safety regulations, client care and consultation and correct working practices, this is a subject that only needs the input of ideas rather than teaching. There is no right or wrong way once the basics of nail technology are understood and carried out.

There are very few technicians who want to take their craft and skill to the extreme lengths of this type of nail art and even fewer clients who require the service. From an employment point of view, this skill will not make a technician more employable than one without it. A good and intelligent technician who truly understands their products and their application could work out how to create the real fantasy of 3D nail art. For the right technician, it is fun, supremely creative and essential if high level competitions are to be entered.

3D nails   Odyssey Nail Systems

There is the rare occasion when this type of nail art is required for media work in the commercial world and, as long as safety is observed for all concerned, anything goes!

SUMMARY

This chapter has provided information on how to prepare and promote nail art services. It moves from simple steps in nail art to advanced techniques, including airbrushing and embedding.

chapter 13

MEDIA WORK AND SPECIAL OCCASIONS

Learning objectives

In this chapter you find out about:

- **opportunities for special occasion work as a salon-based technician**
- **the type of technician suitable for work in the media**
- **how to start out in the media**
- **how to create images in preparation for this work**
- **the roles in media work**
- **usual technician activities in media work, procedures and tips**
- **how to plan and provide a nail service for fashion shows**
- **how images can be created from a brief**

INTRODUCTION

As described in the introductory chapter, there are opportunities for technicians to use their skills outside the salon. These could be in connection with the salon, for example, a wedding party might like their nails done at the bride's home, or a local fashion show where the salon can be represented. But there are also opportunities for technicians to use their skills to complement other creative disciplines. Examples of these opportunities could be:

- Fashion shows with designers, hair artists and make-up artists
- Photographic work for advertising or editorial pictures
- Visiting technicians (different from a mobile technician).

For straightforward home visits, for example for a wedding party, the usual arrangements for a mobile technician would apply:

- have a full, safe and hygienic kit

- have protection for your client's furniture

- have appropriate insurance for your car (even if you are connected to a salon, the journey and carrying of a kit needs different insurance)

- have an understanding of what is required of you

- leave sufficient time for the journey there and back (especially of you have more clients booked after the visit).

However, this chapter is more concerned with the role of the technician in a commercial media setting, how to create the opportunities, how to maximise them, how to behave, the roles of other people, tips on how to create the various looks, etc. This area of work has definitely developed into a career where very good living can be made by the right person. The main part of the chapter will deal with the higher profile and wider media work as this is such a growing area. However, there are plenty of opportunities for similar work but looking for local opportunities, for example:

- local photographers who often use a make-up artist for portrait and commercial work

- freelance make-up artists may need help with nails

- wedding shops who offer a wide range of services to their customers.

A good way to approach this type of work is to have a form of business card made up with a few of images of your work. With the latest technology, this need not be expensive. especially with digital cameras. These cards can be taken to various appropriate local businesses and either left for their customers to pick up or used by way of an introduction for you. When creating images for this type of card, try to have a range of examples of your skills, for example, natural nails, artificial nails and nail art.

MEDIA WORK

The media at a fashion show

A technician doing this type of work should be experienced in all the other areas this book covers, that is:

- healthy and safety issues

- correct handling and storage of products

- contra-indications and contra-actions

- a thorough understanding of all relevant products and how to use them correctly and efficiently

- recognition of nail and skin conditions

- providing manicure and pedicure treatments

- application of artificial nails

- various nail art techniques

- client care and communication.

In other words, this type of work is not for the complete beginner! It is also important to

- have the right professional attitude

- be a fast worker

- be able to come up with creative ideas on the spur of the moment

- work as part of a team

- be adaptable to work situations

- be calm

- not be easily upset or hurt

- not be 'precious'!

Media work has been around as long as there have been the various media – television, film, newspapers and magazines. Everyone is aware that every actor, presenter, model and celebrity has someone for 'hair and make-up'. Manicurists have often been around, especially in films but not nearly as many as there are hairdressers and make-up artists. This is a situation that is changing and it is much more common for a manicurist to be part of the team now. (It will be a long time before the role is called anything other than a manicurist!)

Hairdressers may be connected to a salon, but most hairdressers in this type of work are specialist 'sessions' hairdressers who only do media work. Many specialise further and only do film or television work or even further specialise in wigmaking.

Make-up is an essential part of media work and, usually, this is done by a make-up artist who does nothing else. Sometimes they come from stores where they work for specific make-up houses, but usually they specialise in media work only and, like the hairdressers, may only work in film or TV.

It is in this sector that opportunities are opening up more and more for nail technicians. It is quite difficult work to get into and, realistically, it takes some time before earnings are good. But the earning capacity is limitless once a high level of work is reached.

As a general guideline, media work is something like this:

1 *Photographic work* falls into two categories: advertising and editorial.

- *Advertising*: this is work where everyone concerned is paid a daily rate. The rate is agreed at the time of booking and there may or may not be an overtime fee paid at an hourly rate. This is where sessions people (artists) earn the majority of their income. A technician could earn anything between £100 and £1000+ a day. (Good potential pay, but not compared with a top sessions hairdresser who can earn £5000+ per day.) Very few people know who works on specific advertising campaigns as it is not broadcast but neither is it a secret. This work usually follows a relatively strict brief and a sessions team will be booked for their ability and skill to interpret that brief and work well together. Sometimes, individuals are booked because their creativity will bring an extra dimension to the result and their input into the finished images will make a difference.

- *Editorial*: this is work for publications where the names of those creating the image are printed (or credited). Often but not always, individuals are expected to bring their own ideas to make the images more conceptual. This work does not pay! What it does is provide artists with the medium to demonstrate their skills and artistry; all those interested will know who they are and will, hopefully book them for advertising work. Some of the more glamorous publications pay a small amount of money for this work but it is necessary for all artists to build a reputation and portfolio of work.

2 *TV advertising*. This is very similar to photographic advertising in levels of payment, but it has a different set of rules for working conditions, mostly in terms of hours worked and breaks taken. This is a good form of income and hours can usually be more reliable.

3 *Film work*. Like TV, this has strict working times but can be a guaranteed job for large chunks of time. The big downside, however, is that involves a lot of hanging around doing nothing.

4 *Fashion shows*. Unfortunately, there is not a great deal of money in fashion (very surprisingly!) and reasonable payment for a fashion show is rare but not unheard of. Payment will depend on how much in demand the artist and their team is. The more usual arrangement is via sponsorship where a company pay the artists to 'do' the show. This may be just the expenses incurred or it may be this plus a little extra for them. Sometimes a company will sponsor a designer to allow their artists to be involved. In return for this, the company can get press coverage for their products. It is an arrangement that suits all but generates little in the way of earnings for the artists. What it does do, however, is get the artists in situations where their skills can be seen. Networking is essential for progress.

How to get work in this area

This is rather a chicken and egg situation: a technician needs examples of work to get more work, but cannot get examples without doing the work in the first place!

ANECDOTE

As an example of the hours that can sometimes be worked, I have worked on several high profile campaigns and specific numbers of days are booked for the job. The required number of images must be achieved and this is an industry where every individual strives for perfection. My worst ever job in terms of hours worked was a 5-day job with a start time of 9.30am each morning. The finish times for each day went something like this: midnight, 1am, midnight, 2am, 5am. What a 'killer', but the overtime pay was great at double time for every hour after 8 hours!

This is the case for everyone in the industry. Models need to have a portfolio of pictures before they get any work, so 'test' pictures need to be taken at their own expense in order to demonstrate how they look in front of a camera and how versatile they can be.

Those artists who want to work in the image industry need to prove what they can do and need a similar 'book'. A traditional way for hair and make-up artists is to try to assist a working artist in order to gain experience and meet people. This can also work for technicians, as there are now many technicians who work in this field.

Agencies exist that specialise in booking artists for media work. These usually specialise further in to areas of media, for example, those that book film work are different from fashion and beauty work. These agencies have a list of artists whom they represent and, depending on the flexibility and popularity of the individual artists, may cover may aspects of media work.

Agencies can be a good starting place for a technician wanting to work in this area. Many agencies now have technicians among their artists or would like to do so. There may be opportunities to assist a working technician and eventually progress to working in their own right. A technician who can produce a good portfolio of images, either genuine or as a series of test pictures, should get a good response from the right agency.

As with any research, a good place to start looking for relevant agencies is on the internet where a search on hair and make-up agencies should turn up a list. To date there is no agency specialising in nail technicians and the association with other artists is very valuable.

Central to the success of a technician working in any media or special occasion work is their portfolio of images. If a technician is serious in pursuing this area it is worth spending time and money on the creation of a portfolio or 'book'. If these do not occur naturally in the work a technician already does, they must be created and, like the suggestion of a business card earlier in the chapter, they should show a variety of skills.

A good place to start in order to get ideas is the glossy magazines. If you are hoping to earn money from this work then think 'commercial' and see what is used in popular magazines. Also look in the more 'trendy' magazines as these may have images and ideas that are more avant garde. Look at the adverts for fashion and beauty products, in fact any advert that has hands visible. Also look at the fashion and beauty features, as these are important for artists.

Start to plan your portfolio by thinking about the number of pictures and what each image will be. Five or six should be sufficient to start with and these need to show a variety of images and the range of your skills. It is certainly worth getting these pictures taken by a photographer as good pictures of hands and nails are more difficult to achieve than you may think. If you have a digital camera, it is definitely worth experimenting with styling, angles of the hands, lighting, etc. Many high street digital photography printers offer the service of improving digital imaging for a relatively low cost. This would only include things like cropping and colour or lighting improvement, so the image must be good to begin with. Any work that is more involved starts to cost a great deal more money.

 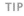

Once you have a small collection of images you are ready to approach the many avenues leading to media work.

In addition to the suggestions already given, some others could be:

- Nail magazines. They are always looking for new talent and new pictures. If you already have a stunning picture they may like it for a cover!

- It may be worth contacting the beauty and fashion editors of magazines (their names and the addresses are always inside the magazine). They usually book artists through agencies but sometimes are looking for someone different and would be willing to give a technician a try.

On any media job, whether it is photographic or filming, the technician is part of the team that is there for the model or actor (the person being photographed or filmed is often called the 'talent'). This usually comprises hair, make-up, nails and styling. Depending on the type of shoot, there can be many, many other people. On film work, the numbers can go into the hundreds, but the technician is not concerned with the vast majority. Occasionally, if a shoot is for hands only, the number involved is drastically reduced, although still may include a stylist and make-up artist.

A guide to the roles that a technician may be involved with:

- *Photographer*. An obvious job, but one of the most important ones. Very often photographers use the same team for most or all of their work. They will certainly have a say in who works on each job. This is not so true in the case of filming as the team is so big.

- *1st, 2nd, 3rd Assistants*. Assistants to the photographer, who can have any number. There are usually between one and three on photographic shoots. Filming involves many different roles assisting the photographer.

- *Art director*. The person concerned with the overall image and how the finished result will look. They work in close conjunction with the photographer.

- *Production*. All filming and most photographic shoots have a production team. These people are responsible for all the logistics of the shoot from booking all the personnel, arranging travel, getting film processed, organising catering and much, much more. Production people usually know the answer to most things!

- *Make-up artist*. Together with the hairdresser and technician, the make-up artist is part of the small team that creates the 'look' for the model. The nail technician needs to work closely with the make-up artist as the look for the nails must work with the make-up. For example, maybe the nail colour needs to match the lipstick, or the make-up look is very natural so it would usually follow that the nails would need to be also. The make-up artist will often have one or several assistants depending on the job.

The make-up artist is usually responsible for any make-up that needs to go on the hands or feet, but the technician should be prepared with moisturisers and some foundation, especially for a hand or a foot shot.

Almost all make-up artists go on set to keep an eye on the make-up and tidy it up between pictures.

TIP ✓

It is often the case that the make-up artist is expected to do the nails. Many make-up artists expect this to be the case but times are changing. Not all make-up artists want to do nails and are not very good at it. They certainly are not able to do the more advanced work. Because of this tradition though, 'manicurists' are often considered to be an assistant of the make-up artist. This is not so, but working together as a team is essential.

- *Hairdresser*. An obvious role but part of the team central to the model. There will often be an assistant too. The hairdresser will be on set to keep the hair looking perfect and maybe use a wind machine to give the hair some movement.

- *Stylist*. This is the person who arranges all the clothes and accessories for the model. They will decide, in conjunction with the client, the photographer, art director and any other relevant person, what the model will wear. This needs to work with the hair, make-up and nails and it will depend on the subject of the job as to which is decided first. For example, in a commercial for a hair product the hair style will be decided first and the styling and overall look will need to fit around that. A fashion shoot will be centred around the fashion so the hair, make-up and nails needs to follow that look. The stylist in a shoot for a magazine article will often be the Editor of that section of the magazine, for example Fashion or Beauty Editor or Director. The stylist will dress the model and be on set to make sure the clothes and accessories look right. There is often an assistant.

- *Set designer*. If a set is being created for filming there is always a designer and their team who have built the set and will be on hand to change it.

- *Props stylists*. This is different from a set designer (who will probably provide the props too). Many jobs involve various props, for example, flowers, chairs, curtains, without necessarily involving a full set.

- *The client*. On advertising work there is always a presence from the client who has commissioned the work. This may be the designer of a fashion line, a brand manager of a make-up product or it may be the advertising agency who are creating the campaign or commercial.

TIP ✔
There is usually not enough time for a technician to work with the model alone and it is normally advisable for the nail work to start as early as possible. Artificial nails may need to be applied, which will take time, and polish needs the longest time possible to dry. Also, the feet may need attention. Therefore it is advisable for a nail technician to work on the model at the same time as the hair or make-up artist. Hair is often prepared first so working with the hairdresser, without getting in the way, is most usual and working with the make-up artist also needs to happen very often. Consideration and team work is essential.

When arriving at a job, it is worth introducing yourself to everyone so everyone knows who you are and you can find out who is who. Every job should be preceded by a call sheet. This will give you information about what time to arrive, where to go and who else will be there.

Every job is different and everyone has a different way of working. If possible, try to find out a bit more about the job, such as: what the look is, are the nails likely to be natural or artificial. Most jobs, unless a hand or nail job, could involve anything, so technicians should be prepared! The people most likely to be helpful before the shoot are the stylist, the photographer or the make-up artist. The main focus of the shoot will be discussed primarily, e.g. cosmetics, fashion, a car, fragrance, etc.

For a hand, foot or nail shoot, what is required must be discussed in detail before, preferably with sight of the model's hands or feet. Although a technician must be prepared for most eventualities, a specialist shot needs preparation as far as possible.

Activities likely on a shoot:

- *Manicure*. This could be for a male or female and requires the technician to tidy the nails and cuticles and make them look as good as possible, however close the camera goes.

- *Pedicure*. Unusual for a man but possible. Very likely for a woman and the technician must always check at the beginning if there is any likelihood of the feet being seen.

● *Painting nails*. If colour is required, a manicure should be given first to provide a good base. Colour may need to be changed during the shoot. Always work with the make-up artist and stylist when deciding what colour to use.

● *Artificial nails*. Artificial nails are often needed, but it is much more likely that they are needed to improve the appearance of the model's nails rather than in their own right. The exceptions to this are shoots for artificial nail products and those requiring an unusual or avant garde image.

● *Nail art or airbrushing*. In the commercial world of media work (as opposed to within the nail industry) nail art and airbrushing are not required very often. Obviously, nail fashions change and unusual designs may be more popular sometimes and may be used to draw attention to or support a theme. From the technician's point of view, it is always good for them and the focus on the subject of nails to do something unusual with the nails but, the most important issue in every job is getting the perfect picture or image on film and that usually involves a lot more than the nails. However, a clever technician will have ideas always available and a kit full of interesting things and be ready to make suggestions that may enhance the image – but will never show disappointment when the idea is not taken up.

General guidelines

● Have a clean, full kit

● Be prepared for most eventualities

● Never be late

● Work as a team where nails are just a part

● If artificial nails are applied *never* leave without taking them off

● Work tidily (however much room others take up!)

● For a job of a few days or less, avoid applying full artificial nails.

Working in studios and on locations does not make for ideal working conditions and technicians often have to work out of their kit. The following set of procedures are general guidelines of how good work can be achieved in less that perfect conditions.

KIT ESSENTIALS

files and buffers

cuticle knives and nippers

hand cream and oil

varnish remover

cotton wool or wipes

selection of colours (as many as you can carry)

tips and adhesive

tip cutters

resin and activator

tip remover

tin foil

nail art products

wet wipes

orange sticks

These are the essentials, but there are many things a technician may like to include, especially if travelling by car as this allows many things and equipment to be if carried.

ANECDOTE

The worst situations I have had to deal with (and they are worryingly frequent) are those where the model has had artificial nails put on previously. Very often they have been put on causing damage to the natural nail leaving it thin, sensitive and ridged and very often have not been removed at the end of the shoot, leaving the model to take them off as best she can – which often means biting them off. This makes models very nervous of technicians and what they are going to do to them.

Manicure and pedicure

1 Wipe hands or feet over with a sanitising wet wipe

2 Apply oil or cuticle remover to the cuticles of both hands or feet

3 Shape nails

4 Remove cuticle and shape nail fold

5 Buff nails

6 Clean under free edge

7 Apply hand cream and leave to be absorbed

8 With cotton wool on an orange stick or a nail oil pen, wipe around cuticles to provide extra moisture and neaten

9 During the shoot, occasionally make sure the cuticles are neat and moist and there is nothing under the free edge.

Painting

1 After preparing the hands and nails, wipe nails over with a varnish remover that does not have any conditioners

2 Very carefully, apply the colour making sure the edges are as close to the skin as possible and very neat. If necessary use a different brush from the one in the varnish to make sure of the neatness

3 Check the varnish in a very good light and if necessary, use a magnifying glass

4 Clean up the edges if necessary

5 Apply a quick-dry top coat

6 Apply a drop of oil to each nail and leave

7 Before the model goes on set, check that there is no damage to the varnish (usually there is!)

8 Reapply a top coat after a few hours to keep maximum shine.

● Make sure the model goes to the bathroom before painting!

● Undo the top button on jeans for her even after you think the varnish may be dry.

● If there is a smudge or dent:

(a) Wet your finger with remover and gently smooth over the dent

(b) Use a quick dry top coat and roughly try to smooth the dent (the solvents in the top coat will soften the varnish a little). Follow this with a good coat

(c) Try a smudge repair product

(d) If all this fails, take the colour off and reapply.

Getting into tight corners to paint nails at a show

TIP

There is often damage to varnish. It takes so long to dry, even with the best quick dryers, that the least-fidgeting models can still have an accident when getting dressed or going to the bathroom.

Artificial nails

Shoots are temporary situations where the models need to look the best they can for a very short time. If longer nails are needed (or a cover up for bitten or damaged nails) they need to be applied very quickly, with minimum fuss and, most importantly, be removed at the end.

There are many technicians who apply full artificial nails (usually liquid and powder) for a shoot. This takes longer than necessary, takes up more space than necessary, the smell usually offends some people and the results take ages to remove.

It is perfectly acceptable to apply a good set of tips and give then some strength with a layer of resin. This gives a result that is very fast and convenient for everyone, can be left natural or painted, colours can be changed if required and they take 10–15 minutes to remove.

The application is the same as for usual tip application with a layer of resin over them. This is buffed to a shine and colour (if required) and oil applied. This technique can be used whatever the length of the nail, even very long nails for an avant garde image and nail art.

The most convenient method of removal under these circumstances is to soak a cotton wool disc in acetone, place on the nail and wrap in tin foil (foil from a hairdressing suppliers for highlighting is ideal as it is in rolls that are just the right width). Leave this for approximately 10 minutes and remove the foil together with the tip. Apply oil to remoisturise. If the studio is warm and the model's hands are warm, by the time the last foil is wrapped the first finger is ready to come off.

Nail art and air brushing

There are no procedures for this other than the safety and hygiene ones. It all depends on what is being done.

FASHION SHOWS

These have a similarity to shoots in that the same people are involved in the central team, that is hair, make-up, styling, designer. They differ in that the time available is usually minimal and the working conditions much worse.

Fashion shows are always carefully planned before the event, but not usually long before. There is always a 'fitting' a day or so before the show. This is where the team get together with a couple of test models and discuss the 'look'. If a technician is involved in a show, it is best to try to get to these fittings even though it takes up more time that is rarely paid for. If the fitting is missed, an opportunity for a suggestion on the nail look is missed and instructions will need to be taken from the make-up artist.

The designer and stylist will discuss what they expect and will have the collection there to see and for the models coming for castings to try on. The hairdresser will try out their suggestions as will the make-up artist. These may change a few times before the final decision is reached.

It is rare for nails to play a big part in fashion shows, but occasionally there is a designer who would like to make a big statement. This is a situation that seems to appear for a short while then go away again. If a *big* statement is required for the nails, then very careful planning needs to be done.

1   Consult with the designer or their stylist exactly what they want. They will usually have a good idea.

2   Create some designs based on their ideas to show them. This can be sketches or drawings, but would be better if it were a selection of ideas on tips. In this way the technician will have the opportunity to try the design out to see if it is practical and the designer/stylist will see the designs for real. It is always best to create a couple of alternatives, especially if a literal interpretation of the original idea is tricky or impractical.

3   Try to find the quickest, easiest and most practical method of creating the design given the time and working condition constraints.

4   Make sure that the producers and the whole team are aware that the application of nails needs the nail team to have time and space to do their work as, in this situation, they are as important as the hair and make-up.

5   Prepare as much as possible before the show so what needs to be done at the show is minimal. For example, prepare tips with the design on ready, if this is possible. They can then just be stuck on to the natural nails. As this is not the close up work of a photographic shoot, minute perfection is not necessary.

Show nails (Raphael Lopez)

TECHNICAL TIP ✔

Do not use nail glue to apply a pre-prepared tip if at all possible. It can take a long time to remove and very often models are rushing off to the next show and do not have time to wait for you. Use sticky pads as these are easily removed with a drop of remover down the back or, sometimes soaking in warm water. These can be obtained from high street chemists or contact the manufacturers of the retail press-on tips.

MEDIA WORK AND SPECIAL OCCASIONS

TIP ✔

Some designers feel that by having a definite nail style it looks like they are trying too much. If this is how they feel then a clean shiny nail is fine.

6 A great deal of airbrushing and application of 3D designs can be done before the show.

7 At the very least, if long nails are required, have them painted or airbrushed and in a variety of sizes. Prepare many more than you think you may need remembering that the middle numbers of tips are used the most. 3D designs can be made before and applied to the tips with adhesive at the show.

8 It is possible to airbrush at a show, but there must be a safe area to do this with an adequate power supply and provision to clean up the fingers after spraying. Space is always at a premium, so this is often not practical and will depend on the venue.

9 Try to check the condition of the nails after the models have dressed as this is when accidents happen. Have replacements ready with pads and adhesive, but remember to take great care of the clothes! Spilling adhesive or varnish on the clothes is not a good idea!

10 Remove all designs after the show. Try to catch the models running out of the door as you will not be thanked for damaged nails and everyone will hear about it.

The more usual situation with shows is that the designer just wants the nails looked after and probably painted a colour. The worst scenario (and it happens frequently) is the requirement for bare nails.

If a colour or colours are appropriate, choose a couple of alternatives for the stylist to decide. Remember to find out if toes will be showing and what is required for them.

Arrive at the venue in plenty of time to get yourself arranged. There may be space to set up a nail area, but this will only work for the early arrivals. Most of the models will arrive without enough time to visit you and you will need to work at the same time as the hair and make-up team.

Making the most of opportunities to get nails done

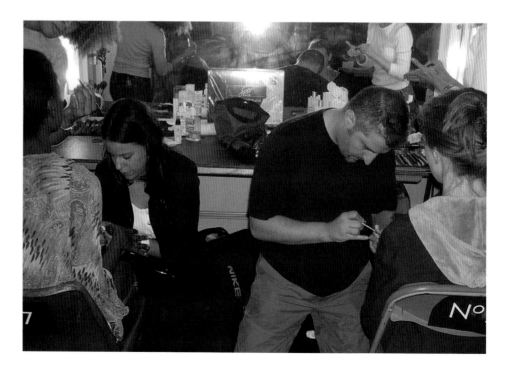

Ask the producer or stylist for a list of models. If there is not one available, go around the clothes rails and make a list of the models that will be on each section. Check you have the right number. This can then be used to tick off each model as they are done so none are missed.

Make sure you have enough assistants in the nail team to get the job done efficiently and without unnecessary people. As a very general guide, one technician should be able to cope with ten models for simple painting. Anything more elaborate will obviously need more, but never more than one to five.

Make friends with the hair and make-up team and explain that you are there to do the nails, you need to work alongside them but should not get in the way.

Get as many models done as soon as possible and, if necessary, get under the table to do feet!

Don't worry too much about the condition of the cuticles, just apply a little oil at the end but not so much that it could get on the clothes.

Any model who arrives really late will be pounced upon by the hair and make-up teams and there will be little or no room for a technician. Also colour so recently applied will be wet when dressing and just get smudged or on the clothes. When this happens, just remove any existing colour that is wrong and leave it at that. If existing colour is almost right, leave it on. Don't forget the toes.

Keep checking that everyone is done from your list and also all fingers and toes.

EQUIPMENT LIST

The kit for this type of fashion show can be minimal. There is little time to do much more than paint.

remover

cotton wool

files

nippers

oil top coat

appropriate colours

TIP

Hands and feet are more move-able and available than heads or faces. A technician at a show is the one who needs to fit in to spaces, not hair and make-up.

TIP

Remember NO colour is preferable to the wrong colour.

Make-up at a fashion show with nails already done (Val Garland and Jade Parfitt)

Painting toes at fashion show

The nail team backstage

IMAGES IN THE MEDIA

It is now a common occurrence for a nail technician to be on a photographic shoot, whether it be beauty, fashion or any other focus. There are also more opportunities for the focus to be on nails. Whatever the focus the brief is important, the team are important and, above all, the finished image is important.

This section of the book takes a small selection of images that have been published in the media that I have worked on. It explains why and how the image was achieved. The images chosen show a range of natural and artificial nails and a range of techniques, including the 'unlikely' in order to demonstrate the versatility of a technician's work.

Media image 1

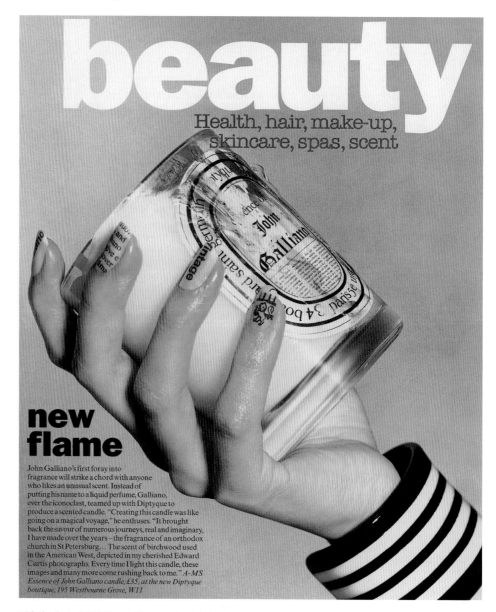

With thanks to *British Vogue*. Photographers: Barbara Metz, Eve Racine

- *Background*: this page is what is called a 'beauty opener' in a magazine. This means that it is the first page of the beauty section. It can be an introduction to a main feature in the section or a point of interest in its own right. This is editorial work.

- *Brief*: this was a page for *British Vogue* and the editor wanted to show a new and unusual candle that had been developed for the very high class manufacturers, Diptique, by John Galliano, designer for Christian Dior. It needed to be held and a very unusual and bold design for the nails were required.

- *Research*: I happened to be working with John Galliano just before the shoot and had the opportunity of asking him where he got his inspirations for the fragrance. He had the candle sent over for me and explained that the main influences were the Russian orthodox church and native American Indians! The candle was very 'heady' and the base of incense very strong. I also asked the editor what she had in mind for the image and she wanted a very unusual image that maybe involved beads and anything else I wanted. Quite a wide brief then!

- *Ideas*: the Russian church and Indian references created all sorts of ideas in my head of Fabergé eggs and feathers, but I had to remember it was for *Vogue* and I had to be relatively subdued! I decided, having seen the candle, that the base colour needed to be exactly the same as the background of the Galliano packaging, which was a deep creamy colour. This could then be decorated with some chains that loop down the finger, black jets, pearls and some airbrushing. In fact everything. But we would see when we got there what the hand model's fingers and nails were like.

- *On the shoot*: this shoot was a good example where all involved should keep an open mind and (hopefully) I have been booked for my ideas and opinions as much as just getting the job done. In the morning I had a bright idea of a completely different look for the nails, but as we had agreed an outline design in principle, that was the one to do first and see if there was time for my alternative.

Having seen the model's hands and nails and discussed the fact that they wanted the candle to look like it had been alight, I decided to use the airbrush to create black half moons over the cream and continue the black up the finger like smoke from a candle. Chains were put down the sides of the nails to drape over the fingers and a few jets and beads applied to the nails. The editor and photographer loved the result and spent ages taking pictures from every possible angle.

I had mentioned my other idea at the beginning and the editor was happy for me to try it if there was time. As the first image took most of the day, there was very little time left, but she felt it was worth a go. My idea was to use the tissue paper that is used in all Galliano packaging that is printed like a newspaper (the Galliano Gazette!) and put it on the nails, using relevant words or pictures where possible. There was a problem as the tissue was waxed and would not soak up the clear varnish but we managed. Once again, everyone loved the nails and many more pictures were taken, but with little time left.

- *The image*: I was hoping the words on the nails would be used because, although the first version was great, the newsprint looked so different and clean. Fortunately that was the one and I love it. There was, however, a bit of tidying up by computer afterwards as the waxed tissue was so difficult.

> **TIP** ✔
>
> Any patterned tissue (not waxed) can be used to create a design on nails. Cut a piece of the approximate size and shape of the nail, apply a base coat and, while it is still wet, place the tissue using an orange stick to press it into the wet varnish. Carefully apply a layer of top coat making sure it soaks into the tissue. When the top coat is dry, trim the edges with a pair of fabric scissors. The pattern of the tissue will be seen and any areas not patterned will be clear.

Media image 2

With thanks to Nick Knight

- *Background*: an image as part of an advertising campaign seen in Europe.
- *Brief*: the image needed to be naturally beautiful and the nails to have a sheer colour but with subtle colours like the inside of a shell.
- *Research*: very little to be done on this one. Advertising usually has quite a tight brief, often with the advertising agency and art director having decided exactly what is required beforehand.
- *Ideas*: any colour used on the nail would depend on the lighting. Coloured lights can cancel out colours or alter them. Colours opposite to each other on the colour wheel cancel each other out and make them look grey: green can cancel red, orange cancels blue. Very bright light will bleach out any colour. As the look is very delicate, lighting will have a dramatic effect.
- O*n the shoot*: for this it was necessary to make the natural nails the best they could look. This involved a very thorough manicure with attention paid to the free edge shape and the cuticle area. Two of the nails were much shorter than the others and, even though the nails were short, every one must be perfectly matched. Some of the nails may not be seen, but the photographer must have all options available and not be restricted by having to hide some fingers. On this occasion, it was necessary to put tiny tips on two of the nails, trying, not only to match the curve of the nail, but also the colour of the natural free edge. No resin

was applied over the tip and nail. When a tip needs to match a natural nail (at this close!) it needs to be as thin as possible with nothing on the natural nail plate. Even the thinnest layer of resin looks different from a natural nail. To make the natural free edges look good and to help with the matching of the tips, a white pencil was used under them.

The lighting was very bright as the droplets of water needed to be captured with perfect focus but still with the appearance of splashing. This meant that the delicate colours of the inside of a shell would be bleached out. A shell has many colours: pinks, blues, yellows. To keep the colours sheer, the varnish had to be the type that has a touch of colour at certain angles. It took four different coloured varnishes applied in stripes to get an effect that was anything like a shell under the lighting!

- *The image*: a beautiful image that does not show the effort that went into the nails! However, the quality of the image, due to the skill of the photographer, makes it stand out. The nails without the (thick) varnish in all those colours would have looked blank.

Media image 3

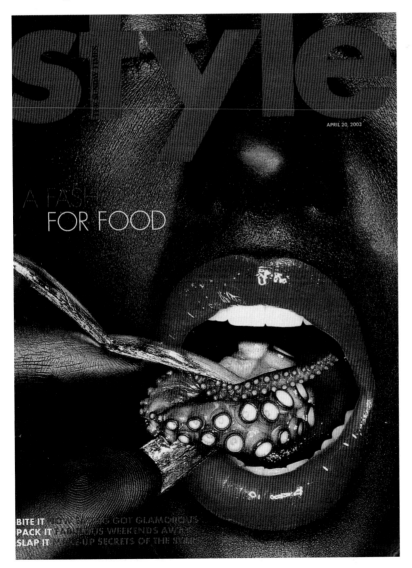

With thanks to photographer Darren Feist and *Sunday Times Style*

- *Background*: this was an image that was connected with a main feature in the magazine about restaurateurs. As with any cover, it needed to be bold and eye catching.

- *Brief*: the information I received was that the picture was connected with sushi, had a Japanese feel and the nails were to be used as chopsticks.

- *Research*: sushi is more Japanese than Chinese so I looked at the styles of Japanese chopsticks. They are usually more pointed than the Chinese version and lacquered, often in black.

- *Ideas*: until the shoot, I was not sure if the nails as chopsticks was literal (i.e. looking exactly like chopsticks) or conceptual (used as chopsticks). I favoured the conceptual version as it would be less disturbing for a cover and long nails play a part in Japanese history and tradition. My main idea was very long, tapered nails with a black lacquer on the top and gold leaf on the underside, in keeping with the traditional chopsticks. I considered decoration with Japanese style writing but, as with almost all images, 'less is more'.

- *On the shoot*: when the team sat around for the brief, I discovered that the image was to have only the colours of black, red and gold, so my black with gold nails fitted very well. Obviously, artificial nails were needed and I spent some time getting the shape right, not too curved and with a smooth and perfect upper arch. With a glossy colour on a nail it is important to spend time on the upper arch as the light reflection on them must be a perfect line (light line). Any irregularities in the surface or shape will show immediately. Painting such long nails with a dense colour like black can be tricky as the varnish becomes tacky and thick very quickly. Keeping the bottle cold and working fast helps. I had applied the gold leaf to the underside of the long free edge first so avoiding the possibility of smudging the varnish.

  The finished nails were amazingly effective and had plenty of time to dry with all the make-up required! They fitted the theme exactly. The photographer spent quite a lot of time taking various angles with hands and mouth (before the sushi was added). Unfortunately for my Japanese chopstick nails, it was really difficult to light the picture in such a way that all detail could be seen and still get the gold underside in and obvious. The only answer was to put gold leaf on the top too so there was sufficient gold in the image to satisfy the brief. That took minutes to do.

- *The image*: well, covers need to be eye catching! I love the nails and the mouth, but I'm not too sure about the octopus! Another picture inside the magazine was similar but with some sushi covered with yellow caviar!

Media image 4

With thanks to *British Vogue* and photographer Robin Derrick

- *Background*: this was another 'beauty opener' image.

- *Brief*: the brief from the Editor was based on the bold 'acid' and fluorescent colours that were popular and different ways of wearing them.

- *Research*: there had been some fashion and accessory lines that fitted with the brief, so it was just a case of finding some of those for colour combinations. This can be done by looking at the 'look books' of the various fashion shows (the easiest place is style.com).

- *Ideas*: there had been some fabulous jewellery around that was layered Perspex of bright vibrant colours. I liked the idea of lines of colour. Also, from campaigns I had already done, there was some interest in the nail itself with regard to the free edge and half moon. Airbrushing would be the best option as this can give accurate lines and vibrant colours. Although with the airbrush there were many possible variations that could have been more graphic, I was keen on a French variation as this was more recognisable to the readers of the magazine.

- *On the shoot*: I arranged for an assistant to help as I wanted the airbrushing to be as accurate as possible so Marco (see his designs in Chapter 12) came along to help. We had a hand model to work with and a Dior bag as the main prop. After trying out several designs we settled on the version as a variation of a French with lines of colour.

- *The image*: a strong image that is fun too. It is not necessarily a look that readers may try at home, but it does demonstrate that French does not always mean pink with a white tip and the bold, acid colours do not have to be worn all over the nail.

Media image 5

With thanks to *Italian Vogue Gioiello* and photographer Justine and model Jemma Fisher

- *Background*: this is part of a jewellery story in a magazine that likes to present jewellery in an unusual and often surprising way. As it is jewellery, there are often rings and bracelets and therefore hands and nails!

- *Brief*: the story was going to have a strong floral set with exotic flowers in a slightly surreal setting. I could do whatever I wanted to the nails!

- *Research*: knowing the photographer and stylist I was sure that something a bit different was wanted. I found out who the model was and knew that she was known for her surreal look. Colour was key to the story.

- *Ideas*: with the strong floral setting, nails could get lost in all the detail plus traditional painted or decorated nails were too 'ordinary'. My only ideas was maybe airbrushing something and take everything! An inspiration would come from the set and what the styling and make-up was going to be.

- *On the shoot*: the clothes styling played very little part in the story and the flowers were dramatic. There was no point in trying to compete with all that colour. The model was to look very natural and any make up should look almost like she had brushed against some pollen, that is, powdery. There were many pictures to take in one day, so changes needed to be fast. I decided to leave her nails natural and airbrush different colour combinations on her nails and fingers, like she had dipped her fingers in all the colourful flowers and some of the colour had been left behind. I did not base the nails as it did not matter if some of the colour came off. There were various combinations: reds, purples and blues; white and blue; blues and yellows.

- *The image*: an unusual picture that is all about matt colour.

Image detail with thanks to *Italian Vogue Gioiello* and photographer Justine and model Jemma Fisher

Media image 6

With thanks to *Italian Vogue Gioiello* and photographer Justine and model Inge Guerts

- *Background*: a very similar to Image 5.
- *Brief*: this story had a '*kabuki*' brief. That is a Japanese feel with strong graphic shapes. There would be lots of images, several models and each look very different from the last.
- *Research*: *kabuki* is a traditional Japanese dramatic art and there are many designs of masks used and graphic shapes. It also involves dance using many strong hand shapes.
- *Ideas*: it was difficult to have many specific ideas without seeing the styling, hair and make-up, but I needed many nails that would be fast to put on and take off. I took my usual vast kit with a few extra bits that may come in useful: beetle wings I found in New York, gold paper doilies, cellophane and glitter pipe cleaners.

- *On the shoot*: myself, the hairdresser and make-up artist managed to come up with about eight totally different looks and I used everything except the pipe cleaners! I had an idea that the cellophane could make long transparent, curly nails somehow. When I tried it the cellophane was too flimsy and the colour not strong enough. Photographers use coloured gels to cover lights for different effects. These gels are like thick cellophane and come on a roll! Strips of this cut to various widths similar to a nail width with one end straight and the other curved could do the job. Because the gel is thick, it was not able to curve on to the nail but it was never meant to look real, so a spot of adhesive did the trick. One hand was left very long and the other cut a bit shorter in order to give the photographer more shapes to work with.

- *The image*: every image in the story was amazing, but this one has made such a feature of the hands and the 'nails' were so quick and simple to do.

Media image 7

With thanks to Robin Derrick and Rimmel

- *Background*: this was an advertising campaign for cosmetics.
- *Brief*: the varnish was a French manicure. It was aimed at the American market, but needed to have a British feel. The image was for point of sale pictures and giant posters.
- *Research*: none was needed because the brief was so specific.
- *Ideas*: the only way to get a perfect French for a picture that size is with an airbrush! The bright white tip is very American, but I thought a British slant on it would be to have a fairly short but more oval shaped nail.
- *On the shoot*: the model needed artificial nails as hers were too short for a nail varnish picture. As before, the arches are very important so that the nail looks like it grew there. I took time to get the white an even length and with perfect points at the side. The most time on the shoot was spent deciding how much denim jacket should be seen!
- *The image*: well it's a French manicure all right! It actually looked fabulous on six foot high posters.

Media image 8

With thanks to photographer Nick Knight, *Dazed and Confused* and model Amy Mullins

- *Background*: this was a very unusual and potentially difficult shoot. The idea behind the story was to show that fashion is not just for certain people, it is for everyone.
- *Brief*: there were to be many different people in the story, all fitting into the idea. A different designer was designing a look for each person.

- *Research*: none could be done as everything depended on what happened at the time.

- *Ideas*: none!

- *On the shoot*: when I saw this amazing model dressed for the shoot I felt she was like a broken dolly that lots of children had played with and loved. Children often put nail varnish on dolls and then it wears off or another colour is put on the top. For these nails, I painted one colour and let it dry then put another on top and over the skin. Before it dried I wiped it off to give the effect. I did the same on the toes. On the legs, I put some foil adhesive in patches then, when it had dried rolled it around and rubbed dark eye shadow into it and around the fingers to make it all look grubby.

Image detail with thanks to photographer Nick Knight, *Dazed and Confused* and model Amy Mullins

- *The image*: this is probably one of my favourites as it is so different in a beautiful but sad way.

Although most media work is usually very straightforward, these images have been chosen to demonstrate how varied it can be. It is almost that all the rules must be known and understood, but then broken in order to achieve something different. But, while these rules are being broken, the care of the client/model and everyone's safety must be put first.

SUMMARY

This last chapter has dealt with an area new to the education of technicians. It has shown where opportunities to work outside the salon exist, how to find them, and how to promote yourself. It has defined various roles in media work and has provided the starting points for many potential areas of work.

glossary of terms

This glossary of terms relates to the words shown in bold in the book on their first use and the context in which they have been used. Many of the words have several meanings. Other definitions can be found in a dictionary or encyclopaedia.

Abductor to move away from the centre of the body

Abrasive material used to shape, polish and remove the surface of natural and artificial nails

ABS acrylonitrile-butadiene-styrene; a polymer from which most plastic tips are made

Absorption in this context, one of the nail 'routes of entry' into the body; that is, through the skin

Acetone a solvent commonly used as a tip remover and nail varnish remover

Acids substances that have pH values of less than 7.0; the opposite of alkaline

Acid mantle a mixture of sweat and sebum on the skin that has a pH value of 5.5 and acts as a protection against bacteria

Acrylates a 'family' of organic chemicals

Acrylics in this context, a 'system' that uses two components, liquid monomer and powder polymer, to create an artificial overlay

Activator one of the components in the 'fibre system'; this is a liquid that speeds up the polymerisation of a cyanoacrylate resin

Adductor to move towards the centre of the body

Adhesion a force that makes two surfaces stick together

Adhesives chemicals that cause two surfaces to stick together; the most common adhesive in the nail industry is cyanoacrylate

After care the advice given to clients following a treatment

AHA Alpha hydroxy acid. Relatively mild fruit acid used as an ingredient in some skin care products. It can assist exfoliation and encourage healthy cell renewal

Albinism a skin condition where the skin cells do not produce any melanin

Alkaline the opposite of acid. 8–14 in the pH scale

Allergen a substance that causes an allergy

Allergic reaction the reaction of the body to an invasion of a chemical substance or foreign body that could be harmful or that the body has developed a sensitivity to. Can be topical (restricted to an area) or systemic (affects the whole body)

Amine a type of chemical compound

Amino acids small molecules that the body uses as building blocks for proteins

Anaemia blood disorder affecting its ability to transport oxygen

Anterior relating to the front

Antiseptic a sanitiser, the lowest level of decontamination, usually suitable for skin use

Aorta large artery leading from the heart

Apocrine gland one of the two types of gland found in the skin. This one is only found in the armpit and groin area and is controlled by hormones

Arteries blood vessels that carry the blood from the heart to other parts of the body

Arthritis a disease affecting the joints

Assessor person qualified to assess the performance of an NVQ candidate

Atom smallest unit of matter that is recognisable as a chemical

Atrium, right and left the two upper chambers of the heart that receive blood from the lungs and venous system of the body

Autonomic nerves nerves that are not consciously controlled

Autonomic nervous system the part of the nervous system that is not under conscious control

Bacteria single-cell, vegetable-like organisms; some are capable of causing disease

Beau's lines horizontal lines on nail plate

Benzoyl peroxide a heat-sensitive catalyst often found in powder polymers

Blue nails a condition usually associated with circulation problems where the nail bed appears blue rather than pink

Brachial artery artery of the arm

Brittleness the condition of a substance that determines how likely it is to break

Bruised nails an area of skin beneath the nail that has suffered some form of trauma causing blood from local vessels to leak into surrounding tissues

Bunion misaligned toe joint

'C' curve the curve of the nail from side wall to side wall

Calcaneus one of the tarsal bones in the ankle

Callus area of hard skin, usually caused by pressure or rubbing

Capillaries the smallest blood vessels that carry blood to all parts of the body

Carbon dioxide a waste product of the body, collected by the blood and expelled by the lungs

Cardiac muscle a type of muscle found only in the heart

Cardiovascular the system of the body that relates to the circulation of the blood

Carpals bones in the wrist

Cartilage a strong fibrous tissue in joints

Cartilaginous joints a type of joint

Catalyst a chemical added to a substance to promote, speed or control the chemical reaction or polymerisation; a catalyst does not take part in the chemical reaction

Cell the smallest unit capable of life

Central nervous system part of the nervous system that includes the brain and spinal cord

Chemicals matter; everything except light and electricity is a chemical

Chemical bond the bonds between the atoms and molecules of a chemical

Chemical reaction a process of two or more chemicals combining to create a different substance

Chiropodist practitioner qualified to give treatment to the feet that has a more medical rather than a cosmetic focus (also known as a podiatrist)

CNS central nervous system

Collagen fibre proteins found in the skin that help provide support to the structure of the skin and surrounding tissues

Constriction a narrowing

Contact area refers to the area of a plastic tip that is adhered to the nail plate

Contamination unwanted or foreign substances on an implement, surface or in a product

Contra actions action to be taken to correct an adverse reaction

Contra indication an indication against performing a treatment

Copolymer a polymer made from two or more different monomers

Corns patch of hard skin on toes, usually caused by pressure

Corrosive substances capable of causing rapid and sometimes irreversible damage to human tissue or other surfaces

COSHH Control of Substances Hazardous to Health

Cross-linker a monomer that links chains of polymers together

Cross-links chemical bonds between polymer chains

Cure polymerisation

Curing the process of polymerisation

Cuticle a very thin layer of skin growing from under the lateral nail fold that adheres to the nail plate

Cut-outs a technique used in unusual nail art that involves cutting away shapes in the plastic tip

Cyanoacrylates the family of acrylates used in adhesives and resins

Cytoplasm the gel-like contents of a living cell that contain the cellular structures

Data Protection Act the regulations governing the recording of personal details of individuals

Decontamination the process of reducing the risk of harm from pathogenic micro-organisms

Dehydrate to remove water from the surface of the natural nail plate

Deoxygenated blood blood returning to the lungs that is depleted of oxygen

Dermatitis non-specific skin inflammation

Dermis lower layer of skin, below the epidermis

Desquamation the shedding of non-living cells

Digestive system one of the systems of the body, deals with the breaking down and assimilation of food

Digital arteries and veins blood vessels in the fingers

Dilation opening, widening

Disease an unhealthy condition of the body

Disinfectant substance capable of killing some micro-organisms and inhibiting the growth of others; second level of decontamination

Disinfection a level of decontamination that kills some living organisms and inhibits the growth of others. Suitable for hard surfaces and implements.

Distal refers to the part of a structure that is furthest from the centre of the body

Distal nail plate the part of the nail plate at the end of the finger; free edge

Dorsal refers to the back of

Eccrine glands one of the two types of gland found in the skin. Found all over the body except in the armpit and groin. Help eliminate waste products and control body temperature

Eczema a skin condition, usually with a genetic basis

Effleurage a movement in massage. A stroking movement

Eggshell nails thin delicate nails, usually curving under at the free edge

Elastin fibre of protein found in the skin that helps the skin maintain its elastic properties and return to shape

Elements the smallest part of a chemical that can recognisably exist

Embedding a technique used in nail art that uses small items within the overlay

Epidermis upper layer of skin, above the dermis

Eponychium the skin fold and seal that is at the base of the nail plate

Ethyl cyanoacrylate one of the acrylate-based family of adhesives, usually used as a nail adhesive

Ethyl methacrylate (EMA) a monomer most commonly used in acrylic nail systems

Evaporation the conversion of a liquid into a vapour

Exfoliation the mechanical removal of dead skin cells from the surface of the skin

Exothermic heat-producing chemical reaction

Extensions artificially extending the length of a finger nail

Extensor extends or straightens

Fabric mesh usually a silk or fibreglass fabric used in a fabric 'system' to provide extra strength

Fan-shaped nail a nail plate that is wider at the free edge than at the cuticle

Femoral artery main artery in the upper leg

Femur bone of the upper leg

Fibre in this context, the 'system' that uses a fibre (e.g. silk, fibreglass) with a cyanoacrylate resin to create an artificial overlay

Fibreglass a fine mesh of fibreglass used to strengthen a cyanoacrylate resin system

Fibrous joints a type of joint

Fibula a bone of the lower leg

Filaments a structure in striated muscle

Flexibility the property of a substance that determines how much it will bend

Flexor flexes or bends

Foiling a technique in nail art that uses a foil to decorate the nails

Follicles found in the skin; the hair follicle is where the hair is formed

Free edge the part of the nail plate that extends past the end of the finger

French manicure a method of painting nails using a white colour on the free edge and a transparent natural colour over the nail bed

French white tips plastic tips that are an opaque white to provide the French manicure effect in artificial nails

Frictions a movement in massage, for active, deeper effect

Fumes particles suspended in smoke

Fungus (fungi) microscopic plant; can colonise or grow on or under the nail plate and skin, and can lead to medical problems

Furrows longitudinal ridges on the nail plate

Gel thickened liquids; can refer to a thick adhesive or a UV-cured material

Gel stage refers to the start of the polymerisation process of an 'acrylic' system when the liquid and powder react forming a 'gel-like' substance before hardening or curing

Glues often used to describe adhesives; its true meaning is an adhesive that is protein-based, usually animal-derived (e.g. bones, hides, etc.)

Grit used to describe the abrasiveness of files and buffers; the higher the number, the finer the abrasive – a level of not less than 240 grit should be used on the natural nail

HABIA Hairdressing and Beauty Industry Authority

Habit tic an habitual action that damages the matrix of a nail. Usually seen on the thumb where the forefinger picks at the nail fold

Hair follicle structure in the skin that produces a hair

Hairless skin version of skin found on the palms of the hands and soles of the foot. Has no hair follicles.

Hairy skin a version of skin with hair follicles

Hangnail sharp piece of nail in the side walls that is separated from the nail plate

Hardness a measure of how easily a substance can be scratched

HASAWA Health & Safety at Work Act

Hazardous substances that may be capable of causing physical or health-related injury

Heart part of the cardiovascular system that pumps the blood around the body

Histamine a chemical released by the body as a defence mechanism to protect against harm from an unwanted substance that causes an irritation or other type of reaction

Hooked (or claw) nail a nail plate that has an extreme upper arch and curves under at the free edge

Hormones a substance secreted by glands that stimulates organs into action

Humerus bone of the upper arm

Hyperidrosis over-activity of the sweat glands of the feet

Hyponychium the distal edge of the nail bed; a seal between the nail plate and nail bed

Infill a treatment than compensates for the natural nail growth after the application of artificial nails. Usually required 2–3 weeks after application

Ingestion one of the main 'routes of entry' into the body; that is, via the mouth

Inhalation one of the main 'routes of entry' into the body; that is, via the lungs

Initiator a chemical that starts the chemical process of polymerisation

Intercellular fluid a clear fluid that bathes all cells of the body and supports cell function

Iron mineral necessary for efficient oxygen transportation by the blood

Irritants substances capable of causing inflammation of the skin, eyes, nose, throat or lungs

Irritation general description of a mildly inflammatory condition

Isometric contraction a muscle put under tension but not altering its length

Isotonic contraction a muscle put under tension and shortening

Keratin protein created by the body and one that is formed when skin cells have become keratinised to form the nail plate

Keratinised the description of a skin or nail cell that has lost its contents and transformed into the protein keratin

Koilonychia flat, spoon-shaped nails usually with a systemic cause

Lamellar dystrophy peeling, splitting layers of the nail plate

Lateral to the side

Lateral nail fold skin on either side of the nail plate

Lateral plantar artery and vein blood vessels in the foot

Leucoderma Patches of skin that do not have any pigmentation

Leukonychia white spots on the nail plate; usually caused by trauma to the nail plate but may have other medical causes

Lifting term used to describe the separation of an artificial nail overlay from the nail plate

Ligaments fibrous tissue supporting joints

Light cured the process of polymerisation using a photoinitiator to start the chemical reaction, usually UV light

Lipid a natural fat produced by the skin; this helps to form part of the intercellular cement that holds keratinised skin cells together

Liquid the most common definition is a physical state, e.g. solid, gas, liquid; in the context of nail products, it refers to the monomer in a two-component acrylic system

Low odour sometimes used in the context of acrylic monomers; means that they have a lower evaporation rate or are not so easily detected by the human sense of smell; does not refer to degree of safety

Lower arch the curve of the lower part of the free edge when viewed from the side

Lunula whitish area at the base of the nail plate where keratinisation is incomplete; often referred to the 'half moon'

Lymph a clear fluid circulating the body via the lymphatic system whose main functions are to fight infection and remove waste

Lymph node structure in the lymphatic system that filters lymph

Lymphatic drainage the manual assistance in the movement of lymph towards the lymphatic nodes

Lymphatic system one of the systems of the body; involved in protection

Lymphocytes one of the white blood cells

Lymphoedema a constriction in a lymph vessel causing localised excess of lymph fluid

Macrophage type of blood cell that destroys harmful micro-organisms

Manicure a treatment involving the skin and nails of the hands and lower arm

Mantle the area of skin that covers the matrix; proximal nail fold

Marbelling a technique used in nail art that mixes two or more colours together

Massage the rubbing, kneading and stimulating of muscles and joints of the body

Matrix area below the proximal nail fold where the process of keratinisation of skin cells takes place to form the nail plate

Medial relating to the middle

Medial plantar artery and vein blood vessels in the foot

Melanin a pigment created by specialist skin cells to protect the lower layers of skin from sun damage

Melanocytes adapted skin cells that produce the pigment melanin

Metacarpel arteries and veins blood vessels in the wrist

Metacarpals bones in the hand

Metatarsals bones in the foot

Methacrylic acid an acid commonly used as a primer in many nail systems

Methyl methacrylate (MMA) monomer no longer used as a component of an acrylic system except as a 'co-polymer' with ethyl methacrylate (EMA)

Mist fine liquid particles produced by spraying

Mitosis the process of cell division and reproduction

Molecule a specific arrangement of atoms to create a specific chemical

Monomer one unit or molecule; individual chemical units that can react to form a polymer

Motor nerves nerves connected to muscles that cause them to move

Mould a term often and incorrectly used to describe nail infections, usually pseudomonas (green infection between the nail plate and overlay)

MSDS Material Safety Data Sheet; forms that provide various information relating to safety issues

Mucocutaneous a variation of skin that secretes mucous for either protection of lubrication

Mucous membrane the internal version of skin that secretes mucous, e.g. lining of the gut

Multiple sclerosis a disease associated with the nervous system

Myofibrils structures in muscle

Nail bed area of skin that lies directly under the nail plate

Nail enamel a term sometimes used to describe a product used to apply colour to the nails

Nail lacquer see Nail enamel

Nail plate the hard layers of keratinised skin cells that form a 'plate' on the end of each finger and toe

Nail polish see Nail enamel

Nail unit the area at the end of the finger that includes all parts of the finger nail

Nail varnish see Nail enamel

Nail wraps most commonly, a fibre system used to overlay the natural nail; can refer to any system

National Occupational Standards the level and detail of the various competencies required by specific industry sectors that make a person capable of carrying out specific work, laid down by the industry sector

Natural nail the finger nail that is formed in the matrix to make a nail plate

Natural nail overlays artificial nail products used to coat a natural nail plate

Neurones a nerve cell

No-light gel a cyanoacrylate-based gel

Non-acetone polish remover solvents for polish removal, usually recommended for use with artificial nails; however, all solvents can damage some artificial nails

Nutrients a substance providing nourishment

NVQ National Vocational Qualification; a qualification based on the National Occupational Standards and strongly promoted by Department for Education and Employment (SVQ in Scotland)

Odour presence of a chemical that can be detected by the sense of smell. Is not an indication of degree of danger or quantity of chemical

Oedema condition involving the inefficient function of the lymphatic system

Oligomers chains of monomers that are considerably shorter than a polymer

Onychocryptosis ingrowing nail

Onychodermal band seal between the nail plate and the hyponychium

Onycholysis separation of the natural nail from the nail bed

Onychomadesis loosening of the nail plate at the proximal nail fold; usually due to trauma

Onychomycosis lifting, discoloration or rotting of the nail plate

Onychophagy the habit of nail biting

Onychorrhexis longitudinal splitting of the nail plate; often associated with furrows

Optical brightener an additive that makes colours look brighter and white look whiter

Organic any substance that contains the element carbon; it does not relate to the degree of safety: virtually every product used in the nail industry is organic

Oval a shape of the free edge of the nail that is rounded

Overlay a coating applied to the natural nail or blended plastic tip and natural nail

Oxygenated blood blood from the lungs rich in oxygen

Palmar arches arteries in the hand

Parkinson's disease a disease associated with the nervous system

Paronychia inflammation caused by damage of foreign body around the edges of the nail plate

Patella bone protecting knee joint, also known as knee cap

Pathogen a micro-organism capable of causing disease

Pedicure a treatment involving the skin and nails of the feet and lower leg

Peripheral nervous system the nervous system of the body excluding the brain and spinal cord

Petrissage a movement in massage; an active, stimulating movement

Peyer's patches structures in the lymphatic system

pH value a measure used to determine the level of acidity or alkalinity of a substance; 7 is neutral, 1 is the most acidic and 14 is the most alkaline

Phalanges bones in the fingers

Photoinitiator a chemical that responds to specific types of light to start a chemical reaction

Pitting a description of the surface of the nail plate that has small dips in it. Often a sign of a skin condition such as psoriasis

Plantar arch blood vessels in the sole of the foot

Plasma the clear liquid part of blood

Plasticiser an additive that increases flexibility

PNS peripheral nervous system

Podiatrist an alternative name for a chiropodist

Polish remover solvents that remove polish from the nail

Polish secures accessories in nail art that stick to the nail using nail varnish

Polymers literally 'many units'; very long chains of chemically bonded monomers or units. It can refer to the acrylics used in artificial nails; it also refers to any other polymer, e.g. hair, that is made up of chains of amino acids

Polymerisation a chemical reaction that creates polymer chains from monomers or oligomers

Popliteal artery artery in the leg

Posterior relating to the back

Powder materials that have been finely ground; in this context, powder generally refers to powder polymers which are tiny beads of a polymer

Ppm parts per million; a general measure of ratio; in this context, it can be the number of molecules of vapour in 1 million molecules of air

Pretailor to shape a plastic tip before application to create a better fit and shape

Primer a substance used to improve the adhesion between the nail plate and artificial products

Pronator muscle movement that turns hand down

Protein chemical substances created by the body from long chains of amino acids

Proximal nearest to the centre of the body

Proximal nail fold the fold of epidermis covering the matrix and extending onto the nail plate

Psoriasis a non-contagious skin condition

Pulmonary relating to the lungs

Radial artery and vein an artery and vein in the lower arm

Radius a bone in the lower arm

Rebalance corrects position of apex when it has moved because natural nail has grown

Receptors type of nerve cell that receives a stimulus

Resin refers to a version of cyanoacrylate used in the fibre system

Resin activator a product that speeds up the cure time of a cyanoacrylate resin

RIDDOR Reporting of Injuries, Diseases and Dangerous Occurrences Regulations

Risk assessment a requirement of COSHH that assesses potential hazards

Routes of entry the three ways a chemical can enter the body: ingestion (mouth), inhalation (nose), absorption (skin)

Sanitisation to kill or reduce the numbers of pathogens to a level considered safe by public health standards

Saphenous vein vein in the leg

Sculptured nails artificial nails created by building the nail onto the natural nail and extending it over a form rather than a plastic tip

Sebaceous gland gland associated with the hair follicle that produces sebum

Sebum a natural oil produced by the sebaceous glands attached to hair follicles that moisturises and lubricates the skin and plays a protective role

Sensitivity a condition that causes the body's immune system to react

Sensitisation the biological process of becoming sensitive to a chemical that usually results in an allergic reaction

Sensory nerves a type of nerve that receives stimuli

Side wall the soft tissue along the sides of the nail plate

Skeletal muscle the type of muscle connected to the skeleton

Ski-jump nail a nail plate that curves upwards from the cuticle area to the free edge

Smile line the curve that is created naturally by the hyponychium or by a coloured artificial overlay or nail varnish

Smooth muscle a type of muscle. Found in arteries, digestive tract, etc

Solehorn epidermis attached to the underside of some natural nails; more often seen on nails that are almond shaped: it has a blood and nerve supply, so should not be removed

Solvents substances capable of dissolving other substances; water is the 'universal solvent'

Spleen organ in the lymphatic system

Splinter haemorrhage small black streaks under the nail plate

Square a shape of the free edge of a nail that has a straight edge with corners and parallel sides

Squoval a shape of the free edge of a nail that has corners and parallel sides but a rounded edge

Sterilisation the process that achieves the complete destruction of all living organisms

Stop point the part of a plastic tip that fits around the free edge of the natural nail

Stratum corneum uppermost layer of the epidermis consisting of keratinised skin cells

Stratum germinativum base layer of the epidermis where new skin cells are formed

Stratum granulosum one of the mid layers of the epidermis where the process of keratinisation starts

Stratum lucidum one of the mid layers of the epidermis apparent in the palms of the hands and soles of the feet

Stratum spinosum one of the mid layers of the epidermis where some cells are connected together

Strength the ability of a substance to withstand breakage if force is applied

Striated muscle skeletal muscle

Subcutaneous layer below the dermis of the skin where fat is stored

Sun damage damage to the skin where the skin has created permanent melanin discoloration, e.g. freckles

Supinator a muscle movement that turns the hand up

Sweat a liquid produced by the sweat glands in the skin; one of the main functions of sweat is to help regulate body temperature

Sweat gland structure in the skin that produces sweat

Synovial joints a type of joint; moveable joint

System in this context, this refers to the 'system' used to overlay the natural nail or plastic tip, e.g. acrylic, UV gel, fibre

Systemic condition caused by one of the systems of the body and affecting many areas

Talus bone in the ankle

Tapered a shape of the free edge of a nail that becomes thinner towards the distal edge

Tapotement a movement in massage; stimulating movement involving tapping

Tarsals bones in the ankle

Tendons tissue that connects muscles to bones

Thixotropic the ability of a liquid to become thinner in viscosity when agitated, returning to its original viscosity when agitation stops

Tibia a bone of the lower leg

Titanium dioxide a white pigment used in white-tip powders

Tonsils structure in the lymphatic system at the back of the throat

Toxic the description of a substance that can adversely harm humans at measured levels

Trauma excessive force

True cuticle the layer of skin that is continuously shed from the underside of the proximal nail fold and adheres to the nail plate

Ulna a bone of the lower arm

Ulnar artery and vein an artery and vein in the lower arm

Ultraviolet (UV) light an invisible part of the spectrum above the colour violet in the visible light bands

Upper arch the curve of the nail from the cuticle area to the free edge

UV absorbers additives that act like sunscreens

UV block a chemical ingredient that prevents UV rays from affecting the product or underlying skin tissues

UV gel one of the 'systems' of artificial nails; it uses a pre-mixed 'gel' and UV light to create the overlay

Vapours molecules of a chemical in air created by evaporation of the substance

Varicose veins a condition affecting the blood vessels. Usually seen in the legs

Vein blood vessels that return the blood to the heart

Vena cava large vein leading to the heart

Ventilation the process of changing the air in an area and therefore removing dust and vapours

Ventricle, right and left the two lower chambers of the heart that pump the blood to the lungs and arteries of the body

Verruca similar to warts, but ingrowing, usually found on the feet

Viruses a wide group of micro-organisms that can only reproduce in living cells and can cause a vast range of diseases

Viscosity the measure of a liquid's ability to flow, that is, its thinness or thickness

Vitamin D a vitamin formed in the body and essential for the efficient absorption and use of calcium

Vitiligo a condition of the skin where it is not able to produce the pigment melanin

Volatile describes a substance that easily evaporates in air

Voluntary nervous system the part of the nervous system that is under conscious control

Warts lumps of usually hard tissue on the skin caused by a viral infection

Wetting the ability of a liquid to spread out to cover a surface

White-tip powder a colour of acrylic powder used to create a white free edge on an artificial nail

Whitlow localised and painful swelling at the edge of the nail plate

Yeast a type of fungus; some yeasts can cause fungal infections

Zones the three areas of the artificial nail referred to when creating the correct artificial structure

index